Forbidden Family

Wisconsin Studies in American Autobiography
William L. Andrews, General Editor

Margaret Sams

Forbidden Family,

A Wartime Memoir of
the Philippines, 1941–1945

Edited by Lynn Z. Bloom

The University of Wisconsin Press

The University of Wisconsin Press
114 North Murray Street
Madison, Wisconsin 53715

3 Henrietta Street
London WC2E 8LU, England

Library of Congress Cataloging-in-Publication Data

Sams, Margaret, 1916–
Forbidden family : a wartime memoir of the Philippines, 1941–1945
Margaret Sams; edited by Lynn Z. Bloom.
316 p. cm. – (Wisconsin studies in American autobiography)
Bibliography: pp. 315
1. World War, 1939–1945–Concentration camps–Philippines.
2. Sams, Margaret, 1916–   . 3. World War, 1939–1945–Personal
narratives, American. 4. World War, 1939–1945–Prisoners and
prisons, Japanese. 5. Philippines–History–Japanese occupation,
1942–1945. 6. Prisoners of war–Philippines–Biography.
7. Prisoners of war–United States–Biography. I. Bloom, Lynn Z.,
1934–   . II. Title. III. Series.
D805.P6S26   1989   940.53'17'0952–dc20   89-40267
ISBN 0–299–12140–2

To Jerry,
without whom I would have had no life,
no love, no story, and to our children
and grandchildren
who made the story complete.
With love, Margaret Sams

To my own forbidden family—
Martin, Bard, and Laird,
and to Sara, most welcome
new family member.
With love, Lynn Z. Bloom

Contents

Preface

Forbidden Family and Literary Tradition

Like other personal writings of distinction, *Forbidden Family* draws upon traditions of autobiography even as it enhances them. It is a love story, an account of a watershed experience, a memoir of wartime internment, an apologia, a confession.

Extraordinary circumstances throw ordinary people into the maelstrom, often with cataclysmic consequences. Margaret Sams, a thoroughly nice, wholeheartedly middle-class wife and mother reared in small-town California, deliberately violated the existing norms of her culture, her religion, and her society. Shortly after the bombing of Pearl Harbor, Margaret's husband, Bob Sherk, who had been working as a mining engineer for a Philippine company, enlisted in the American army, leaving Margaret and their three-year-old son, David, trapped in Manila. Although Bob survived the Bataan Death March, he (along with some 12,000 others) was incarcerated throughout the war in Cabanatuan, a Japanese military prison known as a "death camp" because of its unceasing atrocities and extraordinary mortality rate. Margaret and David, along with some 5,000 other citizens of America, Britain, and other allied nations, were soon rounded up and interned in Santo Tomás, the Japanese camp in Manila for civilians. There Margaret fell in love with Jerry Sams, another internee. In a defiant loss of innocence, she made a decision with irrevocable consequences. She chose to risk her life, her reputation, and all ties with her family in the States to bear and keep his baby. Nothing could be the same afterward. When Margaret had gained enough perspective to recognize the profundity of this watershed experience, she began to write this account.

Forbidden Family is a quintessential apologia, for it represents the author's defense of her commitment to a belief or value system (in this case the primacy of passionate love), and to its short and long-term consequences as expressed in her entire way of life. Like other apologists, the best known of whom is John Henry Newman in *Apologia pro Vita Sua* (1864), the author may be proud or defiant (Margaret is both), but is neither regretful nor apologetic. As Newman said of his own *Apologia,* for it to be "the true key to my whole life, I must show what I am, that it may be seen what I am not. . . . I wish to be known as a living [person], and not as a scarecrow which is dressed up in my clothes. . . . I now for the first time contemplate my course as a whole" (99–101). Margaret's sentiments exactly; to understand the message of her deep heart's core, she believes, is to understand her essence.

The autobiographer's life becomes the medium which is the message. Any author who is a good storyteller—Margaret is superb —by design shapes her experience to reinforce its central theme as it displays her character. As Siebenschuh observes of Newman's *Apologia,* "data often provide drama; dramatic choice is autobiographical statement. . . . [Yet] it is pointless to attempt to categorize [the work] as either data or drama, persuasion or poetry, as appealing primarily either to the reason or the imagination. . . . It makes a multiple appeal. It simultaneously humanizes, personalizes, persuades, and proves" (26). An autobiographical apologia narrating a love story is obliged to function on these simultaneous levels; what is humanized is persuasive. To the extent that the world (i.e., the readership) loves the lovers, it is likely to be persuaded of the merits of their case. But how far can a conventional audience be moved, if the autobiographer's values persistently violate accepted social and moral codes?

Egan points out in *Patterns of Experience in Autobiography* that an age-old narrative pattern emerges as the narrator "makes sense of events in his life by translating them into a mythic shape," a pattern that "begins in equilibrium, is disturbed by disequilibrium, and moves into a new equilibrium." This structure, common to myth, folklore, and confessional autobiography, describes a pattern of "separation, initiation, and return." By "making sense out of one life for others to understand," such an autobiography translates "the unique and inexplicable into the universal" (40–41).

Confession contains the potential for exculpation. Thus in confessing the most profound experience of her life by writing this memoir some five years after the fact, Margaret, Prodigal Daughter, hoped to write herself back into the community from which she had risked exile. This "fallen woman," "scarlet woman," as Margaret continually calls herself, confesses from, as Weintraub says of Rousseau, "a deep urge for self-justification" (298). She hopes, as Rousseau did, that by revealing her private experience to the public, not only her immediate family but posterity will come to understand, to approve, and even to love her "once the veils are lifted" from her inwardly troubled life (298).

Yet *Forbidden Family* is just now finding a public audience, nearly a half century after World War II affected the United States—and Margaret Sams—so profoundly. Several major changes have occurred in our nation's cultural and intellectual life that make this work of particular current interest. Various social and political movements, by and on behalf of women and minorities, have raised our national awareness of the importance of these groups and the individuals who comprise them. This new enfranchisement of women and minorities has changed the ways in which historians, writers, and sociologists (among others) understand and interpret our culture. The study of history no longer concentrates primarily on the activities of kings, generals, and archbishops; it now encompasses accounts of women and men, majority and minority, who participated in events large and small. Women's Studies has become an independent discipline, including among its concerns the interpretation of autobiographical accounts of a great variety of engaging, energetic women. The literary canon, until recently comprised primarily of belletristic works by and about Great White Men (and sometimes their wives), has been democratized to include a far greater variety of writings, among them autobiographies, memoirs, and diaries by all sorts of people. As Gertrude Stein said in beginning *Everybody's Autobiography,* "Alice B. Toklas did hers and now everybody will do theirs" (3).

Love stories have a perennial fascination, for narrator and audience alike. Yet for the autobiography of a bourgeois housewife to present such a candid acknowledgment of passion and sexuality is unusual before the 1960s even in times of peace; to my knowledge, *Forbidden Family* is unique among internment literature of World War II. Although Margaret's juniors who came of age in an era of casual sex may wonder what all the fuss was about, the author, writing with a mixture of guilt and defiance, love and pride, makes it clear why her transgression was horrendous according to her Christian value system and contemporary mores—and equally clear why she'd do it again.

Forbidden Family is not only of psychological interest, but of sociological interest as well. It shows how women played various roles (assigned and elected) in a captive community dominated by men, both the Japanese captors and the American executives. In themes that will be elaborated on in the Introduction and throughout the text itself, *Forbidden Family* anatomizes not only the experience of pregnancy and childbirth in captivity, but the efforts of a single mother to survive under conditions of stress and privation while caring for two young children. That Margaret was literally cut off from home and family, in addition to experiencing ostracism within the camp, balances love against alienation, defiance against the desire for social reintegration.

EDITORIAL PRINCIPLES

The text of this memoir is essentially as Margaret Sams wrote it. Any additions to the original text have been made by Margaret herself, in answer to my queries—usually to supply proper names to fully identify people originally alluded to, or to clear up unclear pronoun references. Nothing has been deleted except an occasional redundant word or phrase.

However, while the words are Margaret's, the punctuation is often mine—mostly apostrophes and commas, added or deleted to enhance the clarity of the text. I have routinely corrected misspellings and provided Tagalog or Spanish terms for transliterated native words in the original text. These emendations are not otherwise noted; any other changes are indicated by brackets [ ] in the text.

I have sought to maintain the integrity of the original text by including supplementary and explanatory material in footnotes rather than trying to incorporate it into the narrative itself. Thus some of the longer footnotes consist of supplementary material Margaret wrote in 1987 in response to a friend's request for more information, or afterthoughts she had when we were reviewing the typescript, page by page, or in still later supplements to early drafts of my footnotes. My previous research in editing Natalie Crouter's *Forbidden Diary: A Record of Wartime Internment, 1941–45* (Burt Franklin, 1980) and in writing articles on the experiences of civilian internees in Baguio, another Japanese camp in the mountains 100 miles north of Manila, during World War II (1980, 1987), has greatly enhanced my understanding of the subject. Of significant help have been extended conversations with former Baguio internees Daphne Bird, Fred Crouter, Natalie Crouter, the Reverend Carl Eschbach, James Halsema, Margaret and William Moule (and Moule's wartime memoir, *God's Arms Around Us*), Betty Rochfort-Boyd, the Reverend Joseph and Winifred Smith, and June Crouter Wortman. In the course of this research I have discovered a dozen other unpublished diaries, memoirs (including Fern Harrington Miles's *Captive Community*, printed by the author as *Forbidden Family* goes to press), and a novel, that corroborate and supplement published sources of information. These are cited as appropriate throughout the text.

Jim Halsema, retired Foreign Service officer and historian of

Baguio and World War II in the Philippines, was the matchmaker for this project. He introduced me to the typescript and ultimately to its author. In addition, he has read and provided information for the Introduction and notes, and made available to me once again the resources of his extensive library on Southeast Asia and World War II. He has also drawn the map that appears on p. xix. Alice Halsema, a cook and hostess in a class with Margaret Sams, kept us well-fed and happy while we worked. With impeccable timing, William L. Andrews, editor of Wisconsin Studies in American Autobiography, called to ask about my work within virtually the same week I'd told Margaret I'd edit her memoir if we could find an appropriate publisher. He has been consistently supportive of this project. Joanna Bowen Gillespie provided an expert reading of the manuscript. Barbara Hanrahan, humanities editor of the University of Wisconsin Press, has throughout our work treated author, editor, and text with a much-appreciated blend of enthusiasm, common sense, and critical acumen. Virginia Commonwealth University, through the good offices of Dorothy Scura, then-chairman of the English Department, and Elske v.P. Smith, Dean, College of Humanities and Sciences, provided research time and supplies that greatly helped my work.

Editors of texts by living authors assume risks that researchers of texts by authors safely entombed in libraries do not have to deal with. The author might write a later book that undermines her earlier manuscript. She might be difficult to communicate with, or turn into an antagonist rather than a collaborator during the editing. Or the author might regard the book as a monument to her own vanity, and impose a heavy hand on the editor's delicate sculpting. Although I would not knowingly undertake a project where these hazards were apparent, I believe these risks are worth the benefits of access to the author's firsthand knowledge and ability to interpret her experience in its cultural, social, and intellectual contexts.

In order to edit a text, I must believe the work is of literary merit and intrinsic worth; I must feel human sympathy with the author; and I must be free to do my own work my own way. No managed news. Fortunately, Margaret Sams has shared these views and our collaboration (much of it over the scrubbed birch table in Margaret's kitchen) has been frank, focused, fun—and incorporated into the interstices of already busy and engaged lives. In coming to know Margaret and Jerry Sams and their children and grandchildren (see Afterword), my sense of family has extended and expanded. To critics who argue that scholarly objectivity is lost if one comes to know and love one's subject, I would reply that no research or writing is objective, nor should it be. Serious work, like marriage, is serious love; one is committed to it for the extended duration, and a mixture of passion and good will makes the rough places plain. This collaboration, for the most part amazingly smooth, has been exhilarating to us both.

My husband, Martin Bloom, has been for me what Jerry Sams has been for Margaret. Our courtship and forbidden (yes!) marriage of thirty intense and happy years has furnished an analogous experience that enables an understanding of the heart of this text and the soul of its author. It has also given us a comparable investment in the treasures that are our own children, Bard and Laird, now doctoral students at MIT. One fringe benefit of our marriage is Martin's expert critique of my writing, another is his instruction in how to make sourdough rolls. Work on this book has been such a pleasure that I'm (almost) sorry it's done. Margaret's story has become part of my repertoire, like the sourdough start from her pioneer grandmother that has been incorporated into our family baking. Indeed, that vigorous memento makes the past a living present—a fitting symbol for the spirit that energizes this love, these lives in the work that follows.

L. B.

Storrs, Connecticut
December 1988

Margaret Sams's Acknowledgments

Without the pushing and prodding of our good friend, Robert Bonney, whom we met after the war, I would never have put pen to paper, even though I wrote this book with our children in mind.

Without the help of Robert Merriam I might not have survived the gestation period in Santo Tomás.

Without the insight and encouragement of Robert Kleinpell I might never have knuckled down to the inevitability of a long, long incarceration.

Without Robert Sherk I would never have gone to the Philippines and become friends with all these wonderful men.

Without the encouragement of Hal Greer, formerly of the Eleventh Airborne, I would not have taken this manuscript out of the drawer where it had lain for more than thirty-five years and tried to find a publisher for it.

Without the help of James Halsema, the book might not have been published; in addition to the many other ways in which he has been of assistance, he introduced me to Lynn Bloom, the editor.

I remain grateful, too, to the many other friends who also read this manuscript and encouraged me. The people acknowledged here had a profound effect on my life, and on the writing and publication of this memoir, and receive my unending thanks.

———————————

I would like to extend special thanks to Lynn Bloom. I am grateful to have had the benefit of her expertise in writing the Preface, Introduction, and Afterword to the manuscript and in preparing the notes. She was also responsible for finding the right publisher for the book.

Chicago Park, California
January 1988

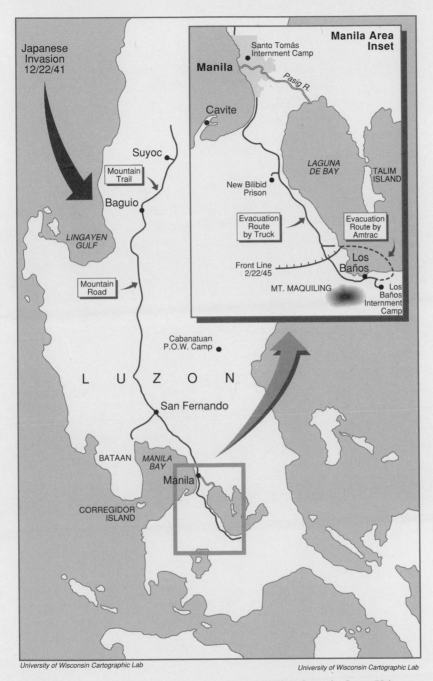

Japanese
Invasion
12/22/41

Mountain
Trail

Suyoc

Baguio

LINGAYEN
GULF

Mountain
Road

Cabanatuan
P.O.W. Camp

L U Z O N

San Fernando

BATAAN   MANILA
BAY

Manila

CORREGIDOR
ISLAND

**Manila Area
Inset**

Santo Tomás
Internment Camp

Manila

Pasig R.

Cavite

New Bilibid
Prison

LAGUNA
DE BAY

TALIM
ISLAND

Evacuation
Route
by Truck

Evacuation
Route by
Amtrac

Front Line
2/22/45

Los
Baños

MT. MAQUILING

Los
Baños
Internment
Camp

The Philippines and Manila. Map compiled from two maps drawn by James Halsema.

Forbidden Family

Introduction

Private citizens caught in a war are unintentional actors in a drama that is being scripted by remote hands even as they are enacting their roles. These private people, accustomed to the pre-war predictability of daily routine and established custom, no longer have recognized roles, determined by merit, competence, or privilege, let alone star billing. In wartime, the drama has moved off the stage and into the streets, where everyone, willing or not, becomes an actor. They must continuously improvise as the unprecedented unfolds.

Whatever these unwitting actors knew before the war, however they lived, must be readjusted, if not abandoned, to accommodate ever-new situations. In their search for stability as well as survival, they must continually cope with the ambiguous, the uncertain. Daily they must take risks unimaginable in peacetime. Yet as they acquiesce to the inevitable they must also assert their individuality, mold their new roles to the new shapes of their hungry bodies, their hearts. To fail is to kill the spirit. To fail is to die.

A confrontation between Japan and the United States had been building since the beginning of the twentieth century. At that time Japan moved into international politics with its victory over Russia in the Russo-Japanese War, three years after "the United States finally 'pacified' the Philippine Islands after a long and

3

bloody struggle which had begun as part of the Spanish-American War." Although the two countries had been on the same side during World War I, the competition between Japan and American allies for raw materials and trade markets in Asia escalated throughout the 1920s and 1930s, exacerbated by the Depression. In the 1930s, Japan, hungry for raw materials to feed its expanding industrial system and increasingly militaristic, moved into China and Southeast Asia, a potential threat to American economic and strategic interests in the Far East (Petillo xi). This threat intensified after Japan joined the Axis in 1940 and proclaimed the "Greater East Asia Co-Prosperity Sphere."[1]

As the political and military situation worsened in Asia in the late 1930s, the strategic importance of the Philippine Islands, significant in any event, increased dramatically. During the early years of American occupation of the Philippines, the United States expanded the Spanish naval bases of Cavite and Subic Bay, built Corregidor island into a fortress commanding the entrance to Manila Bay, and maintained modest army posts at Fort McKinley near Manila and Fort Stotsenburg, as well as an air corps base at Clark Field in central Luzon (JJH to LB 4/1/88). America intended to keep these even after the transition to Philippine independence (begun in 1935 and targeted for 1946) was attained, so critical were they in defending "air and sea lanes stretching from the northern Pacific through Southeast Asia and the Indian Ocean to the Middle East and Europe" (Shaplen 99). However, with military appropriations in disfavor at home, particularly during the Great Depression, little was done to modernize any of these facilities until much too late (JJH to LB 4/1/88).

American Far Eastern foreign policy at this time, directed from Washington with only limited firsthand understanding of how matters really stood (despite warnings from insightful journalist Edgar Snow and others), provided limited support for the nationalist Chinese fighting the Japanese invaders. Only sporadic attempts were made to counteract widespread domestic isolationism that undercut even minimal Congressional appropriations

1. James J. Halsema, hereafter JJH, to Lynn Bloom, hereafter LB, 4/1/88.

necessary for these activities. In the late 1930s, General Douglas MacArthur convinced president Manuel Quezon of the need for military forces to defend his country. Filipinos paid for the expenses of the handful of American advisers and the meager amount of obsolete materiel (such as World War I Lee-Enfield rifles and P–36 planes) and the basic training of young Filipinos that was begun. But these men largely returned to civilian life, reservists who could be recalled in a crisis, and an ineffectual force. Not until the formation of USAFFE (United States Armed Forces in the Far East) in mid–1941 were state-of-the-art American equipment, pilots, antiaircraft and tank units sent to the Philippines. However, between 1935 and 1941 the Japanese had continued their own military buildup, thereby increasing their military superiority over the forces intended to protect the Philippines (JJH to LB 4/1/88).

Although in tacit acknowledgment of the situation all dependents of American military personnel had been evacuated to the United States by early 1941, many other American civilians were reluctant to leave. Some had lived in the Philippines for decades; even for relative newcomers like Margaret and Bob Sherk, their jobs, their families, their homes and material possessions and opportunity for the good life were in the Philippines. The State Department advised the U.S. High Commissioner to the Philippine Islands, Francis B. Sayre, not to "give official notice that American civilians should leave the islands," and if they inquired about leaving, to "reply that no one at the time could foretell whether an attack would occur or, if so, when;" each individual citizen was to "decide for himself" (Sayre 153). The State Department's calculated evasiveness was an attempt to buttress its foreign policy; if Americans fled the Philippines, the Filipinos would feel betrayed by their erstwhile protectors. So, in effect, the American citizens who remained in the Philippines became hostages to national policy, including Margaret, who when she flew to Manila to inquire about whether to leave, was told to stay and not to worry.[2] These people were, as Sayre said, "entrapped" in

2. Margaret Sams, hereafter MS to LB 8/11/87.

the Philippines, itself an undefended, unprepared country, "with no way of escape" when on December 8, 1941,[3] World War II struck the islands with the Japanese bombing of American air fields (Clark, Nichols) in central Luzon, ships in port, and even a military rest camp at Camp John Hay.

The war changed utterly and irrevocably the lives of the protagonists of *Forbidden Family*, Margaret Sherk, 25; her husband Bob, superintendent[4] in a gold mine in Suyoc, 65 miles north of Baguio; and Jerry Sams, 30, an electronics engineer working at Cavite, the American naval base across the bay from Manila.

Margaret Coalson (born February 4, 1916), daughter and granddaughter of pioneer homesteaders, had traveled from her hometown of Beaumont, California, to Manila in 1936 to marry Bob, her hometown boyfriend—tall, dark, blue-eyed, clean-cut handsome. Both had worked their way through two years at Riverside (California) Junior College; Margaret's job mending books in the college library paid $15 a month (enough to cover her expenses if she lived on prunes and oatmeal), and was to serve her in good stead during the war. Like many other young, adventurous, hardworking Americans, Bob and his older brother, Jack, had been attracted to work in the Philippines by the pay and perks (housing, use of a company car, and recreation facilities), particularly because of the hard times at home. Bob, a mining engineer, began as a mine-shifter, "a white man who supervised the work of several dozen perspiring Filipinos who blasted, dug, and hauled the ore to the surface" (MS 2/12/87).

Within months, he had earned enough to send for Margaret; they were married in Manila on the night she arrived. Although she had loved college, an extension of her childhood pastime of reading books, her thoughts of becoming a librarian were sub-

3. Because of the day's difference demarcated by the International Date Line, at the 180th meridian.

4. The hierarchical order, top down, was: general superintendent, mine superintendent, mill superintendent, "shifter,"—all white men in the 1930s—and the Filipino natives who actually used the shovels. Today Filipinos fill all these positions (MS to LB 12/18/87).

ordinate to growing up and gaining independence. "Education was incidental," she admits, "I simply wanted to be a nice wife for someone, have a nice home, nice children and a nice husband. I also wanted to travel." The Sherks journeyed to the isolated mining camp at Nyac, 55 miles north of Baguio (itself 155 miles north of Manila), where Margaret was the only white woman in a community of diverse Filipino tribes that ranged "from the peace-loving Benguets to the head-hunting Bontocs." There she learned to accommodate to the varied cultures markedly different from the safe, predictable, middle-class life of California. With the help of Velasco, a Filipino boy-of-all-work, Margaret transformed the primitive mountain dwelling provided by the mining company into a home, whitewashing the walls, making curtains, baking bread. She set up a small clinic among the Igorots. The isolated newlyweds read a great deal, big boxes of books sent from Baguio and Manila, and Margaret learned for the first time the meaning not of fear (that would come later), but of horrendous loneliness. David, born in April 1938, solved that problem.

Two weeks after the war began, on December 22, massed troops of the Japanese army, under the direction of General Masaharu Homma, landed on Luzon, just north of the Lingayen Gulf, and rapidly marched southward, threatening to cut off Baguio from Manila. The American army warned the Sherks and the rest of the isolated enclave of American mining families at Suyoc, Mountain Province, where the Sherks had moved after David's birth, of the invasion and told them to get out while they could. The Americans were preparing to blow up the Mountain Trail, the only road to the south and what appeared to be safety. Anyone who stayed would be forced to flee north into the remote mountains, far from civilization (JJH to LB 4/1/88).

In Baguio, the Sherks joined the fleeing masses of native Filipinos, leaving their peaceful Shangri-la and heading south toward the chaotic metropolis of Manila, a city of 632,000 under siege by air. In their company car they took what they were advised to take—two suitcases of clothing (with a photograph album crammed into one) and a Christmas present for David. But no food, bedding, or medical supplies. Like other Americans, they thought the war wouldn't last long; "yellow peril" was a contradiction in terms. Like other Americans, they thought the Imperial Japanese Army would be a pushover for the invincible American troops, buttressed as they were by the "invincible fortress" of Corregidor. MacArthur, whom they trusted implicitly, had said so. But his assurance of victory was predicated on the assumption that the Japanese would be thoughtful enough to wait until April 1942 to attack—when his preparations would be complete (JJH to LB 11/21/87).

Momentous, even catastrophic, events often begin casually. In Manila, the Sherks, typical of wartime's displaced persons, were without a home, without friends, without employment, without money, except for the twenty dollars Bob had won in a poker game. They had banked all their savings in the States, and Manila banks were prohibiting withdrawals, in any case. Bob was patriotic and he needed a job to support his family; the Army was looking for engineers on Bataan. So off he went, newly inducted, on New Year's Eve, 1942, to meet his fate.[5]

"I felt as if I were a widow," said Margaret. "I was on my own, with no one on earth to protect David and me." A week later, she and David were interned by the Japanese on the campus of Santo Tomás University, in the process of being converted to a civilian internment camp for between three and five thousand people.[6] Thousands of people, accustomed to the privileges, free-

5. In 1942 some 14,000 American and Filipino survivors of the Bataan Death March were imprisoned by the Japanese in the infamous military prison of Cabanatuan, fifty miles northeast of Manila. Official U.S. Army historian Robert Ross Smith, quoted in manuscript in Vince Taylor's *Cabanatuan: Japanese Death Camp: A Survivors* [sic] *Story* (Waco, TX: Texian Press, 1985) says, "The [peak] total enrollment at Cabanatuan was approximately 12,000 Americans" (p. 179, n. 17). By February 1, 1945, the camp population had diminished to 516, all sick or maimed. Another 1,200 had been sent to Japan to work in Japanese mines.

6. The exact population of Santo Tomás, like that of other internment camps, fluctuated considerably, as internees were released to (or recalled from) hospitals, hospices, and private homes in the community, or transferred to other camps. Hartendorp's initial figures were provided by the Santo Tomás

dom, and elevated social status that automatically accompanied being white (unless one was a drifter, an alcoholic, a prostitute, or otherwise socially problematic) in a prewar oriental society, were dumped, with their pathetic baggage and crying children, into university classrooms, each expected to house 20–40 crammed-in people. Toilets were scarce and inadequate, and dining facilities were non-existent for months; people had to eat in the halls or outdoors because of lack of space. Once the children were in bed for the night (at 7 p.m.), their mothers had to share the common space—a hallway—with the guards. The "guards" in the annex were a few internee men—*not* Japanese—stationed there to provide the women with moral support and protection, if needed (supplied by MS to LB in phone conversation, 11/30/88). There was only one dim light, under which they read, knitted, smoked, talked. As everyone scrambled to find a niche, Margaret realized that she was without real friends—"I knew no one except the half dozen people from Suyoc." Yet she had to protect herself and her child in this indifferent, if not hostile, environment. Indeed, there was little choice if she and David were to survive, for the Japanese provided no food for the internees during their first six months of confinement.

Internees from Manila, especially white male business executives with money, friends, and former servants still living there in a partially functioning economy, had easy access to food, medicine, and the amenities (soap, needles and thread, flashlight batteries) that made confinement manageable. Such men comprised the central committee, the internees' governing body (see Stevens, 18–19). Though well-intentioned and hard-working, they saw camp life essentially from this privileged perspective. To those with money, a fee-for-service economy seemed reasonable; if someone cuts your hair, babysits your child, mends your shoes, you pay them. Those without money, however, do without.[7] With

---

executive committee cable to the American Red Cross, March 12, 1942; later figures were generated by the camp's internal census lists (see n. 27, p. 90).

7. This capitalistic organization was typical of most Japanese internment

no savings, no income, no mail for three years, no contacts on the outside, and no network of friends or allies inside, Margaret in her proletarian status had no resources except her own strength, skill, wit, and resilience. She was also very pretty.

There was no script, no model, and no rehearsal for the ever-changing role of wartime internee. Its uncertain configuration was dictated by the press of numbers (How many mothers and children could fit into how much space in the classroom converted to barracks? How many grams of rice was each entitled to when supplies grew scarcer and scarcer?); by the progress of the war (leniency toward the internees when the Japanese were winning, starvation and brutality when the Japanese were losing); and by Margaret's own strength and state of health at any given time. *Forbidden Family* illustrates, among other things, Margaret's resourcefulness in interpreting and playing her ambiguous role.

In all the camps every able-bodied person was assigned a job and expected to work anywhere between two and six hours a day, though many people, such as the camp officers, kitchen staff, and medical personnel worked more, while mothers caring for infants and young children had fewer formal duties. In Santo Tomás, for instance, providing meals and maintaining sanitation and health required the daily efforts of over six hundred people; the garbage detail was almost as popular as helping in the kitchen because of its proximity to salvageable scraps of food. Jobs were determined by camp needs, gender, and specialized skill or training, not by one's prewar social status. Thus women generally taught classes for children or adults, and served as clerks and

camps in the Philippines except Baguio, which by internee decision was communal with all services except dentistry (Baguio's only dentist was an uncompromising—and uncooperative—capitalist). However, Margaret says, "I never paid for David's or my haircuts, and no one baby-sat for me except once when I was in the hospital. I never had my shoes mended. I never saw a cobbler, and my shoes simply wore out" (to LB 3/31/88). For significant differences between the effects on internees of capitalistic and communistic social organizations, compare *Forbidden Family* with Natalie Crouter's *Forbidden Diary,* an account of the captive community of 500 Americans and British in Baguio internment camp.

stenographers; men dug and tended the camp vegetable garden and grounds, served on the patrol guard, and worked as porters, carpenters, and building custodians. Stevens proudly notes that "the vice-president of . . . a large electric supply house could be seen daily in one of the toilets gravely handing out the four sheets of toilet paper to which each candidate was entitled . . . [while] a bank manager [washed] dirty, bedbug infested mosquito nets . . . for months" (24–25).

Margaret's job was to mend camp library books. She earned 12½ cents apiece, enough to provide David's nursery school and supplementary food. She learned how to defend her few square inches of territory. She became skilled at trading and bartering. But as a single parent with a small child, she could never overcome the long hours of standing in line (a task couples shared) "to get your food, to wash your hair, to take a shower, to get soap—when they had any." David spilled everything he tried to carry—precious food—so Margaret could entrust him with nothing. Indeed, for the first nine months of the war she remained especially vulnerable psychologically, desperately isolated and alone amidst the hordes. Confinement and deprivation, like suffering, breed narcissism, and Margaret's world contracted to the narrow confines of Santo Tomás and her own immediate problems.

But in mid-September 1942 came a chance meeting with Jerry Sams, with cataclysmic consequences. Margaret thought him "one of the most handsome men [she] had ever met." His photograph, taken at the time with his clandestine camera—one of the countless contraband items with which he delighted in violating the rules—shows a handsome man indeed. Margaret learned that he had grown up in southern Illinois (Ava) and Chicago, that he had served in the Marine Corps (1930–31) and in the Coast Guard (1932–35), as a radio operator and later a member of the intelligence service. Before the war broke out he was employed by the Civil Aeronautics Authority; as a civil service employee of the navy he was working in 1941 as district engineer of the 16th Naval District in the Philippines. She also learned that he had a wife

in Albuquerque. Jerry learned that she had a husband, in Cabanatuan, and a son.

Jerry was an operator, a risk-taker, not content to accept a passive role in a rigid system. He made things happen, and he made
them happen his way. Inside the camp he broke and bent the
rules at will. Jerry connived and concocted a privileged existence
in camp, shared with a few, envied by many less resourceful than he.

The six months before Jerry was sent to Los Baños, another
internment camp under construction on the site of Los Baños
Agricultural College forty miles away, were in Margaret's opinion
"the only good months of the war"—certainly not from a military
perspective, but from her point of view as an internee. These
were the only months she was relatively well fed. The only months
she was able to relax. The only months she menstruated. Margaret was by nature a risk-taker herself. It was, after all, risky to
go halfway around the world, even to marry a sweetheart. It
was risky to live in an isolated mountain mining outpost in an
alien culture, far far away from family and friends where even the
amenities of middle-class America were over fifty-five miles away,
in Baguio.

But riskiest of all for Margaret, accustomed to filling wholeheartedly the roles of good girl, dutiful daughter, model wife,
and devoted mother, was to fall in love with Jerry Sams. Such
a love was the source of great moral conflict for Margaret, despite
the fact that with the onset of war most of the foundations of
her life and her sense of identity had vanished into an abyss of
uncertainty. She knew she was still married to Bob Sherk—a good,
honest man whom she might never see again. She could not deny
that she was also deeply in love with an imaginative adventurer
who tapped her passionate, romantic nature in many unexpected
ways. Still, marriage, she believed, was for life, divorce was "the
work of the devil," and adultery was unthinkable. A woman who
violated this prohibition was, in her opinion, "scarlet," wicked,
a pariah to be cast out of her family and shunned by society.
According to the double standard of the day, and the language
of *Forbidden Family*, the man escaped these strictures, the guilt,

and most of the responsibility. Thus the woman had a double burden to bear.

That Margaret chose to bear this burden, to violate her own deeply ingrained ethical sense, and to live with the consequences of her actions can only be partially explained by the exigencies of war. Her realistic appraisal of the uncertainties of war, "no one knew what the next day held; we might be dead, we might be liberated, anything might happen," may have been arrived at after the fact, perhaps even while writing *Forbidden Family,* to justify the *carpe diem* view that "Right now, this minute, is the important thing. Live it. Enjoy it if possible." This was surely a pragmatic policy for precarious times, and in clear conflict with her conception of marital fidelity. But there might never be another chance.

Extraordinary times encourage extraordinary risks. Margaret, in taking the chance, ran the risks and accepted the responsibility—first, for her passionate attraction to Jerry Sams, and second, for her desire to consummate their love by bearing their child. *Forbidden Family* registers honestly and movingly the difficult process by which she came to make these decisions, but it never pleads or seeks to excuse, for Margaret's motive in writing her memoir was not guilt but love, her love for Jerry Sams and for the daughter whom she bore under the most extraordinary of circumstances. This daughter deserved to know how and why she came to be born out of wedlock in a Philippine internment camp during the most dreadful days of World War II. She deserved to know how much her mother had wanted her, how far her devotion had taken her, and how convinced she had been through it all that this child was worth the ultimate risk.

The story of Margaret's resourcefulness and determination during her pregnancy is one of the most intimate and absorbing parts of her narrative. It is enough to say here that her patience and strength were rewarded on January 23, 1944, when Gerry Ann was born without complications in a Manila hospital, with an old Spanish doctor, wheelchair-bound, and Mickie, Margaret's sister-in-law, in attendance.

Rearing an infant in internment camp required constant ingenuity and improvisation. But once the baby's daily routine was established and her survival was assured—to the extent that anything was certain in the unpredictable arena of war—Margaret could concentrate on her next major problem, her relationship with Jerry. He had been separated from her, transferred to Los Baños, throughout her pregnancy. During the winter of 1943–44, Margaret had lost touch with him, and had not been able to inform him of Gerry Ann's birth. Remaining true to her own nature, Margaret had to take the risk and find out where she stood; and on April 6, 1944, when the baby was less than three months old, "against the combined advice" of Jerry's best friends, Margaret took her children and moved to Los Baños Internment Camp, forty miles southeast of Manila. Like many long-anticipated but uncertain reunions, the abrasive reality was a shocking contrast to the romantic expectations. The barracks were primitive, especially the open latrines, hot, dirty, malodorous, and full of flies. As the Japanese began to realize that they were losing the war, they took out their frustrations on the Los Baños internees through increased restrictions and harsher punishments. Internees throughout the Philippines were being starved to death during the last five months of the war, particularly during the final weeks when they endured 800 calorie-a-day diets. These consisted largely of lugao (gruel made from otherwise inedible rice grains, laboriously husked by the internees), and talinum, a slimy green spinach substitute, and resulted in numerous cases of beriberi, anemia, and other diseases caused by severe dietary deficiencies. The Japanese even murdered two internees, Pat Hell and George Lewis, caught in the act of returning to Los Baños after foraging expeditions during the camp's final desperate days (see pp. 248–49, 251; Arthur 145–46).

Under such repressive conditions a short-wave radio was invaluable for receiving broadcasts from territory controlled by the Allies. Such a radio was in the 1940s the principal means of contact with the outer world for prisoners, civilian or military, held incommunicado as the internees in the Japanese camps essentially were.[8] The internees in Santo Tomás and Los Baños, like prisoners everywhere, were starved for contact with the outside world, from which they were insulated as well as isolated by the Japanese policy of deliberately cutting off sources of information not under their control.[9]

Mail from abroad was infrequent, censored, restricted to the postcard-sized official forms, and consequently terse and uncommunicative–frustrating if not depressing to send and to receive. Many internees received no mail throughout the entire war; Margaret got only three letters, in the spring of 1944, after two years without word from home. The mail that did arrive was delayed intolerably; she received a letter telling of her father's death more than a year after the fact. The clandestine notes smuggled from one internment or prison camp to another carried with them the threat of death–to the sender, the receiver, and the intermediary. As *Forbidden Family* reveals over and over, these messages, too, were frustratingly brief, general, and uninformative.[10]

The Japanese tried hard to wear down their captives psychologically, by giving them whatever would depress, discourage, dishearten them. To get uncensored, "free" news became the internees' challenge. Shortly after their occupation of the Philip-

8. "Even radio was new enough that few Filipinos had one, and I imagine that even fewer Japanese had them. Not all Americans had radios either, in the United States in the 1930s" (MS to LB 12/18/87). "Today's prisoners can also use TV" (JJH to LB 11/21/87).

9. Even English language newspapers printed in Japan and more candid than the Manila *Tribune* were seldom allowed into the camps (JJH to LB 11/21/87).

10. Notes were smuggled between civilian internees in various Japanese camps in the Philippines (Santo Tomás, Los Baños, Baguio, Bacolod, Cebu, Davao, Iloilo), and between civilian internees and military prisoners. Notes were carried clandestinely by American POWs and Filipino truck drivers and others who traveled between two or more internment and/or prison camps. To write, smuggle, or receive a note could be punishable by death. It is not surprising that many of the notes were cryptic and conventional, almost formulaic; if discovered, the more noncommittal the notes were, the less likely their author and receiver would be identified and consequently punished.

pines, the Japanese tried to control access to the sources of news by ordering owners of all short-wave receivers (the only devices able to pick up outside broadcasts in English) to have their machines "reconditioned" by removing the short-wave circuits, though Filipinos (but not internees) could keep medium-wave receivers. The penalty for violation was death (JJH to LB 11/21/87, 4/1/88).

Yet the air over the Philippines crackled with short-wave signals. The Filipinos themselves had numerous short-wave receivers hidden throughout the islands. Until 1944, when the Japanese curtailed most contacts between Filipinos and internees, camp visitors and vendors smuggled in news when they entered Santo Tomás (and other camps to a much more limited extent) on authorized visits (Hartendorp II, 522–23).

But risk-taking internees, such as Jerry Sams and Dana Nance, the camp physician, preferred to go right to the source.[11] For Jerry, a clandestine radio filled many functions. As the provider of access to the outer world, the radio was therefore the source of some power—overt power to those few who knew the possessor, but far more covert power through his largely unrecognized (though perhaps suspected) capability of transmitting genuine information and rumors (or a mix of true and false) throughout his restricted world. The possessor of this power was therefore somewhat godlike; as a presence unseen but strongly felt, he could influence people, control moods, even provide an antidote to the captors' news and/or propaganda.[12] He became glamorous, because of both the power and the omnipresent danger of detection.

11. As did Jim Halsema in the Baguio camp, whom Nance designated to listen to his secret radio before being transferred to Los Baños.

12. Jim Halsema comments, "As noted here, an important objective in the use of secret radios at Santo Tomás, Los Baños, and Baguio was to combat Japanese propaganda by circulating news as 'more or less dependable rumors' and by confirming the validity of items in the Japanese-controlled media that the listeners knew to be true. We soon learned that Allied radios were occasionally guilty of slanting and suppressing unfavorable news (e.g., BBC's 'an orderly withdrawal to previously prepared positions' was a euphemism for 'an ignominious defeat'), and we checked KGEI (San Francisco) and BBC (London) against Radio Saigon and a Soviet-controlled station that continued to

The radio thus became the source of continuous excitement in an extremely regimented, routine existence. To have a radio was to have the potential to stir things up, for better or for worse.

Jerry Sams had an additional advantage. In addition to possessing a radio, he was one of the few people who knew how to build it, even how to make the tubes. "He asked for only one tube to be smuggled in from Manila," says Halsema in admiration. "Only an electronics genius could have built a radio (from innocuous materials in camp) that was capable of picking up signals from stations across the Pacific (to LB 11/21/87). Consequently, though Jerry was often on the outs with the camp central committee in Los Baños, since he was one of the few people who knew how to make something, otherwise unattainable, that they wanted and needed, he was usually insulated from their wrath. He could get away with a fair amount because the camp needed his expertise.

Jerry, with Margaret's help, was also adept at concealing the apparatus amid the ordinary paraphernalia of camp life. But it was also true that, for Jerry to have a radio somewhere in the family cubicle, along with radio parts and other forbidden items, was to keep Margaret in a state of continuous tension and fear.[13]

---

operate in Shanghai's International Settlement. Our dissemination of news was both exciting and a felt duty to camp morale."

Halsema adds, "In the final days of the war, especially after the American return to Luzon in January 1945, it was vital for camp leaders to know the tactical military situation so they could prepare to deal with it. For instance, after the Japanese guards left Los Baños, January 5-12, erroneously thinking an American invasion was imminent, the Camp Committee knew, because of information from Jerry's clandestine radio, that the Americans were not close enough either to rescue them or for the internees to attempt to escape to American lines. Consequently, they stayed in camp with no loss of life, and the Japanese returned on the night of January 13, after the false alarm was over" (JJH to LB 11/21/87).

13. "I did not really mind this. It was worth the tension to know what was going on 'outside.' Having a clandestine radio lost its savor after the bicycle incident [see pp. 266-68] and I was afraid Jerry would have to go over the fence" (MS to LB 12/18/87).

The barracks were subject to random searches which became more and more menacing as the Japanese military situation worsened, the internees grew hungrier, and the more civilized Japanese guards were replaced by Formosans, uncouth and unrestrained.

By February 1945, both Margaret and Jerry had been ill and hospitalized with bacillary dysentery, and were so weakened as a consequence of disease and starvation that "it was almost more than we could do to walk to the hospital." Their desperation was tempered, however, by the news that the Americans had landed on Luzon and were in Manila.

On February 22 heavy bombing began in the vicinity of Los Baños. And at seven in the morning on February 23, while the Japanese guards were unarmed and engaged in ritual calisthentics, the 11th Airborne paratroopers could be seen "gracefully floating down out of a blue-blue sky." By three that afternoon every one of the 2,122 internees, one only three days old, had been evacuated with no loss of life either to themselves or their rescuers, in a raid so successful that it is to this day studied in military history as a classic example of how to do everything right (JJH to LB 11/21/87). Flanagan explains the strategy of this amazing demonstration of military skill and efficiency:

> On the surface the plan was relatively simple: surround the camp during the night before the raid with a force of some 60 [Filipino] guerrillas and 30 U.S. 11th Airborne reconnaissance men; drop a parachute company of about 125 men a few hundred yards from the compound at first light of dawn; have the recon platoon and the guerrillas attack the guards around the camp as soon as the first parachute opens; bring in a battalion (less the parachute company) in amtracs across a large lake and move it the two miles overland into the camp, arriving a few minutes after the parachute drop; round up the internees and transport them back across the lake to U.S. lines; then bring out the attacking force (10–11).

Flanagan reminds us that although the "plan sounds uncomplicated, the execution easy," the raid had to take place 25 miles behind Japanese lines, where thousands of Japanese troops lurked within "marching distance" of Los Baños. "Nevertheless," he exults, "it worked. The paratroopers, the guerrillas, and the recon platoon hit the camp in unison; they wiped out the guards or sent them scurrying to the hills; they rounded up the internees and forced them . . . to move swiftly to the amtracs" (11).[14] As a result of "intricate and resourceful staff planning," disciplined and experienced troops, "heroics by fractious guerrilla bands," and tactically sound ground command, the strategy, under the aegis of Major General Joseph M. Swing, worked without a hitch. Even under extreme time pressure to remove to safety the "excited, hilarious civilians, suddenly free and unaware of the dangers" before the Japanese troops in the area retaliated, the raid was completely successful.

Their survival assured, Margaret and Jerry had other problems to cope with immediately, some large, some small. In what condition would Bob, a POW since the Bataan Death March, emerge from three years of torture and starvation in a Japanese military prison? Would he be too frail psychologically to cope with a divorce? Could Margaret ever make peace with Bob, or atone for having hurt him? Even if both spouses agreed to divorce their partners, what assurance did Margaret and Jerry have that their liaison, which bore the cachet of being both clandestine and risky, would survive once the pressures and privations of wartime internment were removed? What would the effects of a predictable, unromantic, workaday existence be on this adventuresome couple? Would Margaret and Jerry ever be able to gain for their forbidden family the social sanctions she so desperately desired?

14. "Armored . . . amphibious, road-running tractors . . . [which] carried a crew of three men, mounted .50 caliber and .30 caliber machine guns on pedestals on the front, were powered by a 9-cylinder aircraft engine mounted forward of the guns, and could carry up to a platoon of fully loaded soldiers with all of their ancillary equipment in the open bay," including jeeps or howitzers. "On land they lumbered along at about fifteen miles per hour, but on water they slowed to a five-mile-per-hour wallow, churning up a wake of white water and making an ear-thumping racket that precluded an undetected arrival. Their only hope for anonymity, secrecy, and privacy was surprise" (Flanagan 131).

Would Margaret's mother welcome home her prodigal daughter? Would her sisters and brothers, some of whom were still away at war, and who knew and liked Bob, receive the new couple into the family? *Forbidden Family* answers these questions, and does so in memorable fashion. Written nearly forty years ago to explain herself to her daughter, the autobiography of Margaret Sams testifies today to the heroism and dignity of an American woman who not only survived the harsh test of war but who forged out of its grim necessity a new understanding of the person she was—and was proud to be.

The Wartime Memoir
of Margaret Sams, 1941–1945

LOS BAÑOS INTERNMENT CAMP

WITHIN THESE GROUNDS UP TO THREE THOUSAND AMERICANS AND OTHER NATIONALS OF THE FREE WORLD WERE INTERNED BY THE JAPANESE MILITARY, SUFFERING GREAT PHYSICAL PRIVATION AND NATIONAL HUMILIATION FROM MAY 14, 1943, UNTIL LIBERATED FEBRUARY 23, 1945, BY THE AMERICAN FORCES UNDER GENERAL DOUGLAS MacARTHUR.

FEBRUARY 1954

AMERICAN ASSOCIATION OF THE PHILIPPINES

Prewar

For two specific reasons I have wanted to write Jerry's and my story. First, we think, it is a love story deserving the name. Second, it may help our children judge us a little more dispassionately when the time comes. Until then, we can only show them by word and deed that our love has been good; therefore we should not be judged in haste. At the same time we hope to teach them that living according to the established rules and regulations of our society most certainly has its compensations and advantages.

I want to make it very clear that we offer no apologies or excuses for our actions during the years we spent in Japanese internment camps. What I do apologize for, humbly, is my lack of writing ability. After having been liberated for seven years many small incidents have left my mind. I think it is time to write our story if I'm ever going to.

Parts of our story will come as a complete surprise to some of our friends and all of our acquaintances—for which I am indeed sorry, but I will not tell the story unless it is all told, and honestly told.

The first few pages of this story I have written for only one purpose: to calm the fevered brows of some dear friends. These friends felt that I was doing myself and my readers (if it ever comes to that) an injustice in not letting them see a bit of my own background before the war years, as a possible means of showing what may have led up to the internment camp experiences. Frankly, I think I have done myself an injustice in writing them, for the war years were the interesting and exciting years, the years people might possibly want to read about. I seem to me to have been a singularly uninteresting, dreamy, romantic, even a silly girl.

Presumably, from my forebears who each generation went a little farther west, I have inherited an instinctive desire to see all, hear all, taste all, smell all; in other words, I have inherited an itchy foot. My mother likes to quote me, at the tender age of four, as saying, "Mama, every time I see a train I just want to get up and go." It is a desire still unquenched. The desire burned strongly in my grandparents when they died at a ripe old age. Perhaps it will still be as strong in me when I die. I recognize it in our children already. It is born of many things: a desire to see, to know a little more, to understand more fully. To have seen, and to be able to remember and to picture far places in one's mind's eye, is the only thing that cannot be taken away from us on this earth. Senility even robs some of us of that quiet joy. It is, unquestionably, a desire for the romantic, the unpredictable, the unusual. The popular conception of this desire is "escapism," I believe, with which conception I do not necessarily agree. It's a desire to get all from life that there is to be had in one short lifetime. It is an instinct over which I have had very little control, nor have I wished to control it. Rather, I have fed it with daydreams, with hopes, plans, and all the reading which I could possibly cram into an otherwise full day.

I was born in Oklahoma, as a far-reaching result of my great grandfather's desire to go west when that territory was opened up. He had raced that day in April 1889, along with the other hundreds, but the new adventure held him for a while only. A few years later California called him even farther west. When I was nine months old, my own father and mother went to Colorado, which at that time was being opened up for homesteaders. When I was five my parents were convinced that opportunity lay even farther west and we too went to California where we remained during my formative years of grammar school, high school, and junior college. Here again my desire for strange sights, sounds, smells was being fed, for we lived in a small Southern California town, on Route 66, and always, day after day, year after year, people traveling to adventure, to the unknown, to the beautiful, were always before my eyes.

Until 1933 my life had been that of a very average, very ordinary, small-town Southern California girl. A little more strict, in some respects, and a little more protected and sheltered; my viewpoint was narrow, but no more so than that of most of the other townspeople. I thought then that my home town [Beaumont, California] was probably a very good example of any small town in the United States. Since then I have completely reversed my opinion. It was a very good example of any small Southern California town, within a radius of a very few miles, that is. We were brought up with no prejudices. We had no racial or religious problems. Most of us went to one or another of the seven or eight small churches of which our town boasted. There were no people who were too poor to go to school. With one or two possible exceptions there were no people wealthy enough to send their children away to boarding schools. Mexicans went to school with white children. I don't ever remember hearing a discriminating word against them. All of us in a freshman history class chose names of children in foreign countries to whom we were to write "to cement better foreign relations." All through high school I corresponded regularly with a Japanese boy who wrote beautiful letters, in not too good English, and from whom I received several small gifts.

From a scenic point of view our town was beautiful. There were spring days when the surrounding mountains looked so close and so lovely that one ached to be able to paint them, at the very least walk to the top of them. Those mountains have put something into my soul that only mountains can satisfy. The years I have spent away from them, I have missed them much more than the people with whom I grew up. Today I can see those mountains in my mind's eye, and I can almost smell the clean oak-and-sycamore-tree fragrance of them. I can see the vacant lots in town, golden with poppies, and I can remember searching the roadsides for the elusive "Johnnie-jump-ups," and I can hear the birds saying "Bob-White, Bob-White" as I walked across a well-worn path. Those were lovely years in retrospect, and the things I seem to remember most are the colors that surrounded us. The heavenly pinks and whites of the peach and cherry orchards in bloom, the wonderful perfume of the narcissus that bloomed around the foot of the almond tree on my birthday. It always rained that day and I can hear the drip-drip of it yet, and I can smell the pungent smell of the wet eucalyptus leaves which the rain always brought out. Who could forget, who has seen it, the glistening white world that we found the morning after a snow—white from the top of the mountains right down to our very door steps? The snow never lasted more than a day or two, but it was doubly appreciated (by the children anyway) because of its short life.

I remember the color, and feel, and smell of the fog which came regularly and at a given season every year. As a matter of fact, the foggy weather usually came at the right time to split and ruin the glistening red cherries which hung thick and heavy on the overburdened trees. Two cents a pound we got for picking cherries, and I can still feel the soft powdery dirt that settled all over one, from one's head to one's heels. I loathed it then, the being dirty part of picking cherries, but there was something wonderfully satisfying about sitting on top of a ladder in a leafy green world, with nothing to do but pick and eat cherries (to say nothing of trying to tear up and hide the spurs that one inadvertently broke off) and to dream about the many wonderful things that could be bought with the cherry picking money. The Depression was a part of a way of life, and could not affect nor alter the beauty that one found on all sides of one.

And there was the library. I wonder if Mr. Carnegie could possibly have known what his gifts were to mean to the world? To me there was no other place that could compare with our town library. It was here that I could find anything I wanted. The street was lined with acacia (soft and feathery yellow in spring) and olive trees, and it was on the way to the library that I learned my first four-letter, ugly words. Words written boldly on the sidewalk with the juice of young olives. Who writes words like that, I wonder, and when? If one is a girl one pretends not to see them. The cool quietness of the library is something never to be forgotten. The floor, the tables, the librarian's desk, all gleamed with a well-polished look that was a joy to behold. The rows and rows of books beckoned one. And there was always a perfect bouquet on the desk. The art of flower arrangement should be taught every librarian. The feeling of contentment, of *belonging* that I found in that library would warm the cockles of Mr. Carnegie's heart. Not long ago I visited that same library, and my childish memories have not played me false. It is still a lovely world, a refuge, inside that building.

There is much more social life in a small town than a city-dweller is ever willing to believe. School and its associated operettas, plays and athletics (which I took terribly seriously), church, wiener roasts, moonlight rides on the desert, picnics, bicycle rides, books, and baby-sitting played a major part in my life for several years, but there was always time to dream the inevitable dreams of the teen-ager. How was I ever going to meet the "right man" in our small town? He was not among the boys I dated, there was no question about that. I had the usual crushes, but instinctively I seemed to know that they were temporary things, merely a preface to the big affair for which every girl longs. I dreamed of a man, not a boy, and a man who would not be contented to live in our town the rest of his life. All the boys I knew seemed perfectly satisfied to work in service stations. As a matter of fact, I know now that they were very *glad* to work in service stations, just as I was glad to baby-sit whenever some Depression-ridden parent could afford the fifty cents it took to pay me for an evening's sitting. To the boys, as well as to me, it meant the difference between having a class ring, or a year book, or an extra pair of shoes. Who knows, perhaps to the daydreaming boys I seemed perfectly contented to baby-sit for the rest of my life.

For years it had worried me that I had no burning desire to be any particular thing when I grew up. I simply wanted to grow up and be a nice wife for someone, have a nice home, nice children, and a nice husband. I also wanted to see things. It is only now, since I am older and have a bit of a sense of perspective, that I am no longer ashamed that I never did want to be anything except what I am: a wife and a mother. However, since I had made up my mind that I was going on to college after I finished high school, I did a little soul-searching and decided that I wanted to become a librarian. In the fall of 1933 I entered Riverside (California) Junior College. I wanted to go to school, not so much for an education's sake, I am bound to admit, but for the sake of getting out of the nest, for the sake of trying my own wings, having to work, for the sake of seeing new faces and hearing new names. Not that I dared say any of that to my family, of course. Education was incidental, I shamefully admit.

In those Depression days, girls going away to school were taking all sorts of jobs. The most popular one, at that time, was working for one's room and board. One registered with the dean of women, who had applications from various and sundry women in town who wanted a built-in baby-sitter and mother's helper, all for the price of a bed and an extra mouth to feed. For many of the girls it worked out beautifully, but for me it did not. I was "placed" with a Mrs. Haufman. I hated the entire four-month sojourn, though I had to admit that I was seeing another side of life, and I was learning things I would never otherwise have known. Mrs. H. was an excellent cook, but pickled herring I still do not care for. Mrs. H. was deaf, and so naturally talked very loud. She and her husband did a great deal of quarreling, and discussions of all aspects of their private life I could not help overhearing. Undoubtedly there have been many worse first experiences away from home, but I dreamed about mine for months after I was gone.

The fact that I am stubborn and that I had met Bob kept

me from quitting school. Not that I hadn't known Bob Sherk most of my life, for we had gone to school together for several years. But that first day at college when I felt a complete alien, I had seen one familiar face out of the milling hundreds and it was exquisite relief to walk up to someone I knew and say "Hi." Bob had felt very much the same way, apparently, and from that day on we saw each other more or less regularly. We had dated a time or two in high school, but had found no mutual likes or dislikes except each other. Now, all at once, I saw Bob with different eyes. I found that he too wanted to see the world, that he wasn't contented to stay in our small town and work either for his father or in a service station, that he too loved to read and dream. Romances have started with much less. Ours was not the fiery kind, but it was good and solid and comfortable. We knew that we would have a good life together, for our aims and ambitions and dreams were synonymous. We'd have several nice, healthy, intelligent children. Bob was working toward a degree [in mining engineering]. He was tall, with dark hair and blue eyes, a nice smile, a good student, and an excellent football player. He had to work, as almost all of us in school did, and it was not what I call a picnic. He and several other boys were batching together. Occasionally, on my afternoon off, I'd meet him down town and we'd go to a movie. We each paid our own way, naturally.

When I quit working for the Haufmans and the dean of women asked me if I'd like to go to work in the library for fifteen dollars a month, I was elated. I rented a room not too far from Bob's and lived the rest of the year, almost literally, on prunes and oatmeal, which I decided had the most food value for the least money.

Bob's and my courtship progressed slowly, but on a good sound basis. Occasionally I went to a dance with one of the other college boys, because Bob did not want to break training rules. We loved the wonderful spring days and took our full quota of cuts (as who hasn't on wonderful spring days?), took our books and a nickel hamburger apiece to the park, and read and talked and slept in the sun. The second year of school was much the same, except that we had decided that four years of school were much too long to wait to be married. We did a few foolish things that year, but on the whole got the maximum enjoyment out of the moment, I think, and we lived on a minimum amount of money. That was the year that Bob and the boys with whom he lived "borrowed" a hundred-pound sack of potatoes from a vegetable market. My conscience hurt me very little, as I recall, for my stomach was much too eager to be comfortably full and I was only too glad to cook them a dozen different ways for the boys, as long as I could have a share. That was also the year Bob bought a Model T Ford which ran nicely on level ground, but would go up a hill no way except backward. Bob got a gold football that year, which I very proudly wore. I won a letter and a gold-and-pearl encrusted pin on my own athletic ability. Those were good years for us, in spite of the Depression which Mr. Roosevelt said was over.

Between terms I had my first long trip alone, and my first trip to San Francisco. In those far-off days, baby-sitting paid fifty cents a night, no matter how long the nights were, but I finally saved enough money to visit my great-grandmother (with whom I had corresponded since I was a little girl) and my mother's cousin, an artist, who lived in San Francisco. I couldn't have been more pleased with a trip and I couldn't have had a better guide. Dorothy and all her friends went out of their way to help me have a good time, and I felt as if I were in the never-never land. There was only one thing wrong with it. I had to begin to grow up and evaluate what I had always known, and what I was seeing for the first time. I had grown up among hard-working people who believed in a way of life that was entirely foreign to the life I saw in San Francisco. The people whom I was seeing were artists and I felt completely the country cousin, completely gauche. I was more determined than ever to see more of the world (not that I particularly wanted to be a part of it, I only wanted to know about it), to see plays, hear concerts, do the things that I heard them talking about in San Francisco, for I loathed being talked down to. I should have missed Bob more than I did, but I was completely absorbed in being a sponge. I soaked in impressions at every pore. I saw Fleishhacker Park, where Dorothy had just completed a mural which I thought very good, all the art museums, the aquarium, the flower market at four o'clock in the morning, from which I went home with seven dozen roses contributed by generous growers. An aunt of my mother's grew flowers for the market, hence my trip into a world that was otherwise inhabited only by growers and large wholesale buyers. I went to Seal Beach, to Mills College to see a group of aesthetic dancers, to Fisherman's Wharf, to Chinatown for my first bird's-nest soup, to Italian restaurants, to French restaurants, and back to the Hill where Dorothy and her husband (a sculptor) and so many of their friends lived. Just to round out the picture, years later, in Santo Tomás, I met a woman from San Francisco who had known Dorothy and her husband when they were all artists together in that strange Bohemian world which I still do not entirely understand.

Because of a war which was being fought when I was born, for reasons which are already vague to my generation, the pattern of Bob's and my life was to take a shape which I would not have recognized as anything except someone's wildest imagination. Because of a man who fought in that war, a man of whom I had never heard until Bob and I became engaged, I was to meet another man in another war, and the pattern was to be altered again.

Bob's Uncle Pat was sent to Manila during the first world war, and of that phase of his life I know nothing. Eventually, when I knew him, he was middle-aged, of average height, piercing blue eyes, sandy complexioned, and he had a will of iron. Because he too had had dreams and ambitions, and saw opportunity there, and because he stayed on after the war and eventually "married the country," both [his nephews] Jack, Bob's older brother, and Bob had grown up with an insatiable desire to see the Philippine Islands. Uncle Pat had realized many of his dreams, why couldn't they? Pat was a self-educated man with a brilliant mind. Over the years he had attained a great deal of wealth through hard work and a keen knowledge of when and what gold-mining stocks to buy. As I understood it, he believed the Philippine Islands were no place for a white woman. He put all women in one class, I was told. They all took to bridge tables, drink and amahs [nursemaids]. Much later I believe I finally convinced him that there are exceptions to that rule.

During our second year at school, Jack came home from the Philippine Islands where he had been for two years. Jack was a great deal like Bob in a sandy-complexioned way, and (to us) he simply reeked of success. He bought a car, he bought clothes, he went everywhere and did everything that Bob and I would have liked to do. Among other things, he got himself engaged to Mickie, a tall, very thin, dark-haired nurse. Mickie was a few years older than I was, and eons ahead of me in experience, and I always felt most ineffectual around her. No doubt I seemed like a child to her, and as a result, there was no basis on which we could form a friendship.

Jack was certain that Bob could get work as a mine-shifter in the Philippines. Many new gold mines were being developed at that time, and there was quite a demand for mine-shifters. A mine-shifter, in most cases, was a white man who supervised the work of several dozen perspiring Filipinos who blasted, dug, and hauled the ore to the surface. A mine-shifter had many other duties as well, but these were foremost. The mines never shut down, which meant that every eight hours a new crew and a mine-shifter went down in the mine to take their turn. Every two weeks the shifts were rotated, for everyone hated "graveyard," as the eleven-to-seven shift was called. A mining degree helped a man, but it was not essential to success if one were intelligent and a diligent worker. We were much too excited about the possibility of a job to pay too much attention to Jack's oft repeated "get as much education as you can, while you can." We began to make concrete plans immediately, since Jack promised before he returned to the Islands to send enough money for Bob's passage in the very near future. The money was to be repaid as soon as Bob had a job, and the job he was to get on his own. In the meantime, as soon as school was out, he was to get some firsthand mining experience. This was a rather stiff assignment, but he did manage to spend a few weeks with an old "desert rat," the only mining man we knew, and he did do some "panning" up around Coarse Gold. True to his word, Jack sent the money and Bob sailed for Manila early in January of 1936.

I was desolate for a while after Bob left, for I had no desire to go back to school. Work is an antidote to almost anything, and after I went to work in a doctor's office, with an occasional evening of baby-sitting for the sake of variety, I was kept busy and more or less happy. I am convinced that sooner or later all knowledge that one acquires is put to use, for the following year I put everything that I had learned at the doctor's office to good effect by establishing a small clinic of sorts among the Igorots in the Mountain Province of the Philippine Islands. I was the first white woman most of them had ever seen. Eggs, bananas, and good faith were my reward.

Bob wrote wonderful letters which were full of strange words and echoes of strange sights and sounds. I didn't do a great deal of living that year, merely put in time until I too could go to the Philippines. I read everything I could find on mining camp life. Mrs. Overbeck's book is a classic on life in a mining camp and can be enjoyed by all, whether one has ever seen a mining camp or not.[1] Many years later, after she was dead, I was to become acquainted with her husband in the best place I know of to get acquainted with people, an internment camp.

Bob had been gone for several months when the letter arrived which said that the future was secure enough for him to take a chance on my coming also. Having been born in 1916, it was inevitable that the Depression of the 30s made a tremendous impression on me. I was at an impressionable age and yet it did not make me, as it did so many others, willing to give up my

1. Alicia O'Reardon Overbeck, *Living High: At Home in the Far Andes* (New York: Appleton, 1935). A geologist's wife recounts her experiences in Bolivia.

heritage of boundless opportunity for that detestable word—
SECURITY—as it is known and understood by the great majority
of people. I was delighted to take a chance on our future.

For the next several months after the arrival of Bob's letter,
with my steamship passage included, my feet never quite touched
the ground. Nothing was quite real, it was a storybook sort of
world. Everything required of me then was new and different.
A birth certificate, a passport with the magic name Washington,
D.C., on it (in those days that name still held magic), visas must
be acquired for my entry into Chinese and Japanese ports, a new
vaccination and inoculations of various kinds must be had, trunks
bought, clothes bought, parties given and received, sheets and
napkins must be counted and packed, the silver must be chosen,
the old beaus must be kissed "good-bye," and then another trip
to San Francisco, with my family this time, where letters, tele-
grams, and red roses were waiting to wish me bon voyage.

There were a few qualms at the last moment, as I recall. My
father had said very little about my going so far away from home
and, although I knew he hated it, I hadn't realized until he held
me in his arms, there in my tiny cabin, just how disturbed he
was. My father was the least demonstrative of men. He didn't
have tears in his eyes even then, but he was trembling as he kissed
me. He still said nothing to unsettle me, but nothing could have
sobered me more. He was a rock upon which I had always leaned,
almost unconsciously, the most dependable of all people. Because of his wonderful example (as well as the fact that I think
I must have been very blind) I had a completely false conception of the world. I thought that, with a few exceptions, all men
were more or less like my father and his friends, that all boys
would naturally be like them, once they became men. My father
and his friends never showed anger or swore in the presence of
ladies. Honest to the nth degree, courageous, strong physically
and mentally, virile, he loved to hunt and fish, wouldn't have
considered telling any woman except his wife (in strictest privacy,
of course) an off-color story; in short, my father was a man in
the very finest sense of the word. We were never allowed to dis-

cuss our neighbors in our home. It was assumed, apparently, that people were all doing their best; therefore they were not to be discussed, let alone censured. There were a few unstable characters around town, and I knew they were not in the least like my father, but I thought they were exceptions in the world. It wasn't brought home to me for years that my father and his kind were the exceptions.

I was on the high seas and plenty seasick before I had time to wonder, seriously, if I were on the right road. Did Bob still really want to marry me, did I really want to marry him, was he changed, would I be sorry for the decision I had made? Mickie had gone several months before, and apparently was quite happy and contented there, but Mickie and I were not at all alike.

A sea voyage is a liberal education in itself and mine was no exception. There is nothing else that can be compared with it. There is especially nothing like one's first sea voyage. I was putty and everything left a thumbprint. There were beautiful days, dull grey days, stormy days, and there were days when the water was like beautiful green glass with not a ripple on it. There was deck tennis on the top deck with the captain, shuffle board, bouillon, hot and savory, served on the deck at ten o'clock in the morning, and there was tea every afternoon. One day we saw the Aleutian Islands off in the distance, cold and forbidding-looking. There was the inevitable romantic young man who wrote love letters and pushed them under my cabin door, and there was a handsome Englishman of whom I couldn't help being very much aware. There were days when porpoises played, and once there was a spout of water on the far horizon which meant that a whale was there. I had an indescribable feeling as we passed a ship in the night.

The first sight of the Japanese Islands was exhilarating, for the islands looked like tiny, floating, thick pieces of emerald moss. Our first Japanese city was Yokohama, and then came Tokyo with its unmistakable sound of clickety-clacking wooden-soled sandals. In their bright kimonos, the Japanese women were pretty as they hurried along the streets, many of them with babies strapped to their backs. I had dinner in Tokyo at the Imperial Hotel (with the entrancing Englishman, to whom this was old stuff), and I shall never forget it because it was my first experience at hearing many languages being spoken on all sides of me. Until that time I had heard only American-English and Mexican spoken—for I knew not a soul in my small home town who wasn't at least a second-generation American. This night a different language was being spoken at each table around us. For the first time in my life I felt that I was really seeing and hearing the things that I had always longed to see and hear. It did not matter in the least that I could understand (with some slight difficulty) only the man with whom I was sitting. It simply added to the glamour of the setting. The beautifully dressed men and women, the surroundings, and the fact that for the first time in my life I was in a foreign country did the rest. There are no taxi drivers who can compare in speed with the Japanese. We were rushed madly from one place to another in outmoded Rolls-Royces, and we could never make them understand more than "maru," which means ship. This, to the taxi drivers, meant that we were tourists; therefore, we were to be shown the sights with thoroughness and dispatch.

Kobe came next, and it had no market which I did not investigate and enjoy. We crossed the China Sea on an unforgettably lovely night, with the moon coming up out of the sea and a square-sailed Chinese junk sailing across the moon's silver path. Who can remember Shanghai without remembering its glamour and its horrible smells, and its tall Sikhs who gave one a wonderfully protected feeling, and who can forget the beauty of Hong Kong with its good substantial British buildings, and who can forget the misery and hunger that stared up at one from the faces in the sampans which clustered thick as leeches around our ship? And who can forget the horror of the first rickshaw ride, for to me it was horrible to sit there and realize that this poor thing running his heart out for me was a human being—just as I was? I had to stop my packing, the night before we arrived in Manila (almost a month since we had sailed from San Francisco), to go up on deck and watch the most beautiful sunset of my life. I am certain that I shall never see another one to compare with it. In that land of beautiful sunsets, the heavens were a magnificent panorama of color. The beauty of it lingers with me yet. Tomorrow, it seemed to say, a whole new life is before me. Jack, Mickie, Uncle Pat, and Bob were waiting for me the next day as we slid gently into our berth at the "longest pier in the world," and I could not possibly know the heights and the depths of emotion I was to reach there in that land so far away from my native land.

I had gone to the Philippines expecting to live in Baguio.[2] I believe it is still called the summer capital, and it was a most beautiful small city. Bob was working as a mine-shifter at the largest gold mine in the islands, which was very near there. Shortly after I arrived, he was offered a job on a prospect more than a hundred kilometers up the Mountain Trail—back in the "boondocks." We felt that it would be a wonderful opportunity for him to get needed experience in his profession; there was a raise in it for him, and he would be his own supervisor. He accepted with alacrity.

My first experience with a typhoon came shortly after we arrived in Baguio, but I've always thought that growing up on the edge of the desert stood me in good stead, for neither a typhoon nor a hurricane (I've since lived in Florida, which is the land of hurricanes) has ever seemed any worse than the winds we had every fall; and where I came from people just said "hmmm—

2. Baguio was then and remains the lovely summer capital of the Philippines, 155 miles (a five-hour drive in the 1940s) from Manila. Ringed by the Luzon Mountains and nearly a mile high, with a temperate climate far more comfortable than Manila's summer heat, it was particularly healthful—free of malaria because anopheles mosquitoes do not live at that altitude. Its 1940 population of 24,117 included 21,857 Filipinos, 1,213 Japanese and Chinese, and 449 whites, mostly Americans, with a few British and Spanish. The nearby mining communities, of which Itogon, Benguet, and Balatoc were three, had a population of 35,179, of whom 345 were Japanese or Chinese and 115 white (*Census of the Philippines, 1939.* I, part 3, Manila, 1940).

quite a breeze today, eh?" Hurricanes and typhoons are much more uncomfortable, because rain goes with them. And what rain! We waited in Baguio for weeks after the typhoon was over before the trail was cleared and we were able to go up the mountain toward our future home. On the way up we learned why it had taken weeks to clear the trail, for in the first place, it was a trail in every sense of the word, and in many, many places the road had been entirely obliterated by half a mountain falling down across it.

At that time we knew nothing about mud, but we learned, the hard way, never to leave the prospect without several boys, each with a shovel. We learned to go prepared for the inevitable, and I always went with plenty of reading material to while away the hours of pushing, hauling, lifting and shoveling that it took to get us out of the prospect on to reasonably solid ground. And what a hue and cry they made, those native boys, as they dug us out. The world over "husa, dua, *tutlo*" (one, two, *three*) seems to be the get-ready signal for any big push. I wonder if they were really as happy and fun-loving and carefree as they always appeared to be.

It hadn't occurred to me, or to Bob either, I think, that I might not be dressed properly for the trip in to the prospect. A conservative suit, a hat, high-heeled slippers, and silk stockings seemed conventional enough to me, but one can imagine my chagrin upon arriving at Kilometer 100 to find that there was no way into the prospect except a very narrow, very muddy foot-trail up, over and down the other side of the mountain. The smell of Shanghai had been nauseous to me, but the smell of that small native roadside barrio that we found at Kilometer 100, our branching-off spot, was appalling beyond words. In time I became used to the smell of fish, excreta, rank native tobacco, red betel juice spittle, [and to the sight of] naked, undernourished, bloated-stomached children, dogs so starved and disease-ridden that they no longer looked like dogs, pigs and chickens always under foot, and everywhere the smell, completely unforgettable and undefinable, of unwashed bodies, in which the smoke and grease of countless camp fires had permeated not only their skin but the very air. Later, because of my nose, I often knew of the imminent arrival of visitors before I could see them. I have never seen such beautiful mountains, however, and the brilliant green of the perfectly kept rice terraces is something that I shall always remember.

After considerable dickering, as is the custom in all Oriental countries, I bought a pair of men's tennis shoes. Nothing else was to be had, and though they turned up at the toes, they were preferable to my own high heels and silk stockings. And so we walked over that beautiful, damnable mountain to get to our new home. It was situated at the bottom of an enchanting pine and tree-fern covered mountain canyon. The house was built of stone, and was perched precariously on the edge of a small, singing, clear river, which in the rainy season became a muddy, raging torrent. The way was made clear before us, and following after us were red-G-stringed Igorot cargadores who carried all our worldly wealth on their muscular bronze-brown shoulders. Their knotted muscular legs never seemed to tire, whereas my own legs were screaming for rest within the first ten minutes.

All the old timers in Baguio were Uncle Pat's friends, and as a result we had met most of them before we left Baguio. Those men were rather sweet, for the most part, and they had one and all assured me that the house we were to live in was the very best one they had ever seen on a prospect. "The best house I've ever seen on a prospect" rang no bells of warning. I had never been in a mining camp, for Bob and I had lived in Baguio until it was time to go to the prospect, nor had I seen a prospect, but somehow my fertile imagination pictured a mansion. I may say, without fear of contradiction, that no one has ever been more surprised at what she found. We did have running water, and we did have a bathroom of sorts. Aside from that we had a wood stove, a table, two chairs, and a mattress.[3] Well, homes

3. "Our first house was made of river rocks, with a galvanized iron roof and a cement floor—the Filipinos lived in nipa [palm-leaf thatch on bamboo

have been started with less, I suppose, and it was a distinct challenge. I love trying to make something out of nothing, and I succeeded after a fashion. Many tears were shed, of course, but I was very proud of the final result. A whole book could be written around those first few months, but I shall spare the reader my growing-up pangs.

In all the disappointments, there was one marvel that still puzzles me. We arrived at dinner time and there was nothing for it but to get dinner for Uncle Pat (who was to visit us a few days), for Bob and for me. At the exact moment I was looking with great trepidation and loathing at the ugly, squat, black beast called a wood stove (*The Egg and I* hadn't been written yet), a native boy opened the door and came in without knocking and started to build a fire. After it was built, he brought in a box full of wood and left. After dinner, as I was getting ready to clear the table, the same boy opened the door, came in and started to clear the table, and immediately began to wash the dishes. No words were said between us, for I could not speak his language and he, at that time, could not speak mine. For all I knew it might be some sort of Philippine magic, and I liked it, and who was I to break the spell by talking? For weeks Velasco came in every day as if I had rung a bell for him, and for weeks I did not mention pay and neither did he. Finally I could stand it no longer. We came to an understanding and I paid him a certain set wage on a certain day of each month. As long as we were on the prospect, Velasco came every day as faithfully as if I had gotten his solemn promise to do so. I even learned to like that wood stove, for it was cold in the rainy season in the mountains, and it was nice to get up on a cold morning and rush to the

---

frames] huts with dirt floors. It was dark inside because of the overhanging eaves and the fact that it had no windows on one side. It had one bedroom, a 'bath' that was just a john, a kitchen with a cast iron stove, and a dining-livingroom area. I could do what I wanted to decorate it, but count Bob out. I painted and put woven mats on the floor. Eventually we had a bed, chairs, books, pictures, lamps (kerosene), and a flower garden—my first one" (MS to LB 8/8/87 and 11/10/87).

kitchen where Velasco had the fire crackling and the kettle sim-
mering. I never did set an alarm clock there, for I knew that
Velasco would awaken me as he came in the kitchen door; in
summer and in winter the time was the same—six o'clock, time
to get up! Velasco and I never had a real conversation, for we
never learned enough of each other's language, but he was a fine
boy, of that I am sure.

I even learned to bake bread in those far-off days, there being
no corner bakery; eventually it became very good bread too, but
before I broke down and bought a cook book and learned that
yeast had to be put in it, it was a sorry mess!

The nearest American community was an hour's drive away
from us, after the road was put in. Eventually our mining company bought a car for us, and in it we occasionally paid a visit
to Suyoc, a small gold mine, which boasted thirty white men,
women, and children.

Life on a prospect, the smallest of all mining communities,
can be anything one chooses to make it. Rather like heaven, or
hell, or something in between. There are millions of people who
would rather be dead than attempt such a life, and to say that
I was completely unprepared for my new role is a masterpiece
of understatement. Bob and I were to become acquainted all
over again, we were to adjust to each other's likes and dislikes,
we were to eat, sleep, read, play, love, learn, and work together.
There was no one there to see to it that Bob went to work at
a certain time each day, or indeed if he went to work at all, and
there are millions of chiselers who are looking for just such work.
I need say only that he lived up to every possible ideal that I
could have had for a man, and I was full of ideals. We were the
only white people in a community of Filipinos that embraced
practically all tribes, with the possible exceptions of Moros and
Negritos. There were Christian lowlanders from all provinces,
each speaking a different dialect. There were Igorots of all varie-
ties, from the peace-loving Benguets to the headhunting Bontocs.
I must be honest and admit that headhunting was no longer in
vogue, although there were at least two heads taken during the

years that we lived in the Mountain Province. There were Kalingas from their remote and little-known province, and there were the Ifugaos of rice terrace fame. We learned many things from them and they, perhaps, learned a few from us. I even learned, by observation, to tell from which tribe a man came by the small bodily and facial characteristics that distinguished one tribe from another.

At Christmas, the Bontocs and Ifugaos honored us by dancing for us their age-old tribal dances of love and war. Can I ever possibly forget the flickering light of the campfire, the dancers capering, gesturing, leaping in mock battle, with one hand holding a fierce-looking spear which flashed in the firelight, and the other hand holding a protecting shield? Knowing that we were an hour by car from the nearest Americans made the performance infinitely more realistic than when I was one of many Americans watching the same performance in the light of day.

We climbed and climbed and climbed to attend a wedding, once, on the very top of a far mountain. With our fingers, we ate babuy (pig), which was served on a banana leaf, and drank the wedding couple's health in tapuy, a rice wine which was dirty looking, and horrible to taste.

Can I ever forget another day, a day when a native boy climbed a tree to get a gorgeous spray of white orchids for me, because I was the first white woman he had ever seen?

In the middle of the night, a few weeks after our arrival at the prospect, a runner brought us news from Suyoc that the Sackdalistas were having an uprising and we were to prepare for them. It seemed a little too fantastic to Bob and me, who were used to nothing more than the Saturday afternoon version of an uprising [for entertainment], so we locked our doors (tell me, how does one prepare for an uprising?), sent the runner to warn the Filipinos, who were terrified at the mere thought of it, and went back to bed. After all, this was the 20th century, wasn't it, and such things just didn't happen. In all our lives we had never seen anything more uncivilized than an occasional drunk, and I'd never even seen that until after Repeal [of Prohibition]. The next day, before Bob went to work, he told me to take the car and go to Suyoc to see what all the excitement had been about. I laughed at him when he told me to take Velasco with me "just in case you need protection," but I took him just the same. On the way over I turned to Velasco and said, kidding him I thought, "Velasco, if we *do* see anything, how are you going to protect me?" He, with complete seriousness, said "Oh, I have the axe, mum." That almost startled me out of my complaisance, for Velasco was the soul of kindliness. We didn't encounter anything that even resembled an uprising, but I am sure there are still people who remember that "damn-fool American woman" who didn't have sense enough (and I mean that literally) to stay at home and keep out of trouble. Having just turned twenty-one, and having too recently come from a very civilized small town in the United States, I could not so quickly become afraid of threats. What a lot I had to learn. I've even learned to be afraid, though I thought then that only cowards are afraid. Fortunately the uprising did not reach our isolated province, and we all relaxed after a day or two. Thereafter, however, Velasco became my self-appointed protector and when I was forced to stay alone on the prospect he was a never-ending source of comfort to me. He always brought his bed and slept in front of my door. Presumably the axe was handy in case of emergency. I no longer kidded him, because it obviously was a very serious matter to him.

Before Bob and I were married we had decided that we would wait at least two years before we started our family. The first Christmas we spent together we decided that we had made a wrong decision, for we were lonely and we suddenly realized that without children there is no real reason to celebrate Christmas. After discovering our mistake, we set about rectifying it, and we promised ourselves that by the next Christmas we'd have a baby. I was horribly, yearningly homesick for my family, and I knew that a baby would help heal that wound. Nature doesn't always cooperate with one, so it was the following April [1938], after months of being ill, that I had David. When David was a few days old, the nurse came in and told me why I had been so sick. When she said "eclampsia" she seemed to think that I would understand, but it was a word with no meaning for me, for I had never heard it before.[4] The doctor was very proud of himself for not letting me die, and even proud of *me* I think, for he often pointed me out as a sort of "unpickled" specimen, "the only one of its kind" sort of thing.

The coming of David meant the end of our prospect days because I was afraid to be so far from a doctor with such a precious bundle. We moved to Suyoc, where I had made a dear friend, Jean Heinrich, and there we lived quite happily. We prospered, and David grew and was a well-fed, happy, little boy until Pearl Harbor day, almost four years later.

4. Eclampsia is a toxemia of pregnancy characterized by high blood pressure and convulsions.

A typical section of the Mountain Trail by which Margaret and Bob
reached their first home (Courtesy of E. S. Diman)

A Mountain Province view (Courtesy of E. S. Diman)

Mountain Province roads and rice terraces (Courtesy of E. S. Diman)

A prewar Igorot home (Courtesy of E. S. Diman)

Margaret, Bob, and David at their home in the Philippines, autumn 1941

Margaret and David shortly before their internment

Santo Tomás

On the seventh of December, 1941, David, Bob and I were still living in Suyoc. The bombing at Pearl Harbor was a nasty shock to the whole world, but more of a shock to people like us, stuck way out in the boondocks, I think, than it was to people at home in the States. People [in the States] had been having the papers play the situation up to its utmost, and our papers had not done so. Naturally we had all wondered if we should go home when the army and navy families had been shipped out, but when I had asked in November, at the high commissioner's, if we should go or stay, the answer was "Stay, by all means, Manila is the safest place in the Orient."[1]

It was the morning of the 20th of December, just two weeks later, that I was awakened from a sound sleep to be told to be ready to evacuate our home in one hour. We were to be allowed to take two suitcases, inasmuch as there were three of us. The Japanese, we were told, were coming our way through the only road in that part of the province. The [U.S.] Army wanted to get us out and then they were to blow up the road behind us.

At this point, the picture that we left behind us that morn-

1. "In November [1941] I got on the plane in Baguio and went to Manila to the High Commissioner's to ask whether we should stay in the Philippines or return to the United States. After he said 'Stay,' I went back to Suyoc instead of taking David to the States" (MS to LB 8/8/87).

ing almost seems fantastic. Most of us had lived in the Islands for a number of years and had gradually absorbed a different way of life. There were servants, nice homes, beautiful linens, silver and teakwood, beautiful Chinese rugs, and copper objets d'art bought so cheaply in Hong Kong. Some of the servants we had had for years and they were almost like members of the family. The sun was just coming up when the runner arrived to tell us to get ready to leave. Bob could be of no help to us for he, along with the other American men, had to help blow up the mine, bury the bullion, and destroy anything that the Japanese might be able to use. When the runner came to the house that morning, the day's washing was being done by the lavandera, the living-room rug was rolled up for the house-girl to clean, the garden-boy was in the house "skating" the floors.[2] To be told to leave within an hour made packing rather difficult. I thought we would probably stay in Baguio for a few days, or possibly hide out in the mountains for awhile, and then we would return after the scare was over. Naturally the Americans would whip the socks off of the presumptuous Japanese within a month at the very most!

At the last moment I ran back to the house to get a Christmas present or two for David, just to be on the safe side in case we didn't get back for Christmas. The Christmas presents were all stacked on the top shelf in my closet. When I reached up for one or two small presents that I could slip into my coat pocket, they all came tumbling down and the contents went every way. It made me almost physically ill not to be able to stoop down and at least pick them up and put them in their proper boxes, whether I could take them with me or not. However, it was impossible, and I stumbled through the wild disorder of unmade beds, hurried packing, spilled Christmas presents, and crying servants to join the Americans who were waiting for me below. Each

---

2. The floor-skater puts half a coconut husk on one foot (or two if he's an expert) and glides over the bare wooden floors, thereby polishing them with the coconut's thick, fibrous outer covering.

car had at least one man and one gun, with which he was supposed to protect the women and children from the Japanese Imperial Army. At the time I did not think it in the least incon-
gruous. That is how naive an American can be about, if not his
superiority, at least his invincibility.

I wonder if the smell and the feel of a city from which all its
citizens are fleeing can ever adequately be described. When I read
of the cities that are being evacuated in Korea today, I can always see Baguio as we found it the day we were evacuated. Most
of us had left without our breakfasts and, as there were many
children in the group, the first thing that we had to do was to
get the children something to eat. This we did at the Country
Club, which was empty except for a few servants. A strange feeling it was too, to see it naked of all the Americans who had
made it their after-work headquarters. As I recall, we weren't
even asked to sign a chit for that luncheon. Strange indeed!

While the children were being fed, some of the men in the
group were at the army headquarters trying to find out what the
army wanted us to do, now that we had left our homes and
were in Baguio. The orders for our evacuation had apparently
come from Manila, because the army in Baguio knew nothing
about us and certainly didn't know what to tell us to do. They
had their own problems, some of which were obvious. Signs of
the Japanese bombing during the first day or two of the war
were still very much in evidence, but somehow they could not
make the game that we were playing seem any more real to me.
It seemed, even after ten days of war, almost impossible that the
Japanese could have done the damage which we saw. The trouble
with me was that I could not make this war seem like anything
more than another part of a story which we had been hearing
all our lives. We had not been able to help hearing, in the background, the sound of bombing which came from Manila every
day when we turned on our radios. And yet it sounded like little
more than excellent sound effects. The point is that no matter
how sympathetic and understanding one may be, one cannot actually feel a thing until one is in it—up to one's ears. Then it

is no longer a story, but very real, though possibly it is no more understandable. After much delay and discussion we decided to make a try for Manila, since we were told that the road to Manila was to be destroyed also. Later we learned that the roads were never destroyed, as they might have been, and we always wondered why not,[3] but at that period we were believing implicitly what our Army told us. At that point we wanted someone, *anyone,* to tell us what to do, for we were at a crossroads and there were no maps, no sign posts, no one to help us.

Most service stations in Baguio were already without gasoline, since there had been a rush on them for hours. We finally did find one which still had gasoline, but a long line was ahead of us. For what seemed like hours, we waited and prayed that the gasoline would not run out before it was our turn. During the interminable wait we watched the exodus of a people. In every conceivable manner they were hurrying to get down off the mountain into the lowland provinces. We saw very few Americans. Most of them were already gone. Those who remained behind were later interned at the Baguio internment camp. One almost never, under any circumstances, sees a Filipino alone. A Filipino always has a "companion." That day there were not only companions, but mothers, fathers, sisters, brothers, wives, children, chickens, and occasionally someone leading a pig on a rope. Dogs were left behind to fend for themselves. That day the wheel came into its own, as I suppose it always does in a mass evacuation. There were calisas, caramatas, caratelas;[4] there were cars, trucks, taxis; and there were people rolling wheels of cars, and occasionally someone came along rolling just a plain tire. And all of us, Americans and Filipinos alike, had just one thought in mind.

3. The roads to Manila weren't destroyed because Manila had been declared an Open City on December 22, 1941, and was consequently neither attacked nor defended after that date.

4. "A *kalesa* (in Tagalog), or *carromata* (in Philippine Spanish) is a two-wheeled horse cart; a *carratela* (Spanish) is a four-seated, two-wheeled carriage drawn by a single horse, a less prestigious vehicle, as say, a Chevette is to a Buick" (JJH to LB 11/21/87).

We all wanted to get out of Baguio, a city that would very shortly be without food if the road from Manila were blown up. And so that endless day wore on, a day that was to change the entire course of many of our lives, though we were not to know that for many months.

We left Baguio shortly after noon. The Army gave us their blessing, and assured us that if we were lucky, and hurried, and "hit the ditch" every time we saw an airplane overhead, we could probably make it to Manila. We were also told that our chances would probably be better in Manila than they would be in Baguio. They told us the Japanese were landing all along the coast, along which the road ran for miles, with only sand dunes, in many places, to hide the coast from us. We hurried, and we were lucky, and we made the long trip without loss of life, but it was a hectic day and marked the beginning of many more hectic days. We all grew considerably older that day, for we began to know the meaning of fear.

Every few kilometers we were stopped by sentries who informed us that we would have to go to the American headquarters and be "cleared" in order to proceed. Most of the American soldiers we saw didn't know where they were supposed to go, let alone where we were supposed to go. However, as night drew closer we were also drawing closer to Manila. And as it began to get dark we began to meet the army, a long procession moving OUT of Manila—which should have warned us. It didn't even ring a bell. We were letting them attend to their affairs, and we were trying desperately to attend to ours. At midnight, about an hour before we reached Manila, we were stopped once again and told that an air raid was in progress in Manila and to proceed "cautiously." Though we didn't laugh, that was funny. We had been traveling at a snail's pace in the pitch blackness, because we were not allowed to use our lights. And when a whole army is being evacuated with trucks, guns, tanks, and personnel in one long continuous stream on one side of the road, and one is traveling toward them on the other side of the road, one continues cautiously, I assure you. Not only that, as we got closer to Manila we were halted every few hundred yards and asked the password before we were allowed to go on. Bob, the man in our car with the gun, rode on the fender of the car to cope with that situation and to tell the man driving the car when to stop for the next sentry. As we got closer, we could hear the bombing that was going on in Manila, and a strange sort of blended fear and excitement began to rise within me.

Through darkened, deserted streets we finally slipped into Manila, and went directly to the Manila Hotel, thinking that we would stay there as we had done so many times in the past. It came as a distinct shock to us to discover that Manila was full of people, all seeking refuge in the "safest place in the Orient." We made the rounds of the hotels, and finally found a little rat-trap that had nothing much to offer except a bed and a mosquito net. After our grueling day we were willing to settle for almost anything. It was a comfort to have a roof over our heads, and we crawled exhaustedly into bed. We had hardly gotten settled when we were awakened by the weird wail of the air-raid siren. When we registered we had been told that during an air raid all guests were required to go to the air-raid shelter. The so-called shelter was nothing more than a very poorly ventilated cellar under the hotel and I would have felt a million times more safe outside under a bush. That was my first introduction to rampant fear in the human animal. I shall never forget, when we heard the first bomb hit, the sight of a man (whom I knew) pushing his wife down on the floor out of his way so that he could get under the nearest safe-looking object. Granted, it's a terrifying feeling to be shaken around by falling bombs, but we are brought up to expect something better than that under duress. Or perhaps I'd just read too many stories of bravery and valor, and hadn't really awakened to the fact that fear can do terrible things to the human animal. It was the beginning of many rude awakenings life had in store for me.

The next three days we spent in trying to find out what the consensus was in regard to Manila and the Japanese, in trying to get some money from the mining company for which Bob worked, and in buying a few clothes. When we left home, we hadn't realized that we would be in Manila. All the clothes we had were heavy (in the Mountain Province we had a fire in the fireplace every morning and every evening of the year), and we all had prickly heat as a result of not being used to the heat.

Christmas came and I thought life was abusing us a great deal, for the nearest we could come to a Christmas tree was a branch broken off of one of the trees in front of the hotel. To us it was a symbol; to David I don't know what it was. Just a branch from a tree, probably. We asked the cook at the hotel to make a picnic lunch for us which we took to the park to eat. We had no more than gotten there when we had to hunt an air-raid shelter. The nearest one happened to be the Army-Navy Club. I had been feeling completely frustrated for days, just sitting and watching the Japanese fly at will over Manila, and I could not understand to save my life why we were not doing something, *anything* about it. That day I got my first answer to that question. We *couldn't* do anything about it, for we hadn't the planes with which to do it. (That's what the few men standing around in the club told us.) To Bob and me it seemed unbelievable. We decided that we had just accidentally run into some pessimists. We had no idea how really lucky we were, that Christmas. That night we climbed to the top of our hotel and watched what seemed like the whole of Manila on fire. Actually it was the oil and gasoline being destroyed so that the Japanese could not use it. And *still* we innocents did not realize what was happening. There was talk of an "open city," but who among us had seen or even heard of an open city before; what did it mean? I remembered reading, shortly before the war, a book in which I had *thought* MacArthur had stated flatly that the Philippine Islands could not be taken. I was only too happy to believe him, and who, until he has been shown, doubts the superiority of his own race? After all, Americans couldn't be taken over by the Japanese, no matter how many of them there were and how few of us there were. They simply *couldn't*, for we were Americans!

The Monday after Christmas Bob started looking for work of

some sort. War or no war, a family had to be fed, and we were in a strange city, living in a hotel, running up bills that had to be paid. Someone told Bob that the army was looking for engineers on Bataan. Until that time I had never even heard of Bataan, having lived in the Mountain Province since the day I had arrived in the Philippines several years before. Bob's brother arrived from the southern islands about this time and he also thought that Bataan was the place to be. So did one of the other mining husbands that had made the trek down from the mountain with us, although Bill and Martha had been married only three months.

New Year's Eve, at midnight, the men who had volunteered to go to Bataan were to assemble at a certain pier. I remember walking down to the bay that afternoon with Bob and David, and somehow we had a feeling that the thing might be more than just a job. Bob asked me whether or not I wanted him to stay with us, and I told him to do what he thought best.[5] At midnight, I am told on good authority, the army officials told the men who had assembled to be taken to Bataan what they were up against, and that they would not be coming back until the job with the Japanese was finished. I never saw Bob again. Nor did I ever see Jack or Bill again.

During the week after Christmas we had scouted around and found an unfurnished apartment with which we thought we could manage. We bought the bare essentials: a table (boxes would have to do for chairs) and native bejuco beds.[6] We bought

5. "When Bob left I thought I'd be seeing him in a month or so; the army just had a little mopping-up to do, we were told. I felt he was doing what a man should do. He was drafted into the army on the spot, and was doing exactly what I'd have done if I'd been a man. Yet I had an occasional sneaky thought wondering whether it would really be over that fast. Words can't express what it was like to be without a husband, without money, without friends in a strange war-torn city" (MS to LB 8/8/87).

6. Bejuco (pronounced *bay hu ka*) is a tropical fiber. "A native bejuko bed was a frame with four legs (four legs folded underneath, making a flat package), with the fibers woven between the four sides of the frame. It was cooler than

two sheets for each bed, and a thin bedspread apiece which would have to do for a blanket. January is the cool season in Manila, and out in the suburbs we needed a thin blanket before morning. We decided that three of the mining families could live in one apartment, and two in the other, which was right next door. We bought some canned food and acquired a case of Eagle Brand milk and a drum of salad oil from the bay area, which was being looted of its millions of dollars worth of cargo. It was a sight, that. Everything on earth was in those warehouses, from magnificent Chinese rugs to drums of salad oil, and it was all looted with the army's approval. We could not understand it then, but I assume that the army felt that it was better for the Filipinos and Americans to have it than for it to fall into the hands of the Japanese. Much of it was later rounded up by the Japanese and stored in great piles. I remember passing one huge "dump" which had nothing but flour and cigarettes in it. The flour and cigarettes were inside Rizal Stadium, and the things were stacked to the last tier of seats. There was so much burning of war materials during that last week before the Japanese came that the city was in a black sooty fog. The city smelled of death, destruction, and *fear.*

After New Year's Eve, we suddenly realized that the Japanese were coming, which they did, on bicycles, on January second. It is impossible to describe the feeling one has, watching an army of small yellow men on *bicycles* ride in to conquer one's city. And so we waited, and waited, wondering what was to happen to us now. Were we to be treated as Nanking had been not so long before? We did not know. All we knew was that we could hear the fighting from the direction of Bataan clearly at night, and we could see flashes which meant that there was a battle in progress. I felt as if I were a widow, though I was not to become one in fact for almost three years. I was already on my own, with no one on earth to protect David and me from God

---

a mattress, and made a mattress unnecessary. It wasn't soft, but it was infinitely softer than the cement floor" (MS note 2/87).

knew what. Having a vivid imagination is definitely a handicap, I feel sure, for there were people who never felt the things I did, simply because I had such vivid imaginative pictures of what could be done to us. Waiting for the Japanese to decide what they were going to do with us was one of the hardest waits of my life. Sitting and waiting is dreadful. If one is up doing something, or taking an active part in a thing, life is bearable. Waiting, in idleness, is hell.

We had been warned over the radio to stay off of the streets, and we three women in our apartment had been only too glad to comply. However, even while one's fate is being decided by the Japanese, one must eat. I began to decide right then that eating is a vicious habit and I eventually hated food, simply because life depended on it and we could not get it.[7] When Bob left there were two men left in our apartment, and we finally decided that one of them [Dick Spencer] would have to take a chance and go out and see what he could scrounge to eat. Each family had had no less than a six months' supply of food in our mountain homes but we might as well have saved our money for all the good it did us in Manila. That was on the fifth, or the sixth, of January. Dick did not return. Later we were to learn that he had spent the night at Villamor Hall,[8] where he (along with many other men, women and children) was kept in one room, with no provision whatever being made for them. There were no beds, there was no food, and there were no toilet facilities. Occasionally during the day a guard brought in drinking water for them. To keep women with tiny children under such

7. Margaret was in no way anorexic, but very worried about money: "From the day we left the mining camp we were running out of money. We had sent our money to the United States for banking, but Bob had won 40 pesos, equivalent to $20, in a poker game, and that was the money I had to go into camp with. It was the first time I had *really* thought about life depending on food and I felt terrible that I had no way to get it" (MS to LB 8/9/87, 11/10/87).

8. A collection point at the University of the Philippines in Manila to which civilians being rounded up by the Japanese for internment were taken before being sent on to Santo Tomás Internment Camp.

conditions is inexcusable. The Japanese must have known that they were going to start picking us all up the next day. Why didn't they just send them home to wait until then?

January 7 arrived and we learned early in the morning that the Japanese were picking up all Americans. What they were going to do with us then we could not know, but you may be sure that we went through a mental hell that day. In the afternoon, trucks finally entered our street, and each truck had soldiers and an interpreter. The clomp, clomp, clomp of a booted, sabered, invading, conquering army is a terrifying sound. It had been dreadful to see them ride in on bicycles and in American-made trucks. At close range they made our hearts beat wildly, and we held onto our children with a desperate hold. Up the street, as the soldiers left each apartment, we could see the occupants come out on the street dragging mattresses, suitcases and boxes. The one thing that we were sure of then was that they were not going to kill us, and they were going to take us somewhere. Finally it was our apartment steps they climbed, and it was our turn to be searched and questioned and finally told what to do. My suitcase full of men's clothing required a good deal of explanation, but I finally convinced the interpreter that I was not hiding my husband but that he'd left me and gone somewhere, and I pointed off in the opposite direction from Bataan. What he thought about the situation I did not know, but I felt sure that I would hear more about it later.

From that day on I knew that I was not going to be able to talk to David about his Daddy, for I was questioned over and over about his whereabouts, and I knew that it would not be safe for a three-year-old child to know anything that could hurt us. I felt that the thing to do was to keep David in complete ignorance of anything that might hurt us by being told. The Japanese made it a policy in Santo Tomás to talk to small children and question them; and how are children to know what to tell and what not to tell?

The Japanese left our apartment with instructions that we were to "take food and clothing for three days," and we were *not* to take bedding of any sort. This last instruction was apparently left up to the discretion of the individual soldier. Some soldiers, a little more humane than others, allowed people to take mattresses, mosquito nets, etc. Mosquito nets, as you may know, are a necessity in Manila. There are malaria-bearing mosquitoes, and there are dengue mosquitoes,[9] and there are just plain mosquitoes. All of them sting and make life generally miserable. When we were finally loaded into the truck with our children and suitcases and "food for three days" we were taken to Rizal Stadium where we were again questioned, our baggage dumped on the ground and searched, and made to wait for several hours until the Japanese were ready for us to be taken to Santo Tomás University.[10] When we rumbled through the gates of Santo Tomás, we had no idea that it would be our home for three years and almost two months.

Words fail me when I try to picture the scene that met our eyes as we entered the large front door of the university. I hadn't seen Macy's during a Christmas rush at that time, but as I look

9. Dengue fever is a mosquito-borne tropical disease characterized by almost unbearable pains in the head, eyes, muscles, and joints; it is also called *breakbone fever* and *solar fever.*

10. The Royal and Pontifical University of Santo Tomás was founded as Manila University of Santo Tomás by four Dominican fathers in 1611, by legacy of Archbishop Miguel de Benavides, with St. Thomas Aquinas as its patron saint. Beginning with Humanities, Arts, Philosophy, and Theology, the University added Canon Law and Roman Law in 1734, a School of Mathematics in 1783, a School of National Law in 1835, and within the past century schools of Fine Arts, Mechanics, Commerce, Chemistry, Botany, Agriculture, Medicine, Pharmacy, and Midwifery. It was made a royal university in 1785 by Charles III and a pontifical university in 1902 by Leo XII. The University, the oldest then under the American flag, moved to a new site of 65 acres in 1927; classes were suspended with the outbreak of World War II, on December 8, 1941. When Manila was declared an open city, the American Emergency Committee of the Red Cross obtained permission from the University authorities to use the buildings as a civilian internment camp, and on January 4, 1942 the first truckload of civilian internees was brought to Santo Tomás Internment Camp. (Frederic H. Stevens, *Santo Tomás Internment Camp* [Stratford: n.p., 1946], 8–11, and Elizabeth Vaughan, *The Ordeal of Elizabeth Vaughan,* ed. Carol M. Petillo [Athens, Georgia: University of Georgia Press, 1985], 203.)

back at it the crowds are similar . . . with a subtle difference. There were people, thousands of them, of all ages, types, colors, descriptions. They were all worried to death, and they all dragged, pushed, hauled, and carried everything that was left to them in the world.

And there were the crying children. It was almost ten o'clock when we reached Santo Tomás and, of course, the children had had nothing to eat since we had left the apartment early in the afternoon. Fortunately, we had fed them just before the truck hauled us away, for already we knew that eating was to be [very] important. Just how important we did not know, believe me. The few women from the mining camp tried to stay together as much as possible because, though there were thousands of human beings milling around, we saw no familiar faces. I think, without exception, all of the mining wives from Suyoc had gone almost directly from Manila to the Mountain Province and, except for a vacation once a year, we had stayed there. Though most of us eventually found a few people we knew, that night we saw no one we recognized. We finally found a classroom on the third floor that had a little room left on the floor in one corner, and we dragged our protesting, crying children and our belongings into it. Fortunately, Manila has a warm climate and covers were not an essential item, yet cement floors are always cold, and the mosquitoes were doing their vigorous best to eat us alive. Certainly there was no blanket problem that night, however, for the room was horribly overcrowded and the heat from our collective bodies made the room almost unbearable. I would have welcomed a blanket to put on the floor under David that night, and a few days later one of the mining wives from Suyoc, who had had a great deal more foresight than I had, loaned David and me a quilt to sleep on. Every available inch of space in the room was taken up when we crammed into a corner which was already occupied by a desk. David cried all that night and I wanted to, though I was much too tired and worried to concentrate on [the immediate situation]. As it was, Inga, a German mining wife from Suyoc, and I stayed awake all night trying to fan David and keep the mosquitoes from riddling him. We were lucky to have found a spot on the floor in a room, for during the night when we made the long trek to the bathroom, there were people sleeping, or trying to sleep, all up and down the long halls, with nothing under them except a cement floor and nothing over them except mosquitoes. These were mostly old people, it seemed to me, and they were pathetic beyond words.

The bathroom, it must be mentioned, had five of the most filthy stools that can possibly be imagined to take care of approximately five hundred women and children. I cannot forget the picture of the woman in the bathroom who, somewhere, had found a bucket. She was stark naked and she was taking a sponge bath under the only tap in the bathroom. Before and since I have seen filth, but never have I seen anything that could compare with the sight and smell of that bathroom; and there stood a woman calmly taking a bath, while hundreds of women and children filed in and out—all staring with fascinated eyes. How she could have been so casual about it at that time is still beyond me. Later, much later, I was able to share a shower with ten or fifteen women without cringing, while dozens of other women waited their turn and other dozens marched in and out of the bathroom, but I could not have done it on January 7, 1942. To many men the lack of privacy was as nothing, I am told; to women it was excruciating. [Santo Tomás] University had been used to house Filipino soldiers after the war started, and there was excreta from floor to ceiling, literally. People who have had bathrooms all their lives are careless enough in a public restroom (take a look at any public restroom) but people who have never been in one in their lives can only be described as using one as an animal might. I couldn't help remembering that I was the one who had cleaned my hands with alcohol every time I handled my son, until he was two years old. I was still, until the war came, cleaning his dishes, first with boiling water and then with alcohol just to be on the safe side, in order for him not to get dysentery or any one of a dozen filth-borne diseases that one can acquire in the Orient. And I had let my son in for this! I was terribly ashamed that I could have done this to him, even though I'd done it unintentionally.

I would like to digress here and mention a subject that I am sure ladies would leave unsaid. However, it was so *very* important to us for a while that it seems to me it must be mentioned. As I have mentioned, there were five stools in that filthy bathroom. The women who volunteered to clean that mess will have stars in their crowns some day, I know. Eventually we had what we not too delicately called "toilet duty." I was appalled at the instinctive dirtiness of human beings. It seems incredible that we had to have a woman on duty at all times of the day to see that the people who used the bathrooms left them in a presentable condition. "Toilet duty" was nauseous, but necessary. We had a bucket of disinfectant and a cloth, and after each visitor we wiped the white procelain object with the cloth which had been dipped in the bucket of disinfectant. We used the bare commode, without benefit of seat or lid. I never felt that it was beneath my dignity to clean up after people, as so many women seemed to, but I did despise putting my hand in that awful old bucket of smelly, oily-looking disinfectant. As far as I know, none of our children ever contracted a venereal disease, so it was well worth the time and effort we put into "toilet duty."

After a long, long night our first morning in Santo Tomás finally came, and the immediate problem was food – proper food – for David. One of the few good things I can say for the Red Cross is that they immediately got in a few supplies from the "outside."[11] At this time children were considered first, and I can

11. During the first six months of internment the Japanese provided nothing at all for the internees and no funds for their maintenance; Japanese funds throughout the remainder of the war were inadequate. Thus the internees were initially dependent on either the Red Cross or on their own resources, which ranged from destitution to abundance; most of the 5,000 inhabitants of Santo Tomás were largely dependent on the Red Cross not only for food and electricity, but for "beds or cots, mattresses, pillows, mosquito nets, bedding; all kinds of kitchen and dining equipment; medicines, medical supplies, surgical and hospital equipment; building materials, plumbing and electrical supplies"

never forget how thankful I was to hear someone say that they'd seen a line outside a small building on the compound where they were giving small bowls of warm, cooked oatmeal to children under a certain age. The age limit I have forgotten now, but I was grateful that David was well within it, so we forgot every-thing else to make a wild dash for the line, the first of many interminable lines that we were to stand in during the three years ahead of us. Fortunately we could not know what was ahead of us, and I believe that God must have planned it that way on purpose. When we had rented the apartment we had not bought china dishes. The least expensive thing to be found was white enamel soup bowls. These, with large spoons, we had taken in our box with our three-days' supply of food. After David had had his quota of oatmeal, the next immediate problem was where to wash his dish and spoon so that we could go back to our corner of the room where we had spent the night, and try to organize the situation a little. We finally found a small goldfish pond in which people were washing both their dishes and their clothing. It seemed the only thing to do, so we worked our way through another line and took a chance with a few hundred bil-lion germs and washed his dish and spoon. I had no breakfast that morning (though I was offered a piece of papaya), for I was much too bewildered for my stomach to even stand the thought of food. Nerves, I presume.

When we got back to our room, we found that we had been "looted." The only thing I'd brought along with me, purely for morale building purposes, was a large bottle of Elizabeth Arden's Blue Grass cologne which Bob had given me for Christmas. It

---

(Stevens 84). Stevens details the difficulties in obtaining Red Cross support (in-hibited in part because a number of Philippine Red Cross officials were in-terned, in violation of international law, and because the Japanese consistently interfered with International Red Cross operations, again ignoring international law), and itemizes the actual support provided, which began at 35 cents (U.S.) per day—24 cents of which was for food; this was later adjusted—but inade-quately—to accommodate the runaway inflation that occurred as the war pro-ceeded. See Stevens, 78–89, 135–67, and *passim*.

was gone and so were two of the new sheets that we'd brought along. Later, so many people lost things [that] we had to have a monitor in the room at all times. Some time later we found that the culprits were a group of Russian refugees from Shanghai who were camped in another corner of the room. They probably thought that people who were ignorant enough to leave their things unguarded deserved to lose them, or maybe they didn't think at all. Who knows what they thought; White Russians in Shanghai have lived a precarious life for many years now and habit is a wonderful thing. At that time we weren't too angry about our losses, just amazed and a little disgusted. After all, the Japanese had told us that we would be in Santo Tomás only three days and we could surely get more sheets when we got out. *Not* that we strictly believed. My private opinion was that it would be more like three weeks than three days before we got out. It didn't enter my head at that time that it would take the Americans more than three months (at the very most) to have the situation back under control.

The days wore on and David and I succeeded in acquiring a mosquito net from an acquaintance and a quilt to fold under us so that we wouldn't be quite so miserable at night. The first week or two we slept on top of two desks pushed together and were not too uncomfortable. Why wood is softer to sleep on than cement I don't know, but it is. We spent days scouting the university for an outside faucet which would be a little less contaminated than the fish pond where most of the internees were washing their dishes and their clothes. A mining man from Suyoc finally found one by the monkey cages (the monkeys had been kept for experimental purposes at the university) and though it reeked and the monkeys grabbed our clothes through the bars, by getting up at six in the morning I had it more or less to myself. David was an early riser so it worked out very well. I got him out of the room where other people wanted to sleep because, believe me, there is nothing that infuriates a woman with no children (unless it's an older woman whose one child is grown) more than being awakened by a three-year-old at six o'clock in the morning.

Part of each day I spent looking for my sister-in-law, for I felt sure that she must be in Santo Tomás somewhere. I had known her casually for several years now and I thought that this would be an ideal opportunity to really get acquainted with her. After all, our husbands were both gone and we were sort of a family. Later there were endless alphabetical lists of names, which would have made it easy enough to find her, but it took time for organization to take over. I finally found her, and she was as cool and remote as ever. I mentally crossed off the possibility of our becoming one happy family. Mickie's lack of interest was the beginning of a realization which was to come hard to me. I found that when people are in a spot the one thing that is uppermost in their minds is to take care of SELF and devil take the hindmost. We had a saying for it in Santo Tomás—"I've got mine, how are you doing?" Now that I have accepted that bit of philosophy it seems natural enough, but it did come hard to me then. There is an exception to that rule. Mothers, instinctively, seem to rush to the aid of their young, no matter what the consequences. (Naturally there are exceptions to every rule.) Through [thousands of] years, for the good of society, men have been taught that they should also protect their young. It is not instinct with them, however, as I am sure it is with mothers.

A good example of this came shortly after we were interned. By this time one of the small buildings at the rear of the main building had been turned over to mothers and young children. Single women and mothers with older children stayed in the main building. One night an American plane, piloted by a Filipino, flew very low over Santo Tomás. Most of the mothers were sitting in the dark, talking, talking, talking, until time to go to bed. We were not allowed to go to the main building after dark, where many of the women's husbands were (and there was plenty of griping about that, for which I didn't blame the women) so there was nothing for us to do after the children were tucked under their mosquito nets except sit in the dark and talk the endless talk of when we were to get out, when we were going to get decent food to eat, and the latest rumor. Without exception, when the plane flew low over our dormitory and the anti-aircraft guns started firing from every side of the campus, every mother almost literally flew to her own darlings to protect them with her own body, if necessary, there being nothing else with which to do it. There was no screaming or undue excitement. Each mother had only one thought, and that was to take care of her children to the best of her ability. We were amused then to hear the tales that came from the main building the next day. There were the people who had jumped out of windows and had been hurt in doing so, and there were the men who had pushed their wives, and the wives who had shoved their husbands, and there had been much, much screaming. Many people thought that the plane was the beginning of our liberation, but with the exception of Easter Sunday (or was it the following Sunday?), when a large group of high-ranking Japanese officers was bombed (we heard), we did not see an American plane again for almost two years.

It was during our talk-fests at night, after the children were tucked in for the night, that I first heard about the man in the main building who had a spy glass.[12] He and two other men had been on top of the main building and, with spy glass and watch, had timed the flashes from Bataan and had arrived at approximately the distance away from us where fierce fighting was going on. At the time I gave no credit to this story, for we had been strictly forbidden to go on the roof of the main building, and all such things as spy glasses, knives, cameras, and radios had long since been taken over by the Japanese. For fear of reprisals to my son, or myself, or to the camp as a whole, I had no thought (at that time) but to do as I was told to do. This particular

12. "When I heard about the man with the spy glass I had no idea that I would someday meet him. If someone had told me that someday that man would be my *husband*, I would have been shocked out of my mind, for I already *had* a husband" (MS note, 2/87).

point was dinned into us pretty thoroughly. *Don't* do anything that will hurt the camp as a whole.[13] Later I was to regain part of my natural inclination to do as I felt I should, but at that particular point of internment I was pretty well beaten. A night never passed that someone didn't come in with the latest rumor, or dozens of rumors, and I never ceased to be amazed at them, for it was a death penalty to have a radio and we were not supposed to have news of any kind, except the Japanese papers. These papers were very carefully tacked on our bulletin boards every day, and they amounted to nothing except as a propaganda sheet, and of course it was their propaganda—not ours. The Japanese have a very subtle sense of humor, I believe. Seeing us squirm, figuratively speaking, when we read their papers seemed to give them satisfaction. However, it was hard for us to believe that they could use propaganda so stupid in so many respects and expect

13. Typical of prison and internment camp administration, the Japanese treated the first known attempt at escape with unmitigated harshness, to serve as a *memento mori* for the rest of the internees. On February 12, 1942, three men, Blakely Laycock, Henry Weeks, and Thomas Fletcher, attempted to escape, were captured by the Japanese, and beaten to the point of insensibility. Despite pleas and promises from the internees that they would "urge that no one ever attempt it again," on February 14 a Japanese military court martial sentenced the three to death by shooting, and over internees' protests, they were executed on February 15, in the presence of representatives of the internees' Central Committee (Stevens 241–45).

Shortly after her arrival in Santo Tomás, Vaughan wrote, "There is a shadow hanging over camp caused by the murder by Japanese of three internees who, half in fun, climbed over 'Stic' walls one night. The jest of the young men ended in tragedy. Caught by the Japanese soon after their more or less open escape, the internees were beaten into almost insensibility till their cries for mercy rent the air. Then, that the lesson might be more impressed, the battered, broken forms of the internees were tied up, propped up and shot. The lesson has had the desired effect. No one speaks of escape from 'Stic.' We do not forget that we *are* prisoners and that there is a war of which we are a part. The tragedy of the three young, gay internees has been told me, with slightly differing gruesome details, on at least half a dozen different occasions. The Japanese permitted a special memorial service in the Santo Tomás Seminary Chapel which was attended by about everyone" (Vaughan, 4/19/43, 208).

us to believe it. We did get a certain amount of information from their paper, though. When their papers mentioned a great battle in a certain locality and told us that all the American ships and planes that participated in it had been lost, and only one Japanese plane was reported missing, we pretty well knew that there had been a battle, probably at the place they mentioned, but that certainly the losses on neither side could have been accurate. We gave our own side a lot of undeserved credit in those first days, for we could not believe that the Americans had been almost completely whipped everywhere.

Somehow, right about here, I must get across a point that is going to make me most unpopular. I said something like it to my grandmother once, and she was shocked and thought I had merely had a bad experience and was bitter as a result of it. I feel sure it is nothing of the kind. We Americans have always prided ourselves on our generosity. Every day one can read about this or that charity to which Americans have willingly contributed. We have given millions to Europe, and to almost all the other countries in the world. Perhaps some people have always known what I had to learn the hard way (and maybe it isn't important anyway). Still, I must say it. We are generous ONLY because we have more than enough for ourselves. If it hurt to give, and give generously, we would not be what we like to think of as God's most generous people. When it means going without food so that others can share, the real human nature asserts itself.

Most of the people who were interned in Santo Tomás were what we called "Manila people," which simply meant that they were people who were from every part of the world, and that they had lived in Manila for a number of years. Many Americans had lived there long enough to have grown children who had never been home to the States. They had homes and servants and cars and all the things that money can buy. There were the exceptions, like the out-of-town mining people and the people who were on their way to other countries and were caught there. There were, for instance, a great number of people who had come down from Shanghai and Hong Kong because Manila was "the safest place in the Orient."[14] There were a great number of us, therefore, who had no connections in Manila and, as a result, when the blow came we had nothing to fall back on. The first few days of internment the Japanese allowed the Filipinos to come close to the fence, and those who had money could buy food through the fence. Servants of the Manila people brought food parcels and put them through the fence for their employers. Later, after things became organized, the Japanese allowed us to have what we called a "package line." This meant that people on the outside could send packages of food and clothing to friends on the inside. The packages, however, had to be examined by the Japanese guards. One can imagine how it went. Those who had servants outside received food packages every day (in hundreds of cases complete cooked meals came in) and those who knew no one on the outside *never* received a package.[15] Those first six weeks were rough for these last individuals,

14. In 1941, as relations between the United States and Japan grew tense, Ruth Shipley, the testy, semi-autonomous director of the U.S. State Department's Passport Office, adopted a policy of refusing to issue passports to American wives (and their children) seeking to join husbands in China. Some wives en route to China were stopped in Manila. By the summer of that year conditions deteriorated to the point that Americans already in China, such as the students of the Peking Chinese Language School for missionaries, were urged to seek safety. The Philippines were the closest and cheapest place to go; the summer resort of Baguio had ample accommodations in the off-season. The prevailing sentiment among the allies was that because the Philippines was still an American protectorate and there were a number of American military bases in the Philippines, the Islands would be well-protected. Indeed, MacArthur had pronounced Corregidor an "impregnable fortress" (JJH to LB 11/21/87). For a typical view, see Judy Hyland, *In the Shadow of the Rising Sun* (Minneapolis: Augsburg, 1984), 14–22.

15. "In those first six weeks of not one single hot meal, I bought what I could through the fence, from Filipinos on the outside. It was either canned or fresh fruit, with an occasional fresh vegetable—a tomato or a cucumber. There was nothing else for me to buy. Aside from that I was trying to save enough money to buy a case of canned milk for David, if and when I could. It was considerably later when I was able to mend and bind books for a little cash" (MS note, 2/87).

of which group David and I were members. For several weeks nothing visible was done in the way of organizing a food line of any sort for adults.[16]

My first warm meal came six weeks after we were interned. Quite by accident I ran into a "Manila man," with whom I had become acquainted on board ship on my first trip to the Philippines. Having considerably more than he needed, he was most generous and, since I was a woman and therefore presumably knew how to cook, he asked me to come over to his shanty one night and make some hot cakes for him and some of his friends. He also had a can of Spam, he said. I never have eaten anything any better than those hot cakes were, but after a steady diet of canned and fresh fruit, for which I had been able to make deals, I was horribly sick. [I] sat up all night under my mosquito net, with a bucket between my knees and vomited almost continuously. In our room it was no uncommon occurrence, however, for most of the children had had upset stomachs and diarrhea most of the time since we had been in Santo Tomás.

I had, the first week or two, been fortunate enough to be in a room next to another Manila man—an old Dutchman, I believe he was—who had servants on the outside. He had been most generous with his leftover rolls. I had not at that time fully realized what generosity means and I was very grateful. I still am,

16. A. V. H. Hartendorp, the official Santo Tomás camp historian and a meticulous recorder of details, says in *The Japanese Occupation of the Philippines* (Manila: Bookmark, 1967) that "Starting with serving, gratis, of hot coffee to some 300 people," a small restaurant "ultimately served two light meals a day to over 1,000 persons who were receiving no food from outside the camp" (I, 16). Margaret comments, "Hartendorp implies that this was done *gratis*. It cost money to buy a meal in the restaurant. I had no money, and *I* did not have these two meals a day" (MS to LB 11/10/87). Hartendorp continues, "The central kitchen . . . began functioning on February 1 [1942]. . . . [It] regularly fed from 1,500 to 3,000 people two meals a day" (18). Margaret adds, "It is *possible* that it was only three weeks, not six weeks, until I had a hot meal, but I don't think so. As long as we lived in the Annex our food came from the Annex kitchen. When we moved to the landing it came from the central kitchen" (MS to LB 11/10/87 and 12/14/87).

for he gave them so nicely. Later we were to be a million times more hungry than we were in those first hectic months of internment, but it didn't hurt me any more than those first days when we had come from plenty, [having] so much more than we needed in fact, to nothing overnight with no gradual slackening to take away the hurt.

In the dormitory I was in a room which was full of Manila women and children. An English woman, over in the corner, was in my position. No husband, no money, and no one on the outside. One Manila woman, Louise (who was later to become my very dear friend), received very few food packages because her servants had been threatened by the Japanese and told not to go near Santo Tomás. Louise's husband was also in Bataan. Jean Heinrich, from Suyoc days, and her two children in somewhat the same position David and I were in, were in the room a short while before they all went to Holy Ghost Convent.[17] Mrs. Payne, Louise, and I, with our respective children, were in a spot that I never want to be in again. We would wait at lunch time, hoping against hope that one of the women who was a little more generous with her leftovers would bring them in to us. Many times she did, but by this time such generously given food had begun to take on a bit of a bitter taste. Perhaps I was looking a gift horse in the mouth and it was foolish of me to do so. After all, I can't know for *sure* how I would have acted if the shoe had been on the other foot. However, there were literally hundreds of people in Santo Tomás those first weeks who kept the garbage cans full and overflowing all the time.

17. Under Red Cross auspices, the Holy Ghost Convent in Manila opened a boarding school for children from infancy to twelve years of age in January 1942, directed by a pediatrician, Dr. Fe del Mundo. Beginning with fifteen children, the population eventually expanded to 100. The children were "fed three good meals a day, taught by convent sisters and internees and coached in outdoor sports by American padres" (Stevens 376). Margaret lay awake all night debating whether to send David, and ultimately chose his psychological security and hers over the opportunity for better nutrition ("I will die if I don't have David") (MS to LB 8/9/87).

And there was the handful of us who were literally starving because we were too proud to go to the garbage cans. Later pride was to go, but not yet. The sleepless nights I've spent thinking about the food under the bed across the aisle from me! Why I didn't steal, as many people did, is strictly due to my mother's training, for it never once entered my head to do so, but I could not help *thinking* about the food that was under almost every bed in the room.

David and I walked to the package line every day; not that I expected a package, for I knew we wouldn't get one, but it was something to do and besides I could see all the hundreds of people with their baskets spread on the grass under the trees, eating. Granted, they had only one *good* square meal a day, but they always had garbage left. When people are really hungry, as they were in the last year of internment, there is little garbage and it *is* garbage. It isn't just more food on one's plate than one can comfortably eat. I have always felt that one reason the Japanese did not feed us for the first six months we were interned was because they could see with their own eyes that we had plenty of food; there were the overflowing garbage cans! The men on the Central Committee were mostly Manila men, or men with money, so they probably had no idea (as is the usual case) how the other half was living.[18] Well, so be it—it taught me a lesson I shall not forget, and it made me realize something else.

18. Official camp records, as cited in Stevens, do not account for gifts of food from Manila residents, such as former servants or other employees, to internees, or food privately purchased. Wealthy Manila internees imported food by the caseload; internees with less money and no local connections went hungry. Margaret comments, "I was able to make very little use of the Filipino stalls that were eventually allowed in camp for awhile, for I never had more than a few pesos during the entire time we were interned except for the loans that I was able to make just before the birth of Gerry Ann. I did once buy a piece of dress material and some string to knit socks or bras from the Filipino business house, Aguinaldo's.

"Things like 'bread, ice cream, cake, milk, soft drinks' were out of my world, though I have just read in Stevens (213) that two Japanese were authorized to open stores in the camp and sell these commodities. Maybe so, but not to

When people are really starving they cannot get up on their hind feet and fight. I remember my history but vaguely, but didn't the French storm the Bastille because they were starving? When one is literally starving, one does not leave one's bed, except of dire necessity.

We had been interned about six weeks when I accidentally met our mining camp doctor, a Filipino, in Santo Tomás. Dr. de Venecia had come to Manila with the rest of the staff members and their wives just before Christmas. After setting up an office in Manila, he was kept quite busy by the Filipinos. He had come into Santo Tomás, for what purpose I don't remember, but he was shocked at my appearance. I had already lost about thirty pounds, some of which I didn't mind losing, but I must have looked a fright. Having no mirror, I had no way of knowing. When we were brought into Santo Tomás from our apartment,

---

me or anyone I knew. I question whether or not I would have bought from the Japanese even if I had had money and had known about it.

"Another thing that has boggled my mind is the 'Relief and Welfare Department' [identified in Stevens 214]. David and I never got, or received from them, the first article—unless the one piece of material with which I made curtains in Los Baños came from there. Such things as 'thread, buttons, pins, dress snaps, hooks and eyes' (Stevens 214), not to mention shoes, shorts, and socks all came to me in my mother's package two years after internment. Not one of these items did I ever receive from the Relief and Welfare Department, *ever*. I didn't even know there was such a department until I read about it in Stevens's book.

"Having just read Frederic Stevens's and A. V. H. Hartendorp's records of internment [in addition to the two massive volumes of *The Japanese Occupation of the Philippines,* Hartendorp wrote *The Santo Tomás Story* (New York: McGraw, 1964)]. I now know for sure that what I had surmised was true. Those men had *NO IDEA* in the world that there were many of us who were literally starving. I didn't know there were such items as 'socks, toothbrushes and tennis shoes' (Stevens 214) that could be applied for and received. In fact, I don't believe it. When my nightgown wore out, I went naked; when my toothbrush wore out I continued to use the handle and a few bristles. When my socks wore out, I knitted some more with string, and when my shoes wore out I wore bakias, a wooden sole with a piece of rubber, a strip of inner tube, over the toes" (MS note, 2/87, to LB 11/10/87, 12/14/87).

two of the Suyoc women were given passes to stay out for awhile. One of the women was almost ready to be confined and the other was a nurse, whom the Japanese allowed to stay with Helen and her little girl. Our Dr. de Venecia from Suyoc was taking care of Helen, and when he saw her the next time he told her sad tales of David's and my condition. David had had [gastro]-enteritis two or three times (a camp malady brought on by filth, flies, improper and improperly prepared food). Out of a clear blue sky, I received a package on the line. It was a pie, sent to one of the other Suyoc women and me, and after we had gorged ourselves, we found a note which had been baked under the crust. Helen and Martha said that they would be happy to have David and me come out and stay with them if I could manage to get a pass out of Santo Tomás. The thought of even asking for a pass scared me to death, for it seemed as if only Manila people were being allowed to go out, but I did put in an application and it was [at] a propitious moment, for at this time the Japanese were taking everything in sight in the Pacific war, and as a result they were quite generous with the conquered Americans. If one had money, a house, and acquaintances on the outside where one could go, one could get out with a pass, a red armband, a strict instructions to stay at home and attend to one's own affairs.[19]

19. Internee A. E. Holland worked throughout the war to secure the release from camp, on either a temporary or permanent basis, of between 400-800 people—mothers with babies under one year of age, women within a month of delivering a child, sick men and women over seventy, and hospital cases. As the result of unceasing "long and bitter arguments and discussions," the Central Committee persuaded the Japanese to allow one quarter of these people to return to their own homes (under the equivalent of house arrest), or to be placed in Remedios and other hospitals, the Hospicio de San José (an orphanage, home for old men, and lying-in hospital), Ateneo de Manila and Sulphur Springs (for some British mothers and children), and Holy Ghost Children's Home. In 1944 the Japanese closed eleven such institutions to internees, forcing some 400 "aged, feeble, sick, and crippled internees" back into Santo Tomás, where some "died within a short time" (Stevens 201–8).

Mrs. Margaret S.
Room 65, Annex

I attach hereto Conditional Release for you and David. You will note that the validity is only for 2 weeks, or until April 7th, instead of for 1 month. However this makes little difference. In order to get your Release extended you must follow this procedure:

On April 5th you should come here without David and bring back the attached certificate of release, together with a Doctor's certificate saying that David is in no condition to return to Sto. Tomás Internment Camp and that therefore he recommends that your Release be extended for an indefinite period.

March 25th.

Sincerely yours
A. E. Holland

On a red-letter day David and I walked out the gate and found a carratela, which would take us across the city to the apartment. How air can feel contaminated on one side of a fence and on the other side feel entirely different, I don't know. I only know that there is a difference in the texture, and the feel, and the smell of air that is free (after a manner of speaking) and air that is locked inside a fence with five thousand people.

And what a changed Manila from the one we had known less than three months before. Japanese soldiers: those ugly, little, bow-legged men everywhere. And their flags! Everywhere one looked, another square of white, with a blood-red ball in the center. Somehow I didn't mind the soldiers and their officers driving our American cars and living in our American houses as much as I minded *always* having that flag and that slogan, "Asia for the Asiatics," flaunted before our eyes.[20]

---

20. Throughout the Philippines the Japanese invaders were attempting to enforce their concept of "Asia for the Asiatics." Yet they did not understand the collective impact on the Filipino population of *utang ng loob*, reciprocal and undying gratitude for favors and kindnesses, enhanced by many warm prewar relationships between the Filipinos and their American employers and teachers,

Americans were not supposed to have relations, friendly or otherwise, with the Filipinos, but I must say that I developed more love for the Filipinos during that ride, and several more that I was to take, than I had developed in the previous six years. Maybe it's my contrary nature, and again maybe it's the nature of human beings, to enjoy deliberately outwitting a conqueror. I am sure that the Filipinos liked the Americans while we were locked up in Santo Tomás and the other camps throughout the Islands more than they ever have before or since. Filipinos have been a conquered people for so many generations that it is instinctive to try to outsmart everyone who rules them. The mistake the Japanese made with the Filipinos, in my opinion, was to underestimate their intelligence. If they had used more intelligent propaganda on them, they might have gone wholeheartedly for "Asia for the Asiatics," as at first quite a number of them did. Americans are supposed (in many quarters) to have exploited the Filipinos, and possibly they did, but at the same time the Filipinos were given advantages that they had never known before. As a result they had developed considerably more than the Japanese realized. Filipinos were accustomed to Americans and their ways and, through the years of association, the Filipinos' way of thinking had become somewhat Americanized. The Japanese way of thinking and doing was definitely a step backward and it did not take very long for the Filipinos to realize this. Already, after less than three months of occupation, the average Filipino in Manila was getting a little tired of jumping, and being

---

that exacerbated the differences between the Japanese and Filipino cultures. The Japanese, for instance, publicly humiliated the lower class Filipinos by beating and punishing them in public and even conducting public hangings—all of which were anathema to the Filipinos. Consequently, during the war many Filipinos were far more sympathetic to the Americans than to the Japanese. The presence of Americans in prison camps on Philippine soil served as a further stimulus to the loyalty of their Filipino friends, stiffening the natives' resistance to the Japanese government." (Adapted from Lynn Z. Bloom, "Introduction" to Natalie Crouter, *Forbidden Diary*, xxi. Information supplied by JJH to LB 4/28/79.)

afraid, when some soldier said "jump." And so, the purpose for which this handful of Americans was left in the Philippine Islands began to materialize. [After the war] it was brought out in Washington, D.C., in a session during which the American ex-internees were trying to get Congress to pass a bill for reimbursement of funds, in regard to loss of working days, that we were deliberately left in Manila, in order for the Filipinos to have something tangible to hang onto. If the Americans had all been taken out of the Islands at the time the army and navy families were, the Filipinos would have lost heart, and the Americans, on their return, would have had a tougher fight. As it was, we were there in Santo Tomás, tangible proof that someday the Americans would return. If the Japanese had been just a little smarter in their psychology they would have repatriated us; proof, to the Filipinos, that the war was won, and there would have been no reason [for the Americans] to come back to the Philippine Islands. When I say Santo Tomás, I do not forget Cabanatuan, and Baguio, and the camps in the southern islands. It is an all-inclusive term.

David's and my arrival at the apartment on the other side of Manila was unforgettable. Helen and Martha were very kind to us, and that night they served us the most delicious of meals: fried carabao steak, rice, gravy, a native green (talinum), and banana bread. Oh Lord, how good! And how good to be in a house, with beds (even though they were our native bejuko beds) and a bathroom, with only five of us to use it, and luxury of luxuries—they had soap, a washboard, hot water, and an iron. How wonderful to wear an ironed dress again. What could be more wonderful than having a bed for David, and to know that he was getting clean, decent food, even though native and very plain?

Women, particularly American women, have always prided themselves on their appearance. I have always considered myself rather plain, but I have taken great pride in the fact that I am neat and clean in appearance. Most women are that way, and the thing that hurt our pride, even more than the lack of privacy

and the lack of food, was the fact that we could never look presentable. There were a few women who always managed to hang
onto a little fingernail polish, and a little lipstick, and a little
perfume, but the great majority of us had to content ourselves
with looking even worse than nature intended for us to look.
There were several lovely blondes and redheads in the first few
weeks of internment, and I could not help feeling very sorry for
them as nature began to take them over. There is nothing much
more unattractive looking than a woman whose hair is "growing
out," especially so if she is wearing a soiled, unironed dress. The
fact that there was nothing much that could be done about it
and that most of the other women looked the same way helped
very little. Such a simple, private affair as shaving one's legs becomes a major problem, and one which one feels that one must
meet. How? If one has a husband around, he has a razor; if one
hasn't, what then? *Why* must one shave one's legs? Most American women feel that it is as much a part of their body care as
brushing their teeth. Most other nationalities of women seemed
to give it no thought. Certainly it was a problem that men were
not concerned with, though shaving their faces was a daily problem for three years. Many men, at first, seemed to delight in
having an excuse for not shaving. However, they soon got over
that and a surprising number of them always shaved. I don't
know how they managed the razor blade situation, but I do
know that it must have been a never-ending chore. The little
everyday musts that normally one hardly thinks about take on
an exaggerated importance when suddenly one is locked inside
a fence, with nothing in the world except a three days' supply
of food and clothing. A straight pin, a safety pin, a needle, a
piece of thread, a piece of string, a shoe lace, a bobby pin, a
bottle, a can, a piece of Kleenex, a cup, a spoon, a plate, a washboard, toilet tissue, toothpaste, a toothbrush, a fingernail file,
a piece of paper on which to write, a pencil, a bar of soap, a
razor blade—these then are the things that make the difference.
If one has them, one is wealthy beyond measure; if one does
not have them, one is a pauper. Food, clothing, a roof over one's

head, a bed—these are the essentials, but the others are the luxury items. If one has the last four items, one is blessed, but one is only an animal. If one has the luxuries, one is a human being. Therein lies the difference. Sometimes I think it would be a good thing if more Americans had had to face life on these terms—at least long enough to make them count their blessings.

While David and I were outside, I managed to get a hundred pesos through some mining company people. Swiss were not interned, and this family was enjoying the mixed blessing of being at liberty in a Japanese-occupied city. With most of the money, I bought a case of Carnation milk. Before the war a case of milk had cost a little more than seven pesos. Already, after only three months of war, I felt very fortunate in getting it for sixty pesos. My pride in that case of milk was unbounded, and probably unfounded as well. I felt that even though I had gotten David into an awful mess,[21] I could at least see to it that he had milk to drink until we were liberated. They were the small cans, and I allowed him one a day, and felt sure that there would be plenty!

A few things stand out in my mind about that six weeks that we were outside. We were awakened from a sound sleep one night by the beds rocking violently. There was a strange rumbling noise, and when we looked out the window in the direction of Bataan we could see great flashes of light all over the city, some close, some in the distance. Those closer seemed to be coming from the electric light wires, but all I could think was "Oh, thank God, they're coming at last." I was afraid, but I was terribly excited and happy. By the time we were fully awake we realized that the Americans were *not* causing all the commotion. It was an earthquake, and a violent one. We certainly did not feel secure on the third floor of that none-too-well-constructed building, so we each snatched a child and scrambled for the ground floor. Three times during the night we went through this pro-

21. "Even in circumstances I couldn't control I felt I should have been able to do something. The situation was frustrating to me because I'm a person who takes action, and I don't like to be pushed into something I can do nothing about" (MS to LB 8/9/87).

cedure, though the other two tremors were not nearly as severe as the first one had been.

Fortunately, Manila is accustomed to earthquakes and Santo Tomás had been constructed with them in mind. Nothing there was damaged except the belltower. Having a perverted sense of humor, I was very amused to hear one story about the earthquake. Connubial bliss was denied people.[22] People being what they are, when there are men and women together, ways and means are always found. This particular couple had found an empty room on the second floor. They had carefully locked the door behind them, and were engrossed in each other when the first strong tremor shook the building. They were sure that the building was going to crumble around their ears, and they could not get the door open. All thought of earthly bliss had definitely flown out the window by the time the building stopped rocking.

While David and I were outside, Martha and I took turns going to the native market for food. Somewhere Martha had gotten a bicycle, and we always rode it to do the shopping, for it was a long way to the market. Our diet was limited to carabao meat, rice, native greens, and bananas (because they were the cheapest fruit), but we never had a meal during that six weeks that didn't taste wonderful to me. We even tried making sourdough bread, while the flour lasted. It wasn't too good, but we weren't fussy and it at least resembled bread. For some trivial offense the Japanese had hanged several Filipinos and had kept them swinging

22. Scarcities of food and space dictated this obvious regulation. In January, 1943 the Japanese inaugurated a policy of jail sentences of men whose wives were pregnant by sentencing four expectant fathers to thirty days in jail. In February, 1944, however, the policy was reversed, and women were permitted to sleep in shanties—lean-tos, nipa huts, and other private dwellings on camp grounds whose "construction had to allow for easy visibility" and consequent inspection by Japanese guards (Carol M. Petillo, in Vaughan, 205. See also p. 98 below). Of the 576 families reunited, 137 women were pregnant seven months later (Stevens, 227–28). Stevens identifies 45 births in 1942, 14 in 1943, 14 in 1944, and 2 in 1945 (485). Gerry Ann Sherk does not appear on Stevens's list of births, but she does appear on the Los Baños December 31, 194[4] census.

on a scaffold for a few days as a gentle reminder to the rest of
the Filipinos that they must do as they were told to do. In order to avoid this street, which was on my way to the market
(since I saw no particular reason for stamping that picture on
my mind), I went around the block and ran straight into a Japanese roadblock. Why I should have resented such a simple thing
as bowing to a Japanese soldier I do not know. However I did
mind it, and in order to try to avoid it I rode by the sentry
with my eyes fixed on something on the other side of the road.
I had done this successfully several other times, but this time
the sentry was in no mood for such nonsense, and he made me
come back and stand before him and bow properly. I was happy
that he did not slap me, as they were apt to do. I realize, too,
that this would make a much better story if he had.

Every night while we were out of camp, we women listened
to the news and always the news from San Francisco was good.
"Help is on the way" and all that sort of thing. We didn't have
the slightest doubt but that it was. Our most crushing, heartbreaking experience came so unexpectedly that we could hardly
believe it. One night in May we turned the radio on for the
nightly broadcast. The sixth, it must have been, according to an
article I read recently, and we heard General Wainwright's message in which he told all fighting men to lay down their arms.
The thought of surrender had not crossed my mind. What a
blow it must have been to those fighting men. It was that night
that Martha and I sat on the steps in front of our apartment
and talked most of the night. It was a farewell to our husbands
really (Helen's was in Santo Tomás), for Martha's husband did
not come back either. I do not mean that we did not keep on
trying to get in touch with them, but somehow I felt that night
that it was the end. It was the bottom dropped out of the world.
There was nothing left to hang onto, if our forces had surren-
dered. Few friends, no husband, no home, no money, not enough
food for my child, clothes already ragged and being out-grown,
and now no *country*, I felt; we were indeed whipped.

A few days after Corregidor fell, the conquering Japanese soldiers moved into the apartment house that we six had had all to ourselves. We were worried for awhile, for there is much drinking and celebrating when a battle is won. There is when *any* army wins a decisive point, our own included. I am really glad that I saw that Japanese army at close range. At that time I hated them intensely, but it isn't in me to hate for long, and I certainly could not hate them when I realized that there was nothing there, really, to hate. The "foot" soldiers, as they were called, who lived all around us, wanted only enough rice and fish and soup to keep their stomachs full, beer to make them happy, a wristwatch or so to show what earthly riches they had attained; and they wanted to go home. How could I hate a human being who didn't even know enough to go into the kitchen and turn on a gas stove to cook his rice? The soldiers had brought their own charcoal "stoves" and cooked on the floor, in the middle of the living room. After seeing them in their long underwear, cooking on the living room floor, I lost a lot of my fear of them.

One morning when I was doing David's and my laundry, before the rest of our household was up, I got quite a start when I looked up to see three soldiers coming up the outside stairs of our apartment. I'm not the screaming kind of woman, but I must say I wanted to [scream] when they motioned for me to come with them. There being no one to help me out except two women and three children (all of whom were asleep), there wasn't much point in it. When a Japanese soldier motions with his sword for one to follow, one follows. That is, *I* do anyway. When we got to the bottom of our stairs, they motioned for me to go up their stairs, and I bade farewell to my honor, mentally, for I could see a lot more soldiers at the head of the stairs, and it seemed quite useless to try to run, or scream, or *anything*, except to climb the stairs with leaden feet, and a mind that was frantically trying to figure a way out of this one. I had been doing the laundry in my housecoat (to save the wear and tear on my three already-shabby dresses) and somehow I can't quite meet situations properly when I haven't a dress and my shoes on. Not one of the soldiers could speak a word of English, and I certainly could not speak a word of Japanese. However, there was little doubt in my mind what they wanted of me when they took me to the kitchen and pointed to the refrigerator. It was a gas refrigerator, something I had never seen before, but the instructions for starting it were very plainly printed on it and fortunately I [could] read English. They wanted the refrigerator started so they could keep their beer cold in it, and they wanted to be shown how to use the gas stove! Again, a good story spoiled because I have a passion for the truth. Also, I am glad to say that it is the truth and I'm really glad to disappoint a lot of people, for I have become very tired of people asking me, with bated breath, "Did—uh—anything—uh—terrible—I mean like the stories we've read—happen to you?" And when I say "No, we were only starved" they seem terribly disappointed, as if to say "Hell, anyone can be hungry—I thought it was really *rough* over there." I cannot say strongly enough that I am sure there is nothing as bad as starving and seeing one's children starve. I have not been raped, but I am sure that nothing that is finished in a short period of time can be as bad as starving day after day for three years.

Shortly after Corregidor fell some Japanese "brass" came to town, and consequently we were supposed to hang a Japanese flag on the front door. This was to show our great love and respect for the Japanese people. I was the one to pick up the paper and read the notice, and somehow it made me furious that we should be required to hang a flag on the house—especially so, when Bob and Bill and Jack and Joe were out there somewhere being killed by them. On the spur of the moment I hid the paper, and I did not tell Helen and Martha that another state occasion was at hand. The next day I worried and fretted and every time a car came down the street I nearly had heart failure. Early in the afternoon a Japanese car, full of brass and uniforms, stopped at our door. I have never prayed so hard. "Please God, don't let them hurt our children just because I've been too stubborn to hang out their stinking flag! I promise to hang it out the next time." They clomped in, sabers dragging and hitting each step as they came in. I don't suppose it was the prayer that did it, but they didn't even inquire about the flag. They merely wanted to look at our apartment, and our belongings, and our passes —all of which they did, and then they went their way.

Shortly after this David's and my passes were up, and so back to Santo Tomás we went. The weeks outside had given me a breather, and a chance to make up my mind about a lot of things. Martha and I had spent a great deal of time at a Catholic church, although neither of us was a Catholic, for after the fall of Bataan and Corregidor the fathers were very kind in doing all that they could for Americans. Many notes from captured husbands came through them, and were delivered by them, but they were never able to help Martha or me get any word about our husbands. They had long lists of typewritten names, but though we pored over them diligently we never did have the satisfaction of seeing either husband's name in print. It seemed a discouraging sign. There were two or three groups of American prisoners encamped not too far from us, and we made dozens of excuses for being in that vicinity, in the vain hope that we might see our husbands. We never could get close enough to recognize anyone, and of course never saw either Bob or Bill, and wouldn't have been able to speak to them if we had seen them.

Back in Santo Tomás David and I went to our old room, number 65 in the annex.[23] David was four now, as he had had his birthday during the time we were outside. This time the Japa-

23. Barbara Clear describes the annex as it was in 1942: "In Santo Tomás, mothers served their apprenticeship of baby care in a hard school. They were packed into a small building with 15 bedrooms [converted classrooms], known as the Annex. It was dirty, congested with school benches, inadequate in plumbing facilities. The majority of the 380 inhabitants slept on mattresses on the cement floor, packed unhealthfully. . . . Bedlam ruled and there was no escape for there were no shanties . . . [or] dining sheds [then]. Curfew was at 6:30 p.m. and when the dormitory lights went out at 7, there was no illuminated room in which the mothers could sit. . . . All the bedroom windows leaked. The central passage, which was half open to the skies, was dripping, muddy and threatening flood. Driven into damp bedrooms, the children made the place a madhouse. At night, after the children's 'lights-out,' mothers could

nese allowed us to take our two small native bejuko beds in with us. This was a step up in the world, for we had slept on the cement floor in the annex until we went outside to stay with Helen and Martha. During the six weeks we were outside the camp had organized a project whereby every person was to have a small wooden platform on which to sleep. I believe the platforms were made by the men who were on the carpentry detail. Gradually, in spite of the Japanese, we were beginning to live like human beings.

Another group of men had made long galvanized iron troughs, with a water pipe overhead, which had several faucets protruding from it. Laundry and dishwashing were done in this. Certain times were designated for each chore. There was a separate faucet, with spray attachment, complete with an old bathtub, which was for nothing but hair washing. With one such arrangement for several hundred women, there was generally a line for this privilege. Soap was always an acute problem, and there was never warm water. We discovered a native bark which could be soaked in a bucket of water and used quite successfully [in place of soap]. Many of the women saved tiny bits and pieces of soap which couldn't be used for laundry or dishes, and put them in a bottle with a little water, and this, in time, became shampoo. The last year there was no soap, and there was no bark.[24]

---

only sardine themselves into the small main hallway—which also happened to be the bedroom of the male guards" (in Stevens 376–77).

A year later, when Elizabeth Vaughan and her two children arrived, conditions had improved considerably. She notes 16 sleeping rooms, a "children's dining room, a clinic and a dispensary, a children's hospital . . . [and] a well-equipped playground," but estimates the annex population at 350 children under 12 and 150 mothers (Vaughan, 204–5)—an average of 31 inhabitants per room. Margaret comments, "It should be noted here that the Japanese were not responsible for any of these improvements. Everything that was done was done by the internees themselves" (to LB 12/14/87).

24. In the spring of 1943 three interned chemists and engineers, T. A. DeVore, M. E. McIntosh, and V. E. Lednicky, constructed the electrolytic cell to produce the caustic soda necessary for soap-making, and the flues, pipes, and fans to control the resulting chlorine gas. Santo Tomás Internment Camp

After David and I were settled again, I looked up my old friend Dr. Robert Kleinpell, the most intelligent man I have ever known.[25] He gave me something to think about, for almost the first thing he said was "Margaret, I think you'd better make up your mind that we are going to be in here AT LEAST two years." I was appalled! It was the best piece of advice he could have given me, for it thoroughly awakened me (at long last!), and even though I was thought a pessimist when I repeated him later, I believed

---

then began to manufacture its own soap, using recycled coconut oil residue. They ultimately produced 16,790 pounds of this valuable commodity, which the Japanese soon ceased to supply. The laboratory also made calcium hypochlorite for purifying drinking water, alcohol for medicinal tinctures, and epsom salts, hydrochloric acid, and creolin (E. E. S. Kephart in Stevens, 261, 263).

25. Robert Minssen Kleinpell (born 1905) earned a Ph.D. in geology from Stanford in 1934 and worked in the 30s as a consultant to "many of the great exploration groups of California's early oil boom," including Richfield and Mobil. While an Assistant Professor at California Institute of Technology, 1939–41, he served as senior geologist for the National Development Company of the Philippines. He, his wife Jerry (Dariel Shively), and Margaret Sherk were table companions on a ship bound for the Philippines in 1939 (Margaret had taken David to California for his first visit with relatives while she had an ovarian cyst and her appendix removed), and remained lifelong friends until his death on March 13, 1986. When the war broke out he was interned by the Japanese, for the last nineteen months at Los Baños. There he organized and taught university level courses in geology and paleontology; each class meeting was "a celebration of life and truth, in defiance of written orders governing the camp."

"It was World War II that made a professor out of me," he said. Indeed, "the years of captivity left an indelible mark on this intensely moral scholar — a sense of the urgent seriousness and joy of the educational process and an intense commitment to freedom of thought," which he transmitted to his students. From 1946–73 Kleinpell was a professor of geology at the University of California, Berkeley, director of the Museum of Paleontology, and active in many professional organizations. He was the author of numerous articles and *Miocene Stratigraphy of California* (1938), "a pioneering study" derived from his doctoral dissertation that became "one of the most vibrant works in the history of stratigraphic paleontology." (Ann Tipton Donnelly, "Memorial to Robert Minssen Kleinpell, 1905–1986," *The Geological Society of America Memorials* XVIII, [1987]: 1–3; and MS to LB 8/9/87.)

him and began to reconcile myself to "at least two years of internment." Having a nature that almost requires routine, I began to set one up for David and me, and I started marking off the days.

There were thousands of people at all times during our internment who never admitted that we would be in for more than "another month." There were people all during the three years who asked for, and got, good rumors just before they went to bed, for it "makes me sleep better," they would say.[26] Not having that type of mind, I cannot understand people who have, for I'd rather know the TRUTH no matter what it is.

Everyone who was physically able was required to do some camp detail. If one were suited by temperament or training for some particular field of work, that type of work was there for one. I had put myself through junior college by binding [and mending] books. It was work I liked and understood, and there was need for it. Binding books became my camp detail. (In addition, mothers in the annex were required to do vegetable cleaning for the children's meals and there was *always* "toilet duty.") The Japanese had allowed the YMCA to bring in certain unrestricted books from their library in Manila. There were several hundred of them, and the constant wear and tear on them, with no new books coming in, kept several of us busy. I had always enjoyed working on books, so I did not mind my detail. One difficulty presented itself, however; what to do with David while I worked? I decided that the place for him was kindergarten. There were many teachers in camp. One of these, an American woman who had had a private kindergarten before the war, said that she would teach David and several other youngsters every morning, Monday through Friday, for the terrific sum of four

26. Rumors abounded in the internment camps, born of hope and escapism. These were compounded of wishful thinking, imagination, distortions of fact, and actual, accurate information received either by the Japanese military on their radios, or by internees who had clandestine radios, as Jerry Sams did. Sometimes the internees deliberately altered the information to prevent detection of their source.

pesos a month per child, $2.00 American or sixteen books to be mended.

There were months when that four pesos was as hard to acquire as four thousand would have been in the days before the war. For a short time some of the officials of the mining company for which my husband had worked took it upon themselves to pay each staff member and his family twenty pesos apiece, each month. Since Bob had not been paid for his last month's work, I did not feel that I was receiving charity. While this lasted it helped very much, though it did not nearly cover everything. Forty pesos are twenty dollars, and it was rather difficult for two people to live a month on that amount of money at any time, even though the rent was free! Inflation was well under way, and I remember paying $1.50 for a box of cornflakes. I felt like a heathen spending that much money just for myself, but for weeks I had been having such an upset stomach every morning after my breakfast of cracked wheat that I thought I would go mad. I thought for awhile I must be getting ulcers, or a cancer, or something else equally horrible, but after stretching my box of cornflakes into breakfasts for a month, I no longer had such pains in my mid-section, and even got so that I craved cracked wheat. The more the better, no matter how many little pink worms were floating upside down in it. The worms had revolted us all at first, but after we convinced ourselves that they were really dead, from boiling, we were quite calm about them. The cracked wheat was a load that had been on the way to China from the United States, and got caught in Manila. The Red Cross had been able to talk the Japanese into letting them bring it into camp. What would have happened to the great majority of us without that cracked wheat, I hate to speculate upon.

The Japanese never forced us to work, but successfully running a camp of five thousand people requires a great deal of work. Approximately two hours a day per able bodied person had to be contributed for the welfare of the camp. There were many people who worked a great many more hours a day than that.

The meals, the great majority of them, consisted of a soupy

stew made with vegetables and a little meat, and boiled rice. Until the cooks learned to cook rice in huge cauldrons this was a nasty mess. Eventually they learned to cook it properly. Part of the vegetables were grown by the garden detail, in a corner of the compound. For the first six months that we were interned, the Japanese did not give us one ounce of food. What we had to eat we got through collective or individual effort. After we had been in Santo Tomás for six months, the Japanese suddenly decided to allot us seventy centavos (35 cents) per person, per day, for food. As I have already pointed out, inflation was well under way. However, compared to the last few weeks of internment, we had a princely diet in those days. The great majority of adults were never provided with more than two meals a day, although children, mothers, and hard-working men were allowed three meals. The first year the evening meal quite often consisted of a boiled duck egg, rice, and talinum. The talinum was always overcooked and black-looking. The black juice from the talinum ran through the gluey rice and the blue-looking duck egg (which tasted like fish) [to make] a most revolting-looking dinner. However, no matter how it looked or tasted, there was a certain amount of good nourishing food value in it. To clean the talinum for five thousand people requires hours and hours of tedious work. Most of the vegetable-cleaning detail hated their work, but it was a necessary job and most of the women were remarkably conscientious about showing up for their detail. The garbage detail was another necessary detail, and another thankless job. Anyone who was in Santo Tomás will not forget the picture of the men on the garbage detail pushing a foul smelling, fly-infested cart, calling cheerfully, "Gangway—Gangway."

Hospital equipment and medicine were things for which the Japanese seemed to feel that we had no need. In any town of five thousand people, anywhere in the world, there are births and deaths. Life, in the general sense of the word, goes right on whether one is interned or not. Among the internees there were doctors and nurses, lawyers and preachers, bankers and financiers. There were indigents, and there were Far Eastern representatives of large British and American companies of many kinds. There were Americans, Mexicans, Filipinos, Chinese, Dutchmen, Norwegians, "Free" French, Englishmen, Scotsmen, Irishmen, Russians (only four nationals), Negroes, and at least one Japanese woman who was married to an American.[27] Almost every nationality on earth was represented by one or many people. Among such a cosmopolitan group, almost every trade and profession was represented, from the oldest profession on earth, to the newest. I don't remember the exact number of doctors there were,[28] but there were enough so that people had quite a wide selection from which to choose. After the fall of Corregidor we had army and navy nurses, plus the civilian nurses. The military nurses were required to put in a certain number of hours every week, and I have never had as good care in a hospital as I had in those of Santo Tomás and Los Baños. A children's hospital was also established, and I can speak equally highly of it. For about six months that first year, David and I were hospitalized, alternately, a great deal of the time. The children's hospital was just behind the annex, and we were allowed to visit the children every afternoon. We were so close to the hospital that we could hear the children cry at night, and I must say that it was a comfort to me to be able to hear David. I could get up and go over to the window and look in, and even go in if the nurse in charge thought it advisable.

One of the first things done for children during the very first

27. Stevens's Official Census List as of December 25, 1945 (surely he means 1944, because Santo Tomás Internment Camp officially ended on July 14, 1945) lists a total population of 3,065, including 2,103 Americans, 720 British, 90 Australians, 58 Canadians, 45 Dutch, 25 Poles, 10 Norwegians, 7 French, 2 Egyptians, 2 Spanish, 1 German, 1 Slovak, and 1 Swiss (499–540). By this time some 2,100 internees, beginning with some 800 men in May 1943, had been transferred to Los Baños to relieve the overcrowding in Santo Tomás and other camps.

28. Stevens lists nine physicians and fifteen nurses (114–16), but the medical population fluctuated, as did the general camp population. It should be remembered that much of the major medical care was provided in other medical facilities in Manila rather than in Santo Tomás. See n. 23, p. 84.

few days that we were interned was to make provisions to send a certain small number of them outside to the Holy Ghost Convent, where they were given better food than Santo Tomás could provide. The children lived in a dormitory and were supervised by Americans. A doctor visited them regularly, I believe, and many of the mothers took advantage of the offer. I considered it pretty seriously for a day or two, but decided against it. David was very much at a loss not having a father. Most of the children did have [two parents], and I felt that the security he felt from my being near him was more important, at that time, than the food. Aside from that, I was selfish enough to think that I could not stand having him so far away from me. I never did regret my decision, and every visiting day when I saw the Holy Ghost children come in I regretted it less. I was especially glad I had not sent him when the children at Holy Ghost got lice. Some of them in Santo Tomás did also, and really I suppose it is not such a serious thing, but I felt that lice on David would have been the crowning blow. I will always think that parents' love and protection and understanding (God knows I *try* to understand, though I make a poor job of it sometimes) count for more than all the efforts of well-intentioned people who do not have the child's every interest at heart.

In regard to religious groups the Japanese were quite considerate. By promising that they would not hinder the Japanese war effort in any way, many of the religious groups stayed outside until the last year. The Catholic organizations were the last to be called in, I believe, and the Japanese always seemed to be a little more lenient with them; hence Holy Ghost Convent for a certain small group of children.

As I look back it is hard to remember and realize, for what it's worth, what my frame of mind was that first six months of internment. David never missed a night of wetting his bed [through the entire war]. In an effort to keep the women in the room from complaining too bitterly, because his mat smelled so (there was no such thing as a rubber sheet to be had), I took him up several times a night. David has always been a very sound sleeper, and it was impossible to awaken him. Someone suggested that I might try walking him to the bathroom, instead of carrying him, for that might wake him enough to cooperate with me. One night as David wove his rubber-kneed way through the group of women sewing and reading under the one night light we were allowed to have, a Russian woman whom I knew only by sight jumped up and ran over to us and jerked David up and carried him to the bathroom. "There, there—poor little mannie" she crooned to him, all the time looking at me as if I were a horrible ogre. I was so amazed that I merely stood by and carried a tearful and uncooperative David back to his bed. Every morning there was a puddle on the floor to be wiped up. David was the youngest child in the room, at this time, and that was a constant source of irritation. He was teased unmercifully [by the other children], about everything, from the fact that he had an unusually large head for a boy his age to the bed-wetting.[29]

All days were monotonous in their sameness. Up at six, for David would not sleep later than that, and outside to the wash troughs to do the daily laundry. This took about an hour, and

29. "It's funny today," wrote Margaret Sams in February 1987, "but when it happened I cried. I didn't know very many people who had extra food, so when David and I were invited to lunch one day I was on Cloud 9. I always worked in the library in the morning, while David was in kindergarten, so when 12 o'clock came I dashed back to our room to get David. I was glad to see that he was there waiting for me. I even thought, 'Ah, what a good boy to have his straw hat on.' It was difficult to make him wear his hat, even though his nose was always sunburned and peeling. I hurriedly jerked his hat off to comb his hair—and there wasn't a single hair on that child's very large, hills-and-valleys, squarish head! Nothing but a shiny, naked, not pretty head. He had talked Jim Harper, a barber who was a married man with two children and should have known better, into shaving his head. David's head sunburned and peeled for weeks afterward. I wasn't one bit sorry for him, just provoked with him for making himself look so ugly."

"Incidentally," Margaret remarked to LB, "Women continued to shave their legs throughout the war, and both men and women were very well groomed. No one was ever a dirty hippie; we didn't use difficulties in sanitation as an excuse to be dirty and sloppy the way some flower children of the 1960s did" (8/8/87).

then back to the room to collect our two tin plates and spoons and go to the chow line and get our morning cracked wheat. Then back to the room, and spend the next hour or so cleaning our spot in the room, airing bedding, etc. Our beds had to be watched constantly for bedbugs, and I felt sick the first time I discovered them on David's and my beds. Most of the rest of the beds in the room had had them for some time, and though I had known it was inevitable for ours to get them sooner or later, I felt like white trash the first time I found the nasty little gray creatures. In those first months we were given some sort of disinfectant, to be sprayed on with a spray gun, but they seemed to thrive on it. Our floor was concrete, and each woman in the room was required to mop her spot twice a week, but several of us made it a daily chore. In the first place it took up time, and in the second place I am naturally a fanatic about cleanliness. I learned a lot about women, and cleanliness, from that experience.[30] I'd rather not know it, too. After David's and my spot was cleaned, and David was off to kindergarten out in one of the nearby shanty areas, I went to work in the camp library.

The first year the custodian of the library made the paste for our books from rice flour and water. The second year we used the leftover morning mush, which by that time was nothing more than rice gruel. It was quite adequate as paste when it was cold. There are as many people who abuse books in an internment camp as there are who abuse them outside of one. There were always great stacks of books ahead of us. We became experienced at sewing, mending, pasting, and binding books. Until the last year Mr. Wishard[31] was always able, through what con-

30. "I learned that women tend to be lazy, particularly when they have been used to living in an environment with servants to take care of them. They knew nothing about mopping or cleaning, and cultivated long fingernails that prevented them from working. Even my friend Louise, before the war, never opened a drawer for fear it would break a fingernail—not that we had any drawers to open when were interned" (MS to LB 8/8/87).

31. Glenn Porter Wishard, Central Committee member and former YMCA official, in charge of the camp library, which was composed of books from the

nection I never knew, to get a cheap grade of book-covering material. It didn't last too much longer than it took us to make the covers, but I think most of us were fairly contented while we were at work. Also, it gave us an inside track on the books, and we always had plenty of good reading material. Under the circumstances, to be allowed to work in the library was all I could want. I worked until noon.

Back to the room then, to see what devilment David had gotten into after school was out, before I got "home." Someone usually met me with a sweet smile and a malicious tongue. It seems to me, as I look back, most of that first year when I wasn't in the library I spent in changing David's clothes, and washing David's clothes, and giving him baths. Everywhere we looked there was mud during the rainy season, and David always managed to be in it. We had a woman from Shanghai in our room by that time, an American who had been caught in Manila. Her husband was still in Shanghai. She had two sons, and what her youngest couldn't think of to get into, David could. Usually these two were very good friends but it is inevitable that children, even the best of friends, must quarrel sometimes. Once, during one of these heated arguments, David picked up a rock and threw it at the child and cut him over the eye. I was properly horrified, for David knew better. However, by the time the story had been told and retold to every mother who came into the room that night, and much sympathy had been lavished upon the young victim, I was plenty sick of the whole situation. A week or so later, when the other child did the identical thing to another youngster from another room, I felt that David had been vindicated. Need I say more about what a mean disposition I was developing?

One of my crosses to bear was the fact that I had the spot directly in front of the large double door of our room. The door was always kept open, night and day. I felt that I was ALWAYS

YMCA. These had been censored by the Japanese before they were brought into camp. Some internees brought in their private libraries, and loaned books to other internees for a nominal fee (MS to LB 11/10/87).

on display. I was in no better position than a monkey in a zoo. There was no place that I could dress or undress in privacy, there was nothing that I could do that wasn't viewed by every one in the room and every passerby in the hall. Not only that, at least once a week I'd come back to the room and find my bed all pushed out of place because the women in the room had been trying again, unsuccessfully of course, to figure out some way to give each one of us a little more room. My bed, being in the middle of the room, in front of the door, was the most easily pushed, and after each try it was a little nearer the door. I never once complained about the mess they made of my bed, and of my worldly goods, all stowed under my bed, not because I didn't want to, but because I hadn't yet learned to stand up for myself. If I am ever caught in a similar situation again, I am going to head for the first corner of the room I can get into, preferably by a window. The next thing I am going to do is get a job in a kitchen, the hospital kitchen. Those are two things I learned the hard way, after it was too late to do anything about them.

Lunch, for the mothers, was soup made from whatever had been left from the children's food the night before. After lunch it was bath time, and then siesta. At least 99 percent of the people who have lived in the tropics for any length of time think they will die if they don't have a siesta every afternoon. It is a Holy Rite with them. When I first went to the Philippines I was young and vigorous and I laid down some rules for myself. I did not want to get soft or go "native." I'd been brought up in a family that practically worshipped work, and so the easy life I saw all around me was something I felt sure I wanted no part of. Later I went soft in many ways. A lavendera [laundress] is one of the finer things of life, as I look at it now! People were as fanatical about siesta as they get [about] religion. Naps for children I approve of thoroughly, as a matter of fact I insist on them, but a nap for me I could not see. While David slept I could work on the clothes for awhile, bring them in and fold them and put them away, and later on when the Japanese permitted a few electric irons I could iron during this time, *if* I could borrow an iron, but most of the time I had to hunt for something to do during siesta time. Very often I helped pick worms out of the rice during this time. After David got up it was almost time to wait in line for the evening meal and then time for another bath and then it was bedtime for David. Before we went to sleep I always read to him, or I recited nursery rhymes for him. Fortunately small children like the same stories over and over. This little time each evening, alone under our mosquito net, seemed the only thing that made life worth while. I somehow felt a little protected from the terrible public eye when we had the mosquito net around us, although one could see through it as well as if it hadn't been there. After David was in bed I either cleaned vegetables for the children's chow the next day, had "toilet-duty," or went out "in front," as we said, and listened to the music. Where the records came from I don't know (certainly the Japanese didn't furnish them), but we had a varied selection.[32] At nine o'clock we had to be inside our own buildings to stand roll call. At ten all lights, with the exception of very tiny ones in the bathroom and the hall, had to be off. Another day had been endured.

Everything that we were given (from a lye soap which ate our hands unmercifully, to the few pieces of toilet tissue), we had to stand in line for, and the smart ones soon got small stools which they learned to carry with them while waiting for hours in the interminable lines. In those endless lines many women learned to knit. We all became adept at knitting, and through a Spanish-Filipino mestizo who cooperated with the Japanese, we were able to buy string (ordinary wrapping string) with which we learned to knit socks, panties, bras, sweaters, [and other items]. With the constant washing our clothes soon wore out. Fortunately, the day we had been evacuated from Suyoc I had, at the

32. The evening music was selected and arranged by Cort Linder from the camp music library of 3,000 records donated by internees; it ranged from country and western music to popular big band dance tunes to arias from grand opera (Stevens 197).

very last moment, grabbed three pieces of cotton print material that I had just bought. A fourth piece of material, piña [pineapple fiber], was folded with them, so I took it also. At that time I had thought I was pregnant, and the material had been intended for smocks.

"There are some things that should be left to the imagination," I have been told, but I have been asked about the following problem too many times to be able to ignore it. If you are a squeamish reader you may skip this paragraph. The first few months that we were interned, dozens of women ceased to menstruate. Naturally, they thought that they were pregnant. Doctors gained some interesting information about women's inner workings from that experience, I believe. Nerves and undernourishment were blamed for the fact that many of us never menstruated properly during the three years. No doubt I will be accused of being vulgar in bringing up the sanitary napkin problem, but for those who menstruated it seemed an insurmountable problem. It finally boiled down to another "detail." Each woman who needed them was given a certain number of small flannel cloths. These were made according to a certain pattern, and each woman embroidered her name and room number on each cloth. A bucket of disinfectant was kept in the bathroom. Each and every cloth went into this bucket and was carted away every day, and a certain detail laundered the napkins and returned them to their respective owners. This detail embraced another group of people who will have stars in their crowns.

Because shanties played such an important part in the life of Santo Tomás, I shall try to picture them in some detail. I know of no woman without a man (except a very few who could afford to have them built) who had a shanty. A shanty was built of any and all materials that it was possible to get one's hands on. The first ones were monstrosities of sticks and blankets and cans and ropes and wire and pieces of bejuco, and if [the owners had] been very lucky, a chair or two that belonged to the university. I remember seeing one shanty town during the Depression, and the similarity was remarkable. Later there were to be some really nice shanties, with floors and sawali[33] sides and flowers and shelves and even curtains. If one owned a shanty a semblance of normal life could be lived. After one's spot in the room was cleaned in the morning, if one had a shanty one met one's husband there, prepared what vegetables he had managed to "scrounge" for lunch, cooked them on a charcoal "stove," washed the dishes, swept the floor, did the ironing with a charcoal iron; in short, went about the business of living in more or less privacy.

I helped a very nice man (an Australian correspondent), whose wife was outside having a baby, make curtains for his shanty. He had bought some pink pinapoc (a rough pineapple-fiber material) from some of the Russian women who lived in the annex. Of all the horrible things to have happen to me, I somehow managed to cut the material for his windows too short. It seemed to me there was nothing to do except take my closely guarded small hoard of money and buy more of the same material. I did just that, and kept the other material, which I used to advantage later on. The correspondent and his wife never did know about the change of material and presumably enjoyed the finished product.

Camp rules permitted only three sides to a shanty, since men and women, so the Japanese informed us, must have no sexual relations. I am not sure that this is possible where men and women live in the same compound, but the Japanese seemed to think it was. Rumor had it that the Japanese had proposed to our committee that we have a large tent on the grounds and "men and women can go to it either singly or in groups." I can quote that rumor, for I was horrified at the mere thought. Presumably the committee felt the same way about it, for word went out that there were to be no demonstrations of affection shown by the internees. Husbands and wives were not even permitted to hold hands, so the rules said.

The very highest ambition of my life was to have a shanty, or to know someone who had one well enough so that I could take

33. Thin bamboo peeled and woven in strips.

some of my hoard of brown sugar and make some candy. I never realized my ambition. I did, on a few occasions, use a friend's "spot" in the patio to cook a little extra chow that I had gotten together for David and me. All the smart women without husbands or friends soon became acquainted with unattached males, and a shanty was under way. At first I suppose I must have looked askance at all the "shacking-up," although I think my predominant emotion must have been a mild sort of passive envy that the other women had enough sense to do something constructive about the problem, and I didn't. It still makes sense that men needed women to clean the shanty and cook for them, and women needed men to build a shanty to be cleaned, and to cook for the men. Unfortunately the men whom I knew were busy with their own wives and children, and weren't *about* to put out any extra strength or time on anyone else.

I lost a lot of illusions about men that first year of internment, and I can never forget many things. One of them is the picture I have in my mind of me staggering down a wet corridor with David's mat over my shoulder, taking it outside to look for a spot of sunshine in which to dry it. Ordinarily it was not too much of a burden, but this morning I had just gotten out of the hospital from a particularly vicious attack of dengue fever, and I still felt miserable. Two men whom I knew very well were standing outside the door of our room as I staggered out with the mat. They both knew that I had just gotten out of the hospital. Both of them just turned their backs and went on talking. This helping women business is purely a civilized trait, and believe me, it can fade into the distance at the drop of a hat!

David and I, alternately, spent a great part of the first six months in one or the other of the hospitals. This can be depressing on the "outside." On the "inside" it can be maddening. Also, to complete tearing my morale into shreds, many people were beginning to get letters from their families in the States. They weren't much as far as news went, for they had been strictly censored by the Japanese before they were distributed to the internees, but at least a great many people knew that they still had families somewhere who cared for them. I did not hear a word from mine, and somehow, in my semi-maddened state, it seemed deliberate to me. Also, of the wives whose husbands were in Cabanatuan, I was one of the very last to hear from mine. The other wives had had one or several notes. The notes were short and to the point, but at least they had heard from their husbands. Some of the husbands were dead, but at least they *knew* they were dead. Now, as I look back on my feelings at that time, I think I wasn't adjusting to my environment nearly as quickly as I should have, for I honestly thought that no one on earth cared enough about David and me to be interested enough to even write us a note. As a result of this mental state, when I was finally handed a note (a much handled dirty scrap of paper) from Bob, in July [1942] (I was on a stretcher being taken to the hospital), I could feel very little emotion of any kind, except— "Thank God, he's alive." I cannot adequately picture how depressed I was at this period of internment. Fortunately, a woman from Suyoc took care of David most of the time when I was in the hospital. Once, the day I returned from the hospital, they took David to the children's hospital that afternoon. It's enough to say that by the time Bob's note came I had become a little bitter. His note said that he was well, but that he had had malaria. "Take care of David," he said. I was doing my best, but a poor best it seemed.

About this time the lists were being prepared for the first repatriation ship. I never expected to see our names on a list to go home, but I think it was a little unnerving to everyone whose name was not on the list to be left behind.[34] It was one more

34. Stevens says that in 1942, on three [undated] occasions, "a number of internees had been given the opportunity of leaving Manila for Shanghai" and for alleged freedom from internment, though most did not go. In September, 1943, 127 internees from Santo Tomás, 1 from Baguio, and 24 consular staff members were repatriated aboard the *Teia Maru*. When the repatriates (chosen with great secrecy) left camp, internees indignantly criticized the executive committee for arbitrarily selecting young and vigorous substitutes instead of giving preference to the elderly or enfeebled, or to women and children. Mr. Kodokai,

blow to the morale. Time dragged slowly on, with internees trying desperately to kill it. Sometimes I thought it would have been
easier to have been forced to work long, numbing hours. One
would have been unable to think and look back. There was no
looking forward, for that way lay madness. We tried in every conceivable way, during that first year, to get accurate news of what
was happening on the outside. Twice I got a pie through the
line during those years (both times from the two women with
whom David and I had stayed on the outside), and once I got
news. The news was baked under the pie crust, so it was a sorry
spectacle when we scraped the pie away, but it was such a thrill
to hear something that had actually been said in San Francisco.

August finally came and went with no more word from Bob,
but David and I each had another turn in the hospital. The case
of milk which we had brought back into camp with us was fast
disappearing, though I was determined to make it last as long
as possible. I was terribly conscious of the lack of calcium in
David's diet, and I would have done almost anything for milk.
I was worried about his second teeth, which he was in the process of forming, and well I might have been, for he has spent
a good deal of time with the dentist since our return to the
United States. The day he looked up at me and said "Mommy,
can't I have just one more spoonful of milk?" I thought my heart
would break. Another time I shall not forget either, though it
happened much earlier in internment. We were having an epidemic of gastroenteritis (diarrhea), and to help prevent it a man
stood at the dining room door to see that we took no food out
with us. Later we seemed to become acclimated, but the first
few weeks of internment enteritis was very prevalent. David and
I always ate our rolls, but many people (those who received food
parcels from outside) did not want their rolls and would leave

---

the Japanese in charge of repatriation, partly exonerated the executive committee, though suspicion of favoritism was never fully abated. Margaret comments,
"I don't know about this. I was never given such an opportunity" (MS to LB
11/10/87).

them on the table. These were the rolls, then, that I made a habit of "stealing" and hiding under my dress until we were outside and away from the man at the door. The day David whispered "Mommy, aren't you going to steal the rolls today?" I thought I had reached the depths. Later everyone saved just a little of the meal he was eating and put it under the bed, in order to be certain of having something for the next meal.

September came, with no change in anything except that we were all just a little hungrier and a little more concerned with nothing in the world except our own immediate problems. Never mind the problems of the man or woman in the next bed. Let him take care of himself. Many people who had gone into camp the best of friends by this time were bitter enemies. Many husbands and wives had separated, others weren't speaking to each other, and in some cases were shacked up with other people. Even people who had been married for years found it hard to have a husband or wife constantly under foot. Most husbands go to work in the morning and come home at night. It isn't too hard to get along well for a few hours each evening and a few minutes each morning. To be constantly in each other's company, especially under the circumstances, was much too much for several marriages. Self came first, and if there was any left over then perhaps other people were considered. People whom I had known for several years I never wanted to see again, and no doubt they felt even more strongly about me. I was no exception. Everyone was going through a very serious re-evaluation period. All nerves were stretched to the breaking point, we thought, and yet we did not dare let them break. As soon as I had made up my mind to the fact that no one in the world cared for David and me, I began to rather enjoy doing as *I* pleased, for the first time in my life. I had no one to account to. As long as I had lived I had had to consider either my family or my husband first. Now, all at once I had nothing in the world to prevent me from coming and going and doing as I pleased, within Japanese bounds, that is. As long as I fed and clothed and took care of David to the best of my ability, I was on my own. I owed no man allegiance, and I began to enjoy the sensation. As I look back at it now, I presume that it merely meant that I was losing all the finer feelings that my mother had taught me to hold dear. I was learning that the world is a hard place, and its people harder. And it meant that my child and I were surviving through the efforts of no one except myself. When we were first interned I had thought a lot about God, along the lines that my mother had taught me to think, but it soon became very apparent that He wasn't going to perform a single miracle for me. He was definitely not going to do anything about it at all, unless I helped myself. David went to Sunday School every Sunday, and most Sundays I went to church, but somehow it didn't help me much; I don't really know why. It had always meant a great deal to me before. Even now, I don't know why it didn't mean more to me. Possibly not *enough* faith in the first place.[35]

This brings me up to September 13, 1942, and up to this time a quite ordinary product of average American parents, with training definitely on the strict side. I will try to make no excuses for the story as it is from here on, for there are no excuses. I had wonderfully GOOD parents, in every sense of the word, and I had a GOOD husband, and I was twenty-six years old and knew exactly how one should go about the business of being a model daughter, wife, and mother. I offer no apologies, for I feel none. I feel that what I did was good for *me,* for it made me look life and facts squarely in the face at last, and made me realize that there is nothing in the world important except facing facts and making the best of them. If it's the truth, and one faces it in-

35. Margaret attended Protestant services in Santo Tomás after having been unable to attend church for several years because "in the mountains there was no church, period. Twice a year a priest came to minister to the Catholics," she explained. "Most of the missionaries stayed out of internment by promising to do nothing to hinder the Japanese war effort" (MS to LB 8/8/87).

stead of trying to run away, one has won the battle, and one is no longer afraid. If one runs away, the story is a downhill one.

September started like any other month. The same routine, the same problems, the same hunger, only a little hungrier. Since a shanty was out of the question, the thing I wanted most in the world right then was a washboard. A very few husbands had invented washboards of a kind for their wives, and my envy knew no bounds as I watched those wives scrubbing their daily laundry. I felt that there was practically nothing I wouldn't do for a washboard.

The afternoon of the thirteenth I decided to go to a basketball game which was in progress out on the front lawn. The first year most everyone showed an intense interest in sports. People still had enough food so that sports were a good idea; sports kept them from thinking too much. The men played football during its season, although they played the touch system in order not to get badly hurt and use up much-needed medical supplies. Playing and watching games being played was the highlight of almost every day for several months. I had been watching the game for some time when a latecomer, a man, walked up beside me and said "What's the score?" There was a scoreboard directly across the court, and without saying anything I merely pointed to it. I did look up though, and I thought "Whew—what a good looking man! I wonder why I've never seen him before? I'll bet he's just come into camp." Shortly after this, the game ended. The stranger went his way and I went mine, and I didn't have the faintest inkling that he would change the whole course of my life. The game having been a good one, I decided a day or two later to go again. The same man walked up and stood beside me during the game. There was no conversation, but we exchanged a smile of recognition. When the game ended we walked back toward the main building together and there was a little small talk. At the main building we separated without finding out anything about each other except that he had been in camp the whole eight months, and lived in the main building. A week or so later I was on the second floor in the main building, having just stood in the soap line, when I met Jerry again. This time he walked over to me and said "Do you have time to go for a walk?" I was a little surprised, but also flattered (for I thought then, and still think, that he is one of the most handsome men I have ever seen), and so we went for a walk, and began to get acquainted.

Under certain conditions becoming acquainted is quick work. I told him that I was married and where my husband was. I was no exception, there were many of us, so that did not make me outstanding. I told him I lived in the annex, but until he walked me home to room 65, he had apparently not realized that only women with children lived in the annex. David met us at the door, and took to Jerry at sight. When Jerry left he asked me to come over to the main building that night, after David was in bed. He told me where he lived, and said that he had some calamancis with which he would make some juice for us to drink. A calamanci is a citrus fruit, like a lime. I thought it over a minute and decided for several reasons that I'd better not accept his invitation. For one thing I was on vegetable cleaning detail in the annex after the children were put to bed, and for another I didn't know him, etc., etc. However, the more I thought about it the more I wanted to go over and sit down in a chair. He had told me that he actually had two chairs, something I had not sat on for eight months. Also he had offered me something to eat. It was the first time I'd had an invitation to go and eat someone else's food since my first hot meal in Santo Tomás, which had made me so sick.

I finished my pile of vegetables in record time, and found my way up the stairs to Jerry's stairway landing which I hadn't even known was there. This landing was his "home," inasmuch as he slept in front of the door of the museum,[36] and was custodian of the key to the museum. I felt that I was being quite daring, and I enjoyed it, and I rather liked Jerry. Especially I liked anyone who was willing to share some of his food with me. In my

36. See explanation, pp. 108–9, n. 45, p. 114.

previous experience it was unheard of. Not only that, he'd let me sit on one of his chairs. It was almost too much. When I got to the third-floor landing I found him playing chess with a friend of his, another man whom I hadn't seen before. I was to meet many men on this landing who lived very quietly and discreetly. Almost without exception they were military men who had been caught in Manila, and as a result always had the threat of Cabanatuan, China, Japan, Bilibid[37] — or death, hanging over their heads. Jerry and a friend of his, Don Rudder, lived on the landing. Don was on the entertainment committee, however, and rarely appeared except at mealtime. When I got back to my room for roll call that night, I asked one or two of the women if they'd ever heard of Jerry Sams. One of them was enthusiastic in her praise of him. She told me that her father had been in Cavite when it was bombed and burned, and that Jerry had been responsible for saving the lives of many men. This, of course, added to his glamour. That, and the fact that he was an ex-Marine and had seen much of the world that I still longed to see.[38]

37. References to locations of Japanese military prisons.
38. Margaret writes, "I finally 'made'(!) Jerry sit down and tell me about this reference."
The island of Cavite is connected to the mainland by a causeway. The causeway was the only way on or off the island, except for a ferry which the navy ran between Cavite and Manila.
Jerry's office was on the end of the island, opposite the causeway. The first string of bombs the Japanese dropped all went into the bay. The second string hit the navy yard, which was set on fire immediately and was a burning inferno within seconds. The navy yard had a barge tied up near Jerry's office. It was obvious that no one was going to be able to escape except by water. (In addition to setting all the buildings on fire, the bombs had knocked out all the fire-fighting equipment.) That meant the people on his end of the island were stranded. Jerry and several other men managed to round up the people and get them onto the barge. However, due to the wind and the tide, they could not get the barge to move away from the dock. They would push and strain and back it would go to the dock.
There was a destroyer (probably the U.S.S. *Peary*, says Halsema), a World War I relic, about a quarter of a mile away; they were fighting their own fire

Writing of one's own love affair must always seem a little inane,
no matter how sincere the feelings are. The first evening together,
sitting on decent chairs and talking, became one of many we were
to share. At first I felt no guilt about spending so much time
with Jerry, for he was excellent company and told wonderful sea
stories. He'd been almost everywhere, was five years older than
I, and had had many interesting experiences.[39] Not only that,
he was most sympathetic and could listen to my own woes without being bored.

Almost as soon as I met Jerry he began to do things, *wonderful* things, for me. One of the first things that he offered to do
was to make a washboard for me. And what a washboard! He
made it from pieces of iron, a board, and a large tin cracker can.
Where he got the board or the iron strips or the can or the tools
with which to make it I didn't even ask him, but he bent the
tin can over the iron strips which he had secured to the board,
in the conventional washboard pattern, and I loved it. I realize
I've spent much time raving over a washboard, but if you've

---

aboard ship, for they had been hit by the first bombs. Notwithstanding that
fact, they sent a motor launch over to give them a hand. The motor launch
managed to tow the barge away from the dock. Jerry never did know what
happened to the barge and the people on it, because after the launch was able
to move the barge, Jerry and several other men stayed to fight the fire in
Cavite. (Obviously they made it, or the woman in Santo Tomás would not have
known about Jerry having been helpful in saving them.)

Since the captain of the destroyer had his own problems, trying to keep his
ship from sinking and losing his men, Jerry feels that the real hero of that incident was the captain—who somehow managed to spare a man and a launch
to help them with the barge.

Jerry reminds us, "In those first war-torn days someone was *always* needing
help and there were *always* people around willing and able to help" (MS letter
to LB 10/18 and 19/87).

39. "Jerry represented adventure, excitement, intellectual challenge. Bob
was more conventional, more predictable. The war changed my view of life.
I became more self-reliant, harder, and even more willing to take risks in the
risky situation of internment camp than I had been before the war. It's possible
that even if I hadn't met Jerry I might not have stayed with Bob after the war"
(MS to LB 8/9/87).

never rubbed little boys' mud-covered overalls in your hands, trying vainly to get them clean, you can't know the joy and satisfaction of scrubbing them hard, and actually getting them clean. The next thing he made was a little pail for David to carry his food. What a blessing the little tin pail proved to be. Again, an old tin cracker can came into its own. Jerry cut the can off at a convenient height, folded the edges over and made them smooth. Inside he soldered a partition so that all the food would not run together, for everything that we ate was of a soupy consistency. When he had soldered a handle on to it, painted it and put David's name on it, it was infinitely more precious than a rare work of art. No one can ever know what it meant to me to have these little things, such tremendously important things, done for me. Least of all, Jerry.

Little four-year-old boys simply cannot carry food on a tin plate across a room without spilling it. Carrying it for a few hundred feet, from the dining room to the place where we ate, was impossible. We had tried it every way. I tried carrying my plate and his small share of milk, and I also tried carrying our two plates and letting him carry the milk. But inevitably, no matter how we tried to get around it, whatever he carried he spilled. It was heartbreaking. Women with husbands had trays, and the husbands very often stood in line for chow for the entire family. Standing in line for several hours every day can be backbreaking work. Not only that, little boys are restless and cannot stand still for any length of time. There were always problems. The washboard and the tin pail solved some of the seemingly insurmountable ones.

From the moment I met Jerry, life began to look up. Every once in awhile he would ask me to come to the landing for lunch. Jerry and Don and two other fellows ate together, and they were not too averse to my coming up occasionally; they did not seem to mind at all if I helped with the cooking, which I was only too glad to do. Compared to the rest of the camp these men had a wonderful setup. They cooked on Bunsen burners from the museum. The balcony of the museum had been used as a chemistry laboratory when it was a university. Bunsen burners were great leaping strides ahead of the small charcoal fires that everyone else used. Also, by hook and by crook, they had wangled a REFRIGERATOR. Jerry had made a wooden "house" around it, in order to disguise it from the Japanese, and he had worked on the motor until it was so quiet that it was almost impossible to hear. The door of the "house" around the refrigerator held the signatures of all the internees who used the refrigerator. After the internees signed their names with a pencil, Jerry burned the names into the wood with a wood-burning tool which he made. When the whole thing was finished it was quite attractive. The internee committee knew about the refrigerator and agreed to let them keep it there, provided they let all use it who wished to. There must have been at least forty people who used it regularly. Each person knew his own dish of rice or soup, and came and went at his convenience. For a year and a half I was there almost constantly, and saw people come and go dozens of times a day, putting in and taking out their food, and never once did anyone by intent take the wrong dish of food. Once only, by mistake, the man on the landing below got our rice bowl and we got his. Occasionally there were choice bits of chicken or meat in the refrigerator. I had seen so many ugly things by then that it helped to restore my faith in human nature.

Much later, after I had inherited the landing from Jerry (who had inherited it from Don), a very amusing thing happened as a result of that refrigerator. Jerry's bed, which I also inherited, had been built up on a scaffold over the landing. This was done in order to have the whole landing, approximately six feet by six feet, free for living space. I had gone to bed, leaving two friends below me sitting on the chairs, talking.[40] Much, much later (the lights were all off), I was awakened by a rhythmical sort of soft,

40. "I never smoked, but both of these friends did. The only tobacco that could be bought was horrible stuff that they had to wash and dry (over 'my' Bunsen burner) in order for it to be tolerable. 'Picadura' (we called it 'barn sweepings') had a rank, ugly odor, but for the sake of my friends I endured it the whole time I was pregnant. This night I had climbed up into my bed

slapping sound coming from down below me. For a long time I lay there and could not go back to sleep. The longer I lay there the more wide awake I became and the more curious I became about that noise. Since I had left the two friends below, I thought that they were still down there and finally, curiosity getting the better of my instinctive feeling to remain quiet and not let them know that I was awake I, like the parrot, said to myself "neck or no neck, this I gotta see"–.[41] In a way I was disappointed when I finally eased myself over and peered cautiously over the edge of the mattress and found only Dave Harvey, our number-one camp entertainer, doing a soft tap dance in front of the opened door of the refrigerator. He was very tall and very thin, and as hungry as the rest of us. Apparently he had to have a nibble at his rice bowl before he could go to sleep. Perhaps it was the sight of forty rice bowls that sent him into his soft tap dance at two o'clock in the morning—who knows?

I shall not attempt to explain my falling in love with Jerry, or apologize for it. I most likely would have fallen in love with the devil himself if he had offered me help and food. When I had sympathy and understanding as well, it was inevitable.[42] Added to that, the circumstances were right for it. No one knew what

---

early, leaving the two of them just below my bed, sitting on Jerry's two chairs" (MS to LB 11/10/87).

41. Margaret writes: "'Neck or no neck this I gotta see,' is the punch line of an old, old naughty joke which I've forgotten." She then proceeds to tell the joke, however: "The parrot's owner had just gotten married and when he put the cover over the parrot's head for the night he said, 'And if you make one single squawk I'm going to wring your damn neck.' Needless to say, finally the parrot couldn't stand it any longer and he said, 'Neck or no neck, this I gotta see'" (MS to LB 11/10/87).

42. Margaret observed, "It took a man and a woman to survive with any semblance of civilization in camp. This had nothing to do with the sex urge. I had no one to talk to, no one to discuss things with, no one to confide in." Jerry, who knew more people in Santo Tomás and had access to more food at the beginning of the war, wisecracked in reply, "I won Margaret through my cooking" (MS and JS [Jerry Sams] to LB 8/8/87, MS to LB 11/10/87).

the next day held; we might be dead, we might be liberated, anything might happen and probably would. It made one want to drain the last drop from the minute at hand. Right now, this minute, is the important thing. Live it. Enjoy it if possible. Probably a poor philosophy, but it is burned into me.

Almost immediately Jerry began taking an interest in David. David's response was automatic, for no man had given him a second glance since his father had gone to Bataan. I was grateful. Very often when I came from my work at the library, or from standing in a line for whatever I would find Jerry and David together. For the first time in many months David had a piggyback ride, and he adored it.

Thanksgiving came and went. We were pleased to have had beans on the line the night before, so there were baked beans for Thanksgiving dinner, instead of the inevitable soup. David and I were invited to the landing. One or two other people were invited, and each person contributed his portion of beans to the kitty. It was definitely an occasion, and one for which we were duly thankful.

Around Christmas the mess which Jerry had been sharing with the three other men broke up. Whether it was due to my arrival upon the scene I do not know. I can no longer remember when it was that Don was suddenly seized by the Japanese and taken to Cabanatuan, but it may have been about this time, which probably helped the mess to disintegrate. At any rate, after the mess broke up David and I ate lunch at the landing every day. David had always had trouble with his siestas in the afternoon. There were seventeen or eighteen children in the room now; at this time the youngest was a baby of a few months and the oldest child was ten or so. One can imagine without too much strain the chaos that resulted. Jerry suggested that I bring David up to the landing to sleep in the afternoon, and I was only too willing. At this time I was spending almost every afternoon working on books for the private libraries around camp. The Japanese had allowed several individuals to bring in their private collections of books. It was an easy way to make money. I have forgotten what the libraries charged (I could always read books I was working on), but it was enough so that they could afford to pay me twenty-five centavos for each book which I made readable again. Twenty-five centavos meant the difference between [subsistence and] being able to buy something extra to eat. One could exist on line chow, but one did little more than exist.

One of the things which fascinated me most about Jerry was the fact that he did EVERYTHING that the Japanese had strictly forbidden. I was so sick of the men who were always saying, "Oh we can't do that, it might endanger the lives of the women and children"—that he was like a breath of fresh air to me. I thought then, and I still think (though not as strongly as I did then!) that there were many men who were purely and simply hiding behind the figurative skirts of the women and children. They were afraid to say, "To hell with the Japanese, we are civilians, not military people, we'll do thus and so." I think they found it most convenient to have a skirt to hide behind. I had not known Jerry for more than two weeks when he told me, in strictest confidence, that he had gone over the wall recently to help some guerrillas set up a radio station in the hills behind Antipolo.[43] Through outside contacts he had made arrangements to be met

43. "Jerry went to the Philippines as a civilian employee of the Navy, and was working at Cavite, across the bay from Manila, when the war broke out. On the *President Garfield* were several Navy types, including one young lieutenant, a Filipino who had just graduated from West Point.

"A few months after we were interned Jerry received a message from Bill Chittick, who worked on the package line, that a Filipino man wanted to talk to him. Although Jerry didn't know the man, he went to the package line and listened to what the Filipino had to say—that he wanted Jerry to help the guerrillas set up a radio station. Because Jerry had never seen nor heard of this man before, for all he knew it might be a set-up. After all, the Japanese had already killed three men who had gone over the fence, and we had been given the ungarbled word about what would happen if more people tried it. Jerry felt that we should be doubly cautious. Nevertheless, he told Chittick to tell the Filipino to get in touch with the Lieutenant from the ship and have him come to talk to Jerry. If the Lieutenant could convince him it was a legitimate request then he would consider the proposal. A few days later the Lieu-

just on the other side of the fence. Apparently it was a simple operation to climb up on the roof of the Red Cross bodega and drop down on the other side of the fence into the waiting cara-mata. It carried a death penalty, but was easy enough to do— physically, if one were not caught. Guerrillas escorted him to the spot where equipment was waiting for him. He was outside of camp for eight days. He had left word that if his disappearance were discovered he was to be notified, through a prearranged signal, and then he would remain with the guerrillas. If he were not discovered he would re-enter camp. Suffice it to say that this happened before I met Jerry. At that time Jerry was reputed to be the outstanding man in his field in the Far East. He was a civilian electronic engineer, stationed at Cavite. He was picked up by the Japanese on January 4, and was a member of the first group of people taken into Santo Tomás.

A story that describes Jerry perfectly is the one of his camera, which he used to good advantage. A few days after we were interned, Kodokai, the Japanese commandant, came riding into camp in Jerry's car. Through circumstances even beyond Jerry's control, he had been forced to abandon his car to the Japanese. When Jerry discovered his car it was in front of the Japanese office, with a Filipino driver and a Japanese guard standing by. Jerry had kept his car keys and he raced upstairs to his room to get them. When he got back, the car was still there, and acting as if he had every right to (which, indeed, he did have), he walked up to his car and unlocked the luggage compartment and started unloading. The Japanese guard, seeing him with the key, apparently thought that everything was as it should be. Various of his friends were standing around, and when he unlocked the trunk he started passing things to them. He took out his electronic textbooks, some magazines, his camera, his pipe and a pound can of Briggs, several personal items, and then he locked the trunk and hastily disappeared into the crowd. The Filipino

---

tenant came to talk with Jerry, and plans began that day for Jerry to go out to help the guerrillas" (MS note, 2/87).

driver apparently appreciated the humor of the situation, for he whispered to Jerry "This your car, sir? I take good care of him until after the war, sir." The next time the car came into camp the driver brought Jerry's navy pass,[44] with his picture on it, which had inadvertently been left in the car pocket.

Jerry had a hand in one of the most amusing stories that came out of Santo Tomás. In the early days of internment Tommy Obst and Jerry were night watchmen. Not only did they "watch" at night, they spent many of these lonely hours "visiting" all the rooms that the Japanese had sealed off. In time they became adept at picking locks, and the museum had a wealth of interesting material in it.[45] Of all the things they *might* have taken, they took the one least calculated to win friends and influence people. They brought out a stuffed four-foot iguana. They decided that it would be a wonderful idea to go quietly into the room of one of their friends and slip the iguana into bed with him. To completely appreciate the story, one must have seen a room full of internees. [See photo, p. 189.] I may say, however, that the beds were so placed that there was a passageway between each two beds. The beds touched, end to end, and two beds were shoved together. Thus, each bed had one free side so that the occupant could enter, and get out of, his bed without stepping over the man next to him. Each man had a mosquito net which had to be tucked under the mattress at night. The four corners of the net were tied with string to a central wire so that around the room each net was tied to the net next to it, as well as to the central wire. Thus the nets were a common support for each other. If one collapsed they all collapsed, enveloping the occupant of [each of] the bed[s] in a shroud out of which it was almost impossible to climb. Jerry

44. Needed for his work on Cavite.
45. Including the cases of money that comprised the museum's extensive numismatic display. Margaret worked at bookbinding on half of the balcony that extended around three sides of the museum, and could look down not only on this collection, but onto numerous other display cases. She did not have access to these, nor to the other half of the balcony where another internee was making coconut oil lamps for internee use.

and Tommy managed to slip the iguana under the net without awakening the fellow. Just before daylight their friend rolled over, and in this foggy state of half sleep he saw the iguana leering at him. There wasn't the slightest question in his mind as to what the iguana intended to do to him. Since the iguana had been slipped into bed on the aisle side, that way out was denied him. He leaped straight across the man sleeping next to him, and landed in his aisle, shouting "shoot him, shoot him." There never has been so much excitement in one small room. Every man in the room was electrified with "shoot him, shoot him," and each man tried to be the first one out the door to shoot him. The fact that none of them knew what they were supposed to shoot, and that the Japanese had all the guns anyway, seemed of little importance. The initial leap across the bed had brought chaos to the room, however, for every man was immediately enveloped, and practically smothered, in his own mosquito net. Needless to say Jerry and Tommy were rolling in the aisles!

We who had children felt particularly desolate as Christmas of our first year in Santo Tomás loomed ahead. Everyone felt a little sick about Christmas. Every available man and woman was put on a Christmas toy committee. Literally hundreds of dolls and scooters were turned out, almost on a production line basis. The aim was for every girl child to have a doll, and every small boy child to have a wheeled toy of some description. The boys of David's age received scooters and I think every man in camp who had labored long weeks over wheels was mortally sorry the day after Christmas. No one was safe. There were major and minor accidents for weeks afterward. Every ribbon or piece of silk or lace was gathered to make clothes for the dolls. That first year there were people who had a lot of clothes, mostly people who had lived in Manila who had been allowed to bring in trunks full of clothes. Everyone was asked to give scraps of ribbon, silk, or lace. More closely guarded prizes than these were rouge and lipstick with which the dolls' faces were made up. Visiting the balcony of the museum, where they were stored, was a distinct privilege. There were hundreds of dolls, and each woman had outdone herself. Each woman viewed her doll with great pride, and many of them wanted Santa to make sure certain little girls received their dolls. A few times during those three years my faith in human nature got a lift. Each Christmas it had a boost. Each year there were less and less materials with which to work, but each Christmas children received toys. It didn't matter in the least to the children that the toys were homemade, or that the paint was still sticky, or had run, or that wheels were not perfectly round. Santa Claus himself was on hand to see that each child received at least one gift. Not only that, there was plenty to eat that day.

If I am ever unfortunate enough to be interned again, I pray that Jerry will be with me. He has more imagination in a minute than most people have in a lifetime. He was as determined to make a nice Christmas for David as I was, and we had a lovely one. By devious methods he got two branches from the trees that grew across the fence in the convent garden. These he cut into smaller branches and fastened onto the barrel of a wooden gun which the Filipinos had used for practicing while they were stationed in Santo Tomás. I thought it symbolic to make a Christmas tree out of a gun barrel. He fastened the "tree" against the wall, between the two chairs. In this way we needed branches on only one side. When he was finally finished it was a perfect half of a small tree. David made paper chains to hang on the branches, and Jerry made a star for the top. I was so pleased for David's sake that I wanted to cry when it was all finished. Christmas Eve, after David was in bed, I went up to the landing with the small gifts that I had managed to make and buy. To my amazement Jerry had LIGHTS on the tree. A friend of his had happened to have Christmas tree lights in a trunk. During the afternoon, when Jerry was working on the tree, Robert had come up to the landing and with a kindness characteristic of Christmas he offered to loan them to Jerry. I believe David was the only child in Santo Tomás that year who had an individual Christmas tree. I am *sure* he was the only child who had a tree with lights on it.

As for food, we had a banquet that year, a real Christmas turkey. We were still allowed to receive food parcels from outside, and Jerry knew some Filipinos. With our line chow made over into something more appetizing and interesting, and our turkey, and our fruitcake (which I had made from coconut oil, rinds of fruit which we had dried and candied, casava and rice flour, and some wine for flavoring which some of Jerry's padre friends had slipped in to him), we had a wonderful day. The fact that David had a wonderful day was enough to make me very happy, but I too received a present from Jerry, a large tube of Ipana tooth-paste, and I am not being facetious when I say it was the most welcome present that I have ever received in my life. We made it last a year. The last year of internment we used anything that we could think of, including part of a cake of Ivory soap. By then it tasted almost as good as Ipana.

The landing, and Jerry, became more and more a part of my life, a necessary part. With Jerry's penchant for making some-thing out of nothing, it wasn't long before he made an oven for us. And it wasn't too long after that until we found a few people who had contacts on the outside—and money. These people were men, and they all wanted something decent to eat. I don't think I'm exaggerating when I say that I have a flair for cooking, and what's more important, I have imagination along with it. With these two qualities, and a place to do the cooking, I was just what a lot of men were looking for. Our diet became better and better. Instead of getting paid for my cooking, we took our pay in food. The people for whom I cooked were agreeable, and so we all benefited by the arrangement. Pumpkin pie is something that has never tasted as good to me since internment. There I made pumpkin pie from squash, raw native ginger, bark cinna-mon, coconut milk, and a very dark brown native sugar. The crust was made from a combination of casava, rice, and corn flour, held together with coconut oil. It tasted heavenly to us.

The first six months after I met Jerry were the only good months of internment. At that time the Japanese had things pretty well their own way in the Pacific. They didn't hesitate to say that we would be treated fairly well as long as they were winning the war.

They also said that we could expect plenty of trouble when and if the war effort became difficult for them. One of our commandants told us this one night at a meeting. At the same meeting we were "entertained" by a repatriated Japanese, who regaled us with the horrors of an American internment camp for Japanese.[46] He had come from White Springs, Georgia. Another of our commandants told us that the Japanese did not recognize the Geneva Convention.[47] By that time we were fully aware of the fact.

I had been well for three or four months. Suddenly I was ill again with an infection. This time I went to an outside hospital, but there was not the usual problem with David. Jerry said that he would take care of him. I have no doubt that he took care of him as well as I could have.

After my return from the hospital a serious talk about Jerry's and my future came about quite unexpectedly. I don't know how long Jerry had been thinking along those lines, but I do know that I had not allowed myself to think seriously of *any* future for us after internment. I knew that we got along beautifully together, that I valued every moment we were together, that he was wonderfully good to David and me, and that David was very fond of him. I knew that I hated to think of the time I wouldn't see Jerry any more. However, that might not happen for ten years, or maybe never. After all, who knew what was going to

46. He was probably right. For an analysis of the these camps, see Peter Irons, *Justice at War* (New York: Oxford University Press, 1983).

47. Principal international agreements affecting the status of civilian internees include sections of the Hague Convention of October 18, 1907, the Geneva Convention of July 27, 1929, and the Annex to the International Red Cross Convention of Tokyo, October 29, 1934. These established in detail rules for appropriate treatment of prisoners of war and civilian internees during wartime, including such matters as food, housing, clothing, and medical care; respect for the prisoners' private property, including prohibition of pillaging; the rights of accused prisoners to have counsel and appropriate trial; and the proper treatment of women, children, the old, and infirm. (See Hartendorp, I, 97–99.) However, although the internees repeatedly asserted their rights under these conventions, the Japanese, who had never assented to these agreements, disregarded their claims.

happen the next day? Jerry and I felt that we might be bypassed altogether, and the Americans might go on to China. We knew that we were only a drop in the bucket as far as the war effort was concerned; after all, what are five thousand lives when hundreds of thousands of them are being lost?

I had been brought up to think of divorce as a work of the devil. I had been married with every intention of making my marriage a lifetime business, and I believe that it should be that way. Bob and I had gotten along nicely and well. We had a child to whom we owed a great obligation. I had always thought Bob valued his work and getting ahead in the world more than he valued anything else. I thought, and I am not too sure I wasn't right, that most men are more concerned with the business of making a living, and making a reputation for themselves, than they are about the whims of their wives. I refused to face facts as they were shaping up. I knew that I had a terribly strong feeling for Jerry. I was an adult, twenty-six years old, I'd been married for more than five years when we were interned, and another year had gone by since I had seen my husband. I was confused as to the proper values of most things. Things I'd thought were God's truth, I had found were not necessarily true at all. Almost everything I'd run into in internment was *not* the way it [had been before the war]. One day Jerry and I were talking about children, how people name them, and why. Jerry had been married for several years but had no children, though he had always wanted them. His wife was in the States. I had planned for years to name my second son Jerry, for my favorite grandfather. I had names picked out for my children long before Bob and I were married. When I said my second son was to be named Jerry, Jerry looked at me and said "Named for his father, I hope." It took me fully a minute to realize what he had meant. And that launched a whole new train of thought and conversation. At first I said, "No, absolutely not, I can't even consider it!" But once a seed is planted, no matter how tiny it is, it begins to grow. And so, six months after meeting Jerry my life began to take a new turn.

My birthday had been pretty generally forgotten for the last few years.[48] When Jerry gave a surprise birthday party for me I was elated. The people who were there still marvel at it. Jerry had not mentioned the birthday all day, which was not unusual, but in my family we had always been a little sentimental about birthdays, and I must confess that I felt a bit sorry for myself. When dinner time came and Jerry had not even asked me to come up to the landing to eat our beans together, I almost disliked him. He did ask me to come up after I got David into bed, though. Jerry had invited six people, I believe it was, and they came up to the landing as if by accident. We often had callers in the evening, and I didn't think too much about it. However, when he unlocked the museum, which he never did at night, and asked all of us to go in quietly I began to get an inkling. He had borrowed the camp record player and some records (my favorites) and we danced in the museum on the balcony.[49] We could have been put in irons, or drawn and quartered, by everyone from the central committee to the Japanese, had anyone known, but Jerry asked the invited guests not to talk about it. It was one time when people could not afford to talk about what they had done the night before. Later we had sherbet made from sugar and water and some cake flavoring which Jerry had scrounged, and a kind of cake. It was the nicest birthday I had ever had, and immediately Jerry's stock soared! A few days after that, suddenly—while we were taking a walk, I realized that I couldn't bear to live the rest of my life not knowing where Jerry was, or how he was, if he were sick, well, happy, unhappy, prosperous or poor, and I mentally began to make plans for us after internment. Jerry's mind had been made up from the first day he met me, he says.

Jerry's birthday is May 2, and our world began to crash around our ears that afternoon. I couldn't believe it at first, and yet some-

48. "Bob Sherk was not very sentimental, nor an enthusiastic celebrator of birthdays" (MS to LB, 8/9/87).

49. "In the 10 by 20 foot portion of space that was accessible from the landing" (MS to LB, 8/9/87).

thing inside me knew that it was true from the very moment we heard the first rumor. Life just has to be hard, it seems, and it had become much too beautiful. The afternoon of May 2 the Japanese announced that eight hundred able-bodied men would be transferred, almost immediately, to a place called Los Baños. They were to prepare a camp for all of us. Los Baños was only forty miles or so away, but it might as well have been at the end of the world. The men were to leave very early the morning of the fourteenth of May, a Saturday. For the next week and a half I felt as if I were walking around with a mortal wound. I felt completely certain that I'd never see Jerry again. The Japanese had said far too many things for me to believe that the eight hundred able-bodied men were actually going to prepare a camp to which we were all, eventually, to be sent. I couldn't see why, after only seven short months of knowing Jerry, I wasn't to see him again. I couldn't believe in anything, or trust anything. My philosophy had become: TODAY. What we take today we have; probably we will all be dead tomorrow. And so it was not hard for us to decide that we would stay together on the landing our last night. Jerry's last night in Santo Tomás, probably the last night we would ever see each other. Certainly the last time we would see each other for many, many months—perhaps years.

I had been brought up by very strict parents, and I'd been reading books all my life, and there was no doubt whatsoever in my mind about what the world at large thought about a woman who forsook her husband when he was away at war. As a matter of fact, I was away at war myself. I doubt if that puts a different light on the situation, certainly I have never thought of it as doing so, but I had fallen completely, irrevocably in love and anything except a straightforward course would have been cheating, and horribly distasteful to me.

And so a thing which I would have sworn would never happen to me if I lived to be a million had happened to me with a vengeance. I was in love with a man who was not my husband, and who might never be my husband. It wasn't Bob's fault in any way. My feeling for him had not changed in the least. I still had as much respect for him as I had ever had, and that respect was unbounded. I have yet to meet a more honest, sincere, good person. It was simply that something far more powerful than respect and admiration had come into my life, something that I had no control over, and something which I no longer even wished to control. Out of life I only wanted Jerry. If I had him, I *had* life. In a way it is dreadful for one person to be able to blot out the importance of the rest of the people in the world, but he had done just that. I believed and hoped that I had done much the same thing to him. I had been what the world calls a "good girl" all my life, and I had reveled in it. I had enjoyed being looked up to as a model good girl, and later, [as the model] wife. Now, all at once it seemed very unimportant what people thought. I hated dreadfully to hurt my mother and father and Bob and his mother. For all those people I had love, of varying kinds. I considered David, and I didn't really think whatever I did, as long as I remained true to an ideal, would hurt him too much. Jerry and I are practical people, as well as idealists, and very romantic. Therefore, before Jerry moved David and me, bag and baggage, up to the landing the night before he left, we talked about the possibility of pregnancy. We were fully grown, fairly intelligent people, and there was that possibility. I shall never forget Jerry's way of saying it. "After all, if we do have a child, we'll be just that much ahead of the rest of the people in here."[50] And I, in my ignorance, agreed wholeheartedly. And I do not mean by that that I have ever regretted my decision in any way, I simply mean that I had no idea how *hard* a path I had chosen. I felt "to hell with the world, our love is well worth it," as thousands of others have felt before me. But when one is actually faced with the results of one's decision, a decision one has made in good faith, mind you, one trembles, to say the least.

50. I.e., "We'll get a head start on the family that others would have after the war" (JS to LB, 8/9/87).

Here I must go back and fill in some gaps in this story. In the very first days of Santo Tomás, the Japanese had laid down rules and regulations for us to follow. Many rules! To prove that they meant what they said, when they said it, they shot and killed three British boys who were trying to escape. That put all thought of trying to escape, over our not-too-high fence, out of the heads of most of us.[51] There are many ways of intimidating a people. Some are more subtle than others. One subtle way of intimidating a conquered people is to make them think that their homeland is no longer what it once was. An outstanding example of this everyone who was there will still remember. One morning, during the first hectic weeks of internment, we all read with great sorrow that Deanna Durbin had died, a horrible death when she was giving birth to a child. When the war started I believe Miss Durbin was at the height of her career, and everyone loved her singing. We all felt as if someone near and very dear to us had died, and the whole camp mourned her death. We felt so keenly about it, as a matter of fact, that we had a memorial service for her in the fathers' garden. We all felt as if we'd had a real body blow.[52] A method a little less subtle was to take a man to Ft. Santiago, which happened regularly the first few weeks of internment. These men, if and when they returned, were always most uncommunicative. They merely limped, or stayed on their beds for weeks, recuperating.[53] Such things are excellent for mak-

51. See n. 13, p. 67.

52. "Deanna Durbin was a very young, very pretty movie actress who had a beautiful voice. Why we felt so devastated by her reported death at the time seems strange to me now" (MS to LB, 8/9/87).

53. Fort Santiago was a military prison inside the old city of Manila, dating from 1756 and the Spanish Inquisition. The U.S. Army used it for offices and living quarters before World War II; when the Japanese took over the Japanese military police used it to house prisoners pending investigation. "[A cell in] the dungeon, about ten by ten feet, with its damp adobe walls and floors, contained thirteen men when [another prisoner] was squeezed in. . . . With fourteen inmates no one could lie down. A five-gallon gasoline can was given them for a toilet and emptied once a day. It was not large enough and con-

ing people do as they are told to do. There are, of course, the brave (or the foolish) ones. Radios and cameras headed the list of the must-not-have's.

Jerry, my brave foolish Jerry, did everything that he was not supposed to do, and [had everything he was not supposed to] have. Before Jerry had been taken away I learned that it was he who had picked the lock which had let him and the other two men out onto the roof during those days before Bataan fell, and it was they who had timed the flashes from Bataan, which told them where the fighting was heaviest. For once, the rumors which we had heard in the annex, many months before, were well-founded.

Above *everything*, we wanted news of the war. Accurate news, every day. Not just typewritten sheets copied by the Filipinos and tossed over the wall. As far as we knew there was only one way to get it, and the Japanese had very definitely told us what we could expect if we were caught with a radio. Nevertheless, after I became acquainted with Jerry I heard news pretty regularly. Not right at first, for after all I knew none of Jerry's friends, but gradually I began to hear things that made me sit up and take notice. Things that put new hope into me, and gave life an added spice. Somewhere on the campus there was a radio! Not only that, Jerry and a very few other men knew where it was, and listened regularly to San Francisco. It went thus, as I understand it. Originally, when something went wrong with the radios of the Japanese, they contacted the central committee

---

tinually ran over covering the floor with human excrement. The stench was offensive and suffocating. It was agony to stand hour after hour, day after day, so that many had to sit down in the filth. . . . Many in the cell had been cruelly beaten and were a mass of bruises and cuts. They received no medical attention. . . . The lice, the bedbugs, the cockroaches, and the mosquitoes fairly swarmed from the cracks of the floor and wall." Prisoners were tortured by being "tied" up by the wrists with arms behind and then jacked up so [their] toes just touched the floor. . . . Those who were taken in for questioning were beaten, burned with cigarette butts, slashed or filled with water to almost bursting and then struck a heavy blow in the pit of the stomach" (Stevens, 324–45).

about whether or not there was anyone in camp who could repair them. Naturally, when they were interned, the men who
knew anything about radios had not mentioned it. The central
committee, however, referred them to three men whom they
knew to be capable of repairing radios. Jerry was one of the men,
Robert Merriam was another, and Earl Hornbostel was the third.
When a radio came into camp to be fixed, Jerry and Robert
stalled as long as possible before returning it to the Japanese. In
this way they heard regularly what was going on, for they would
do something to the radio that would assure their getting it back
for more repairs. I was terrified the first night I put on a pair
of earphones. Jerry and Robert had put the radio on the balcony of the museum, in a closet that had housed chemicals in
the university days. I was completely unprepared for the radio,
and weakkneed, but so very pleased that they had trusted me
enough to let me listen. Me, a mere woman! I felt that nothing
could have made me talk about the radio, but it was more than
a little difficult to listen for hours to women quote rumors that
they are positive are true, when one has just listened to a radio
which has said no such thing.

There were only two people whom I trusted enough to tell
the news, and I did so with Jerry's approval. One was our friend
Bob Kleinpell,[54] and the other was W. H. Donald of China,[55]
Uncle Don to David and me. It gave me great pleasure to be

54. See n. 25, p. 86.
55. William Henry Donald was born in New South Wales, Australia, in 1875.
He went to China in 1902 as a correspondent for the *Sydney Daily Telegraph*,
and "helped man the guns that blasted the Manchu Dynasty out of power
in 1912—resigning his position with the newspaper before he got fired." After
a brief stint as managing editor of the *China Mail* in Hong Kong, an offer
allegedly made because Donald was "the only nonalcoholic newsman in Asia,"
he got a job with the *New York Herald* in China. There he met Sun Yat-sen,
"leader of the revolt against the corrupt and tottering Manchu Dynasty," who
soon hired him as public relations advisor. From then until the outbreak of
World War II, Donald "moved in the highest circles in China." After Dr. Sun
died, in 1928 Donald went to Manchuria as adviser to Chang Tso-lin and his
son, Chang Hsueh-liang, the marshal of Manchuria.

able to give them authentic news occasionally, for I believed that they were as happy as I was to know what was actually taking place. It is impossible to put forcefully enough how very dangerous this news gathering was. Everyone was a potential enemy. Not that the internees intended to be. We worried more about the internees talking too much than we worried about the Japanese finding the source of some of the rumors.

A few weeks after Jerry left I was not too surprised to get a note from him, telling me that a certain man in Shantytown had a small radio that he was willing to give away. He had kept it hidden and was getting tired of having to worry about it all the time. The fact that Jerry wanted me to get the radio and send it to him did not surprise me at all. The thing that did surprise me was how he had discovered the fact that this man, whom he did not know, had the radio. I think it upset the fellow, too, when I walked in and casually said, "How about loaning me your radio for the duration?"

I think I should state here that almost everyone had something that he didn't want the Japanese to know about. It might have

---

After returning to China from Wellesley College, Dr. Sun's daughter married Chiang Kai-shek, and soon sent for the newspaperman, who eventually became a chief economic adviser to Chiang and a close friend of the family. One of the high points of his career was the skillful role he played in securing the release of the Generalissimo when Chiang was kidnapped in 1936. When the Philippines were attacked, Donald was working on Madame Chiang's biography, assisted by her secretary, Ansi Lee, and was trapped in Manila en route from his home in New Zealand to China. "They barely had time to hide Madame Chiang's papers and the partly completed manuscript in an apartment" before being interned in Santo Tomás. The Japanese authorities did not realize that Donald was the notorious Australian-born Scotsman whom they had sought throughout China for questioning.

At the war's end, an issue of *Time* magazine published in February 1945 (before Los Baños was liberated) and distributed widely to American forces, erroneously claimed that Donald was among those liberated at Santo Tomás on February 5. This report caused great apprehension that the Japanese would execute him (MS note, 2/87; MS to LB 8/11/87; JJH to LB 11/21/87; and Anthony Arthur, *Deliverance at Los Baños* [New York: St. Martin's, 1985], 25–26).

been nothing more than a knife, which we were not supposed to have, or it might have been a diary, which we were forbidden to keep, or it might have been that one had once been in the armed forces, or in some cases it was simply that one was sending notes through the underground. Money, notes, and food were the important commodities in the underground work. Through the help of one of the camp doctors, Jerry had faked an illness in order to get out to Philippine General Hospital so that he could contact some Filipino guerrillas in connection with the transmitter-receiver that he had set up for them. Many otherwise sensible people were willing to help in any way that offered even a semblance of security. Almost without exception, everyone had something that he wished to keep from the Japanese. All of us were afraid of being discovered at our "dirty work." All of us were afraid, period.

For years I have hoped that someday I might have the courage to write of the feelings of a scarlet woman. I have read many books pertaining to same. I can't adequately write of her feelings; I only wish that I could. I only know that the people who write the stories and the books have not been there. *That* I know for certain. One reads of women who become nuns "giving up the world" and one thinks "How can they? What a terrific decision to make." Believe me, we who have decided to have our "love children" give up the world also. We too have compensations, but we can never be like other people again. I find that I can never hope to make a new friend again, and I am sorry, for too much has gone before which must be explained before a friendship can be started. Only people who were there can understand, and few enough of them can.[56] Those few know me, and under-

56. "I've changed my mind about making friends since I wrote this. I've made several friends since then. A friend is someone I can trust, who knows my story, but to whom it doesn't seem to matter. I can count on a friend for help whenever it is needed. Generally, it takes some time to make a friend because you have to get to know one another. I have friends of longstanding

stand me, and forgive all. The new, would-be friends try to understand, but I am certain that they can never completely comprehend. I have the feeling that they think I must have been temporarily mad. The relative importance of almost everything that one is faced with in life takes on a completely different color and meaning. Things that I had always thought very important suddenly became trivial. On the other hand, it is odd, isn't it, for people to think that one's heart and mind and ideals can be changed because one has made love to a man one loves, although he is not one's husband?

For some, the books tell us, it is the road down. I refuse to admit that it was for me. I think the intrinsic values it taught me are valuable beyond mere words. I think, as a result of my waywardness, I will at least be a more understanding mother to my children, although very likely I will not be a better mother. As far as I know, I am the only bad woman in our family, on either side.[57] It's quite a distinction. My relatives did talk about it in whispers, though they seem to have gotten used to the idea now and have contented themselves with waiting for the years to vindicate their judgment.[58] I am sorry to have ruined the fam-

---

from high school, several women and a man, Bob Zerbach; Bob Merriam from camp considers me one of his best friends" (MS to LB 8/9/87).

57. "The trauma of Jerry's and my life together in internment made me finally grow up. As a result I've been more understanding of practically everything. I don't think I've ruined my life, although my paternal grandmother would have thought so. I was sorry but not shattered when my son David left his wife of 25 years (no children) and married another woman and when my son Ned left his wife of five years (no children) and remarried. They consulted me before they did it. I said, 'It depends on whether or not you want this stress and strain for the rest of your life.'

"Writing the book helped me to *almost* get over internment. It also helped me to *almost* get over feeling that I had done something dishonorable. I cannot picture in my mind how a woman can have an affair and at the same time be living with her husband. I would never have had an affair at the same time I was living with my husband" (MS to LB 8/9/87, 11/10/87).

58. "Some of my relatives considered my relationship with Jerry as a 'tem-

ily tree for them, but I don't believe I will ever say to my grandchildren, as was said to my cousins and me once, when a neigh-
borhood scandal was being bandied about, "Children, I'd rather
see any one of you dead and buried than have a thing like that
happen to you"—the girl merely had a baby six months after she
was married. I ask you, is that the right way to look at it? If
I'd been born a Bontoc Igorot, I would have slept in an olug
and there

> A girl may mate with a number of different men in the olug and
> it is considered proper and virtuous, for as soon as she becomes
> pregnant she will become the permanent wife of the young man
> responsible for her condition. The marriage ceremony will then
> be performed by the oldest man of the ato in which she lives and
> she is not permitted to sleep in the olug any longer. But a girl
> who sleeps with a man outside the olug, which custom has fixed
> as the mating-place for the young or until the girl has proved that
> she is fertile, is considered a public woman and loses caste in Igorot
> society.[59]

There must be thousands of different customs and moral codes
throughout the world. None of them, I presume, would condone my own behavior. I am most emphatically not advocating
my behavior, but I am advocating a little more charity in people's
hearts.[60] Charity is the most scarce of all human qualities. I have
been taught charity. Being too human, I begin to slip back into

---

porary arrangement.'" They were waiting for this relationship to end to prove
them right (MS to LB 8/9/87).

59. Samuel E. Kane, *Thirty Years With the Philippine Head-Hunters* (London: Jerrolds, 1934), 54.

60. By writing this book, of course, Margaret is expecting her readers to
understand her actions, and to be sympathetic to her as a person—attitudes
which would surely mitigate their moral disapproval even if they did not fully
condone her behavior. "I had been trusting and vulnerable before the war. As
a result of my experiences in internment camp, I developed a defensiveness and
a hardness that I didn't have earlier" (MS to LB 8/9/87).

the old rut every once in awhile, until I stop short and remind myself of the days I have known. Having a past has put me in a position to hear many, many stories of other people's lives. Most everyone has a story, some more interesting than others, but all interesting. Most people hide their stories because they are ashamed of them. Therein lies the shame.

During the next few months of internment, I lived in a scared-to-death hell. Jerry had been gone only a month, when I definitely decided that Fate had decided to take us up on our proposition of getting "ahead of the rest of the people." As I look back now, I think I must have known what was in store for me from the very first moment. I waited for two months until I was positive in my own mind, and not just positive that I was scared to death, and then I began to make plans. I had pretty definitely cut myself off from too many internees when I moved up to the landing. Jerry had talked to everyone who was concerned about my change of abode, and had established me on the landing the night he left. Many people said "What right has *she* to that place?" but there wasn't too much that they could do about it as long as I behaved myself, which I had every intention of doing. I had been put in charge of the book binding for the public library, when the eight hundred men left, and I immediately saw to it that the book binding was done on the balcony of the museum. That gave me a sort of right to be on the landing, and an easy place to work. I could stay there all day and work as much as I pleased on the books, which was a great deal, for I was now being paid twenty-five centavos for every completed book. The landing was one of the least conspicuous spots in Santo Tomás, and I loved it for that reason.

For years now, I have been able to sympathize a little with a trapped criminal. After Jerry had been gone for two months and I'd had one short censored note from him, I felt *quite* a little trapped and very much like a criminal. In books the girl always goes away for awhile. In Santo Tomás there was definitely no place for me to go away. All my life it had been drilled into me how people feel about a wicked woman. There was no doubt in my mind about how people, all of them, would react as soon as I became noticeably pregnant. I had had a ghastly time with David. Two different doctors had told me that I probably could not survive another childbirth. It seems ridiculous, but even worse than that possibility was my fear of having eclampsia, which I had had with David. I had become enormous and horrible to behold. I thought I'd *rather* die than look like that again and feel like that again in front of all those thousands of people.[61]

When Jerry left he had asked his friend Robert Merriam to "Take care of her for me." Robert had blithely said "Sure, I'll be glad to" and neither of us had thought any more about it. I saw Robert every day, however, when he came up to get his food out of the refrigerator, and occasionally he cooked there. Also, I was willing for him to meet and talk to his friend there, for I liked her also. Those two I saw several times a day.[62] Louise Miller, from my old room 65, I saw regularly. I had also become acquainted with Mabel, who lived in a room at the bottom of the stairway. Mabel was tall, dark, stately, several years older than I, divorced, and a woman with a mind of her own, and I loved her for it. These four then, whom I had never seen before camp, I saw often. I believed they came up to the landing to use my advantages (which I was perfectly willing to share, for I liked them

61. "I never quite believed those doctors. After my mother nearly died of childbed fever with her first child, the doctor told her she would die if she had more children—and she had six more. I haven't had a physical since Kathy [her last child] was six months old—thirty-three years ago." "I should be ashamed to admit that," Margaret added later (MS to LB 8/9/87, 11/10/87).

62. "Robert Merriam had joined the Navy as a young boy. Before the war Bob worked in Manila as an electronic specialist for a company that installed and maintained movie theater equipment" (MS to LB 8/9/87, 11/11/87).

all) but I had no reason to expect them to stay around after they became aware of my situation. I decided, after many sleepless nights, that I must tell them my story. It seemed to me they would wish to break all contacts with me before I became a public scandal.

I cannot possibly describe how terribly hard it was for me to tell Louise that I was *not* the kind of woman she had thought me. I shook for hours at the mere thought of telling her. After I had made up my mind that I had to, it took several days before I finally had courage enough to go through with it. I perspired, and shook, and felt sick at my stomach, but finally I told her that I had to talk to her. I must have looked almost as green as I felt, for she stopped dead still in the road and said "Well, tell me!" When I had finished, she said the most wonderful thing she could possibly have said to me. She said, "Oh my gosh, I thought it was something *awful,* I thought Bobby and David had had a fight or gotten into trouble." And so then I cried, and laughed, and immediately felt better. Womanlike, the first thing we talked about then was clothes. *How* to clothe my baby? For two months I had had it all to myself. I couldn't eat, I couldn't sleep, I couldn't do anything except wish that Jerry were there with me, and try to act as though nothing was wrong with me. The exquisite relief of talking about it was almost unbearable. Fortunately, it was at this time the Japanese decided that women could wear shorts. Just before Jerry had left he gave me some sport shirts that were too small for him. My ensemble became shorts and sport shirt, worn tail out. I am one of the more fortunate women. I am large boned, and as a result I do not look terribly pregnant.

After I told Louise, we became boon companions. We had always liked each other, but somehow we found that we had many more ideas in common. Why I don't know, except that a barrier was down, and I could talk more honestly to her than I had ever allowed myself to talk to any woman in my life. My motto seemed to be "Why pretend? It's this way, let's go on from here."

Her husband was in Cabanatuan also. Louise had a lively imagination and could see that, as she said, "A thing like that could
happen to almost anyone." There are some of us who rather enjoy, once the terrible shock is over, being controversial, sticking
out our chins.

I wish I knew more about psychology. I'd like to know the
deep-down reason why, as soon as I had told Louise about the
baby, I immediately began to look at the situation with not quite
so much dread as I'd felt before. If she had reacted in almost
any other way I might have jumped off the top of the building.
When she was so matter-of-fact about it, I began to realize that
I wasn't the first woman in the world who had had a child under
difficult circumstances. I don't know why, but from that day on
I began to get a terrific pleasure out of the fact that I was carrying Jerry's child. I, of all lucky people!

My husband and Jerry had to be told about the situation. I
had had two or three notes from Bob by this time. Each note
was cheerful, and each one told me to "take care of David." Notes
between Cabanatuan and Santo Tomás were always in progress.
Sometimes they came quickly and sometimes it took them months.
They were always tiny folded squares of dirty paper, much fin-
gered (and read, I am sure), but all credit is due the people who
risked their lives in getting them back and forth. I had had two
or three chances to send notes to Bob, and I had taken advantage of every opportunity. He had asked for clothes, which I had
promptly sent to him, and I had also been able to send a package of medicine. I don't believe that he ever got either the medicine or the clothes, but that is expecting quite a lot of human
nature when the distress was so dire. At least I had tried, which
was all I could do.

My first note was to Bob, for he was the one person in the
world I would not have deliberately hurt. I knew that he would
be hurt to death, for he truly loved me. I hate people who talk,
with a smirk, of a "Dear John" letter. They don't *know!* The letter
to Bob was the hardest letter I've ever had to write. I wanted

him to know the story long enough in advance so that he could have his feelings under control, before some busy little wife from Santo Tomás managed to get a note through to a husband in Cabanatuan. In many cases the busy little wife was shacked up with someone else, but that was neither here nor there. Bob had known about Jerry from the beginning, for I had written about him. Also, Jerry's roommate on the landing had been taken to Cabanatuan several months before and I had asked him to be sure to look up Bob. Bob later wrote to say that it was the nicest night of his stay in Cabanatuan—the night Don Rudder came to see him and told him about David and me. (More and more I am forced to believe that our lives run in circles, for not three weeks ago, after almost ten years of silence, Don Rudder called me on the phone and later came out to see us.) All this looks cold and hard-hearted in print. I hope you, my children, when you read it will not measure me by the way it looks. You will have had the benefit of several years of Jerry's and my teaching, and you will know that we have always been in love. A rare thing, believe me. I hope you will judge us from that standpoint, not this,[63] but I told you in the beginning that I'd write it as it happened.

Next I wrote to Jerry, for he seemed next in the order of importance. He had been gone for almost three months, and God only knew how he was getting along. By that time I wasn't sure of anything. Maybe he had only been talking when he said that it would be all right with him if we had a child. With a quaking heart I told him that I certainly would not be the one to hold him to his bargain, if he even *slightly* didn't want to go through with it. And on and on and on. And so I settled down to wait for the answers to my notes, the answers to my fate. Our grapevine was much better organized from Los Baños, so Jerry's note came

63. I.e., "from your knowledge of us as lovers and as responsible parents, not from the colder perspective of these written words" (MS in conjunction with LB 8/9/87).

first. It said all that I had longed to hear.[64] By the driver of the bus Jerry sent tiki-tiki (a native by-product of rice, vitamin B complex), two small bottles of calcium, and four hundred and fifty pesos.

With the coming of Jerry's note, and his blessing, I really began to enjoy preparing for our child with a deeper, more shaky, trembly sort of joy than I have ever known before or since. On the other side of the ledger, however, was the fact that I dared not tell the Japanese, and even more I dared not tell the Americans. Also, always nagging at the back of my mind was the doctor's prediction that I probably couldn't live through another childbirth. I was particularly concerned about David. What was to become of him if anything did happen to me? And my baby, what of it? It was a little late to start worrying, but I could not help worrying constantly about the wrong I had done the baby. Jerry might be killed, or his wife might refuse to divorce him. Perhaps Bob would refuse to divorce me. *How* could I make it up to the child? Health is important, but is it as important as a name? In my heart I knew it wasn't, according to worldly standards, but I had already cast the die, and I loved the baby so much, I had such a protective feeling for it, that I would have done anything to protect it from a disparaging word.

I have always put health at the head of the list of musts. If one has good health, everything else should automatically fall into place, or so it seems to me. With all the concentration that was humanly possible I began to try to make the baby a healthy

64. "The essence of the note was, 'I love you. Keep your chin up.' Jerry was a good letter writer" (MS to LB 8/9/87). Jerry himself observes of the terseness and unoriginality of this communication that the note had to be fairly neutral because he didn't want Margaret to be punished if the Japanese identified her as the recipient. Had he been identified as the father of a baby conceived in internment (which of course he eventually was), he could have been punished by imprisonment by Japanese military authorities, who of course had a vested interest in curbing the population (JS to LB 8/10/87 and Stevens 228; see n. 26, p. 54). Vaughan notes, on 4/24/43, "No cines for many months, entire camp being punished for pregnancies of women in Shantytown scandal" (209). (See Hartendorp I, 358–63.)

one. I realized perfectly that I had handicapped her as far as a name was concerned. She, he might never know his father. The least I could do was to make a healthy child. We were no longer given sugar on the line, and soap was no longer rationed.[65] Food in those days was becoming ever harder to acquire. For a pregnant mother the line food was certainly not adequate. I had no one except myself to blame for that, however, so I had to make up for it if I could.

The most important single thing on my list of musts was to get money. If I had money I could buy food and many other extras that we needed. It seems there is always a way to get things if there is enough money. If I had money I could pay for the baby's birth, and I could take care of the inevitables after the baby was born. I was determined to give the new baby clothes, milk, soap, blankets, oil, etc., just as I had done for David. Perhaps I placed too much importance on money, but I rather doubt it. (*Not* but that I despise money for money's sake!) If I had money I could be self-sufficient and wouldn't have to ask anyone for anything for my baby. If I had money I could buy food to put away for the future. I could buy calcium to take before the baby was born, calcium to give to David. And I would like to point out here that it was no simple matter to find out who the people were who had money, and who had calcium or ways of getting it, who had soap they would part with for a price. I could buy clothes for both of the children. Money could not buy security, but it could buy the thing that I needed most at that time, and that was self-confidence. In the outside world, money is always important, but it can never have the importance that it has under those conditions. I had no one to depend on except myself, and my future was indeed black. If I had money, I could take care of us. I made a concentrated effort to contact people with money, and I had to make those contacts quickly, while I still had a reputation that was a good security risk. I felt

65. Because Santo Tomás internees were making their own soap. See n. 24, pp. 85–86.

as if I were getting the money under false pretenses, but I had to. I finally amassed a fortune! Two thousand pesos, for which I signed notes, to be repaid at the rate of four to one. There have been bitter complaints from the people who borrowed money about having to pay it back at such an exorbitant rate of exchange, but I was so thankful to get money at *any* price that I was only too willing to sign anything. Almost all of it I have since repaid. About the time I got my fortune together I received a note from Bob. He wanted money. The note was written before he got my note about the baby. I sent him five hundred pesos. I will always hope that he got the money.

Bob's answer to my note did not come for months. In the meantime there were problems to be met. In the first place, I knew that sooner or later the central committee would have to be informed of my condition. It was up to them, then, to tell the Japanese that they had a wayward woman in their midst—and what were they going to do about it? A few families, for various reasons, had been on the outside during some parts of the first year and a half. Some of the women had become pregnant. The husbands of these women had been put in jail when they came into camp. Our own internee jail, it's true, but nevertheless it was an indignity to be put in jail because one's wife has had a baby, quite legitimately. I felt sorry for these people, but what was *I* going to do? I didn't have a husband to go to jail for me. During one of my sleepless nights (and they were all sleepless)[66] I decided that I would tell the Japanese, if they demanded a man to be punished for my pregnancy, that I had slept with so many men that I couldn't possibly tell them which man was the father of my child. Fortunately I never had to do this, but I might as well have, for I went through all the agony of making up my mind that it was the thing to do. For me, the actual act is nothing; it's the mental whipping I have to give myself to make me

66. "There was never any 15 minute period when I didn't hear that clock striking. I started sleeping better when I joined Jerry in Los Baños" (MS to LB 8/10/87).

decide what course I am going to follow. Sticking to it is easy then.

I went through another mental torture chamber while I was making up my mind to tell Robert Merriam and ask his advice about the situation. Once again I found that after I had told him the story it became almost fun to talk about it. Robert was properly appalled at my situation, but not shocked, and there is a world of difference. A few weeks after Jerry had been taken away Robert had come up to the landing one day and said "Remember, if there's ever anything I can do to help out, be sure to let me know." I, suspecting already, had said "Thanks Robert, I will." He still laughs when he remembers how readily I took him up on his offer.

The head of the committee was a good friend of Robert's, and since I knew the man only by sight Robert offered to take my story to him. Mr. Grinnell has been much discussed, some good, some bad, but I liked him. My contacts with him were brief and to the point, and he was always very kind to me.[67] When Robert told him about the situation he apparently wasn't shocked at the fact that I was pregnant, just shocked that I wanted to go through with it. Seemed a little upset that I hadn't told anyone sooner, so that I could have had something done about it. *That* was shocking to me, but I appreciated his interest. He told

67. At the war's outbreak, Carroll C. Grinnell had been Far Eastern manager of General Electric. He had lived in the Orient for twenty years, and traveled frequently on business to Japan. There he had learned some Japanese and much about the culture, which was very useful in his capacity as chairman of the executive committee of Santo Tomás, elected by the internees on July 28, 1942. He served as chairman throughout the rest of the war until December 23, 1944, when he, another executive committee member, A. F. Duggleby, and two others, Ernest E. Johnson and Clifford L. Larsen, were arrested by the Japanese, and murdered around January 15, 1945. His body was found in a field after liberation, on February 20, with fourteen other bodies "wired together in groups of a few each" (Stevens, 39, 70–71). Hartendorp says, "It was generally believed that Larsen's arrest was a matter of mistaken identity as he was a young man whose role in the camp was a minor one. Johnson, a onetime ship-captain, was known as a man who was frank and somewhat careless of speech" (II, 459).

Robert that he thought I was a "brave girl" and it made me feel like a child who has just had a pat on the head from an admiring grownup. One day he gave me two bottles of calcium. The calcium was my most prized gift, for most of mine was gotten the hard way. I saved the duck eggshells, boiled them, dried them, ground them, and ate them. Excellent source of calcium, I understand, but a bit of a nuisance. Mr. Grinnell was beheaded about a month before Santo Tomás was liberated as a result of his activities in behalf of the internees. Both Mr. Grinnell and Mr. Duggleby (a mining engineer who was also beheaded) were very kind to me during the last few hard months of my pregnancy.[68]

Another repatriation rumor was in the air. I felt sure I'd never get on the list, but I was hoping. Jerry wrote for me to make every effort to do so. I was glad that he was concerned and yet, when each one of my four friends thought I was some kind of a fool for thinking that Jerry loved me enough to marry me, if and when we were ever in a position to do so, I couldn't help worrying about it. Robert tried for weeks to get my name on the list of repatriates, but to no avail. He even gave me the address of an aunt of his, with whom he was sure I could stay until after the baby was born. I knew that even if I were repatriated I could not go home under the circumstances. Also, I still had not heard a word from my family which, in my unhappy mental state, simply meant that they did not care enough about me to write. Certainly I had written to them at every opportunity. Frequently the Japanese gave us cards on which we could write a certain small number of words to our families. The only one my mother ever received came after we were liberated and had arrived in the States. However, I could not know that, and also I could not know that my mother was doing everything in her

68. "Mr. Duggleby escorted me to the outside when I went out to have Gerry Ann and I know he felt sorry for me" (MS to LB 8/9/87). Alfred F. Duggleby, executive committee vice-chairman, was before the war vice-president and consulting engineer of the Benguet Consolidated Mining Company and the Balatoc Mining Company, the two largest gold mining companies in the Philippines (Stevens 19).

power to find out about David and me and to let us hear from her. Some internees received mail regularly, and some never heard from their families.

After the second repatriation ship left, without David and me, I knew that there was going to be no easy way out for me. I knew that I was going to have to face the music in front of the thousands. I didn't mind *after* the baby was born, it was just that I hated to be a spectacle *before* she was born. Every day I got a little larger, and it seemed to me that I was enormous, though I couldn't have been, for I only gained seven pounds during the entire period. I was especially worried when the man who lived on the landing below me stopped me one day and said in a conciliatory tone of voice, "Aren't you feeling well lately? I notice you're getting thin." I assured him that I was feeling wonderful, and thereafter made it a point not to make my trips up and down stairs when he was at home. My landing was on the third floor and I was always light-headed and dizzy when I arrived at the top. In order to make it at all, I had to stop every few steps and let my heart quit beating me to death.

For the thousand years that I was pregnant, it seemed to me that my entire inner workings were in a constantly shaky state. During that thousand-year period I am sure that I never slept more than an hour a night.[69] I never missed the bong that sounded every fifteen minutes from the clock in the bell tower. I'd go to bed and go over and over and over the possibilities of the situation. Mentally I went over each friend, and each acquaintance, deciding which way they would react to my story. I decided to tell two more women because I saw them frequently. I wanted to give them a chance not to be seen with me for some time before the news broke. I do not believe I overemphasize this event, though I realize I have dwelt too much upon it. We had been interned for almost two years, everyone recognized every face, whether they knew each name or not. It isn't

69. "I wasn't much good because of lack of sleep. I was a walking zombie" (MS to LB 8/9/87).

every day that a situation of the kind arises, where there is no possibility of its being kept quiet. There I was, for the whole five thousand of them to look at and talk about and discuss the pros and cons of the affair. "Who was it?" "What will he do about it?" "Surely he won't *marry* her!" "What will her husband do about it?" "What will the central committee do about it?" "What will the Japanese do about it?" For months gossip had been trying to get *someone* illegitimately pregnant. Most of the younger girls had been under fire, but I don't believe that I had ever crossed their collective or individual minds. Mentally I left no stone unturned. The fact that the four people who were standing by me were all worried about whether Jerry had been as sincere in his feeling for me as my feeling for him had been, concerned me no little. Not that I ever let them know that it worried me! Maybe I *was* just another dumb bunny, who knew? The notes from Jerry were far apart, and really said very little except "Keep your chin up."

As usual I went through another siege of quaking, trembling insides the day I told the fourth and last person about the baby. I intended telling the story to a woman from the mining camp where we had both lived for several years. I had thought she might understand, just a little, for we had been friendly for a long time. Her husband had been one of the men who had thought his duty lay with his wife, rather than with the army, so he was interned with her. The woman was positively horrified, instinctively drew back from me, and said "Margaret, I can understand having an affair with Jerry, but to have a baby under these circumstances I cannot possibly understand. For my husband's sake, his reputation in the mining profession, I will not be able to see you again." And she never did, though we stood side by side in many lines after that. "We like Bob so much that we couldn't possibly overlook the situation," she said. That could only make me laugh, for her husband had never really liked mine; Bob had been his superior at the mine, and he had always resented it. Oh well, the four others of whom I could have expected nothing were so good to me that it would take a book for me to give them my thanks. I shall never forget them, and shall always have nothing except gratitude in my heart for them.

Louise, Mabel, and I spent hours discussing baby clothes.[70] What infinite satisfaction there is in making something lovely from nothing, with the odds all against one, as a matter of fact. David had had nothing that could compare with the pretty little ca-misas that we made for the new baby. We were delighted with ourselves for being able to make the things under the very noses of the internees, without them suspecting what we were doing. I can't forget Mabel, a character if there ever was one, jumping up and stuffing material, needle, and thread under her every time we heard anyone coming up the stairs to the landing. She hadn't taken part in anything so daring for years, and she thoroughly enjoyed herself, *after* she got over being sick at the mess I'd made of my life, as one woman put it.

When I was about five months pregnant I began to get a little worried about me, physically, for my legs began to swell, as they had before David was born, and I had a trapped feeling that pre-eclampsia was rearing its ugly head again. I didn't dare go to an American doctor, and I certainly did not dare go to a Japanese doctor, so what was to be done? Robert, Gretchen, Louise, Mabel, and I put our heads together. We came up with several different plans. The plan that appealed to us most was the most fantas-tic, of course. We decided that since Robert had had beriberi very badly, he was the most logical one to go to the hospital with a specimen of urine in a bottle. The doctor had told him that if any of his symptoms returned he was to go to the hospital

70. "Louise Larkin Miller was an internee in my room in the annex; her son Robert played with David. We became good friends—a friendship that lasted until she died in August 1972. Mabel Burris Carlisle was a divorced woman, older than my mother. Before the war she had lived throughout the Far East—Hawaii, Hong Kong, Shanghai, Manila, working in dress shops every-where. When the war started she was engaged to Johnny O'Toole, the first American man I met in Baguio. She loved David, and we became friends. At first she was devastated at my pregnancy, but immediately started making baby clothes" (MS to LB 8/9/87, 11/10/87).

immediately. We four women spent the two hours that he was gone in an uproar. *What* if they should discover that he was pregnant? I had begun to rediscover my sense of humor by that time, although I had thought it was gone beyond recall. Even at this point I think it is an amusing story. They did not discover that he was with child, I am sorry to say, but they did tell him to cut down on salt and to rest more. This advice I heeded, and the results were satisfactory.

I think the thing I worried most about was the fact that the women who had had babies during the previous few months had had to go outside to Hospicio de San José during the last few weeks of the pregnancy. Of all the fantastic things that could have happened to me, it was my luck to have Mickie in charge of that hospital. Hospicio was a small hospital for all the old bedridden men who were interned. Mickie, two army nurses, and two able-bodied men took care of the bedridden patients. The younger of the men, Buster, had gotten the job because his wife, a Spanish girl, was on the outside. Since she was a good Catholic, and the Church and the hospital were connected, he could see her often.

This combination of Church and hospital was a wonderful setup for many undercover businesses, but I shall not go into them in detail.[71] I do know that several Spanish people lost their heads as a result of the help that the internees obtained through this channel. One of the women was most kind to me when I was in Hospicio. She brought several pieces of material for me, with which I made clothes for the coming baby. The impression that remains with me still, however, is that of her fear. She was

71. "People connected with the church were on the outside and consequently could get money from the Chinese or other moneylenders and could send money, or medicine they had bought with it, to the various prisons. For instance Mickie, my sister-in-law who worked as a nurse in the hospital, received money from people she met by prearrangement at church. This money was sent into Santo Tomás, as well as to other camps. Sometimes she sent medicine, rather than money, to wherever it was most needed" (MS to LB 8/9/87, 11/10/87).

always afraid when she came to Hospicio, and yet she came time after time. She had two or three children, and I've wondered so often what became of them when the Japanese killed her and her husband. What is it, I wonder, which makes people risk their lives (and lose them) for people, most of whom they have never seen? She was a good friend of Mr. Grinnell's, and it was through her that he received much of the money that he subsequently dispersed to various trustworthy people. The hospital and Mickie were the go-betweens, in many cases. When Mickie couldn't go to Santo Tomás, Buster (whose Spanish wife was on the outside) was the one to take the money and go to Santo Tomás.

When I was six months pregnant Mr. Grinnell told Robert that I'd have to submit to an examination by one of the camp doctors. It was to be kept very much a secret, and I appreciated all the efforts they took to keep it so. The doctor showed no astonishment, which was better than I had anticipated, and he was kind enough not to have a nurse with him. By appointment I met the doctor in an office in the men's dormitory, and the examination was routine and quickly finished. He told me that he would see Mickie within the near future, that he would break the news to her himself. He was sure that she would take it quite casually. I wasn't so sure, but that remained to be seen.

Soon after the examination Jerry sent his watch and a note from Los Baños. The things came through Ben George, the man who drove the bus between the two camps. George was the most popular man in camp at this time. When he came up to the landing he told me that he had talked to Jerry a few minutes before he had left, and I was thrilled to have firsthand news of him. George had no idea what portentous notes he was carrying back and forth for Jerry and me, and never did know about the baby until afterward.[72] He saw me at Hospicio a week before

72. Vaughan elaborates on the smuggling of messages: "Messages come into Santo Tomás in cigarettes, from which the tobacco has been removed, the message inserted and the tobacco repacked at the end. Cigarettes are delivered in camp in fifties, tied together with a piece of string. The cigarette nearest the

the baby was born, and thought (so he told me later) that I had somehow managed a pass to visit my sister-in-law. George was another person—tall, thin to the point of emaciation, not at all handsome, but most kind—who dealt with the underground for the love of helping and for the love of getting away with something. I wonder if most people don't have that urge, when they are prisoners and forbidden to do almost everything that is the normal course in every day life. I think it must depend upon how afraid they are of the consequences. George always came to Santo Tomás with at least one Japanese guard riding in the front seat with him. The old truck was alcohol burning, and would have made a perfect relic for a museum. (Almost without exception the automobiles and trucks which the Japanese used, whether American or not, were soon converted into charcoal or alcohol burners.) George was in such demand that I was pleased when he came up to the landing with the note instead of sending it up, and delighted when he stayed awhile and talked. He told me that as a standard practice he used a maneuver which never failed. Something would go wrong with the truck, George would get out and go behind to see what was the matter with it and, incidentally, drop off needed supplies for the guerrillas. Then he would "fix" the truck and go on. Why the guards never suspected him remains a mystery, but he was almost caught one time when he was unloading and another car, full of Japanese soldiers, came around the curve behind him. Somehow he made out, as most of us did, and went on with his same routine until

---

knot in the string has the message. Labels on a milk can are steamed off in Manila by friends of internees, news typed on the back of the paper and the re-labeled tin sent in to Santo Tomás. The old method of inserting notes wrapped in waxed paper in the batter of a loaf of bread is still used. The want ads and the personal columns of the Manila newspaper carry select messages to watchful internees. Yesterday I saw a Manila mestizo, called to the Santo Tomás Commandant's office for a conference concerning his pass, drop a piece of crushed paper in a garbage can at the Commandant's door as he entered the office. This 'rubbish,' later salvaged by the boy's English father interned in Santo Tomás, carried an uncensored message and a roll of money" (223).

the truck hauling between Santo Tomás and Los Baños was finally eliminated completely, not too long after this narrow escape.

For months I worried about the shower problem. I had finally worked out a system. David and I got our food on the line at the regular time. However, instead of eating it immediately, as the rest of the camp did, we would save it for awhile and we would get our baths then while the rest of the people were eating. In this way we rarely had more than two or three people taking a shower at the same time we did. There were four or five showers in one room, and four or five people got under each spray. Thus, as a rule, fifteen or twenty people were usually taking a bath at the same time—except during chow time. We almost always had one woman in the bathroom at the same time we were in it, and I've always wondered about her. No doubt she was so intent upon her own problems that she paid no attention to us. Perhaps she was in the bathroom at that time because she too did not want to be looked at. No blemish went unnoticed, and believe me there are plenty of blemishes on the human form divine. Over a three-year period I venture to say that we saw every woman in a state of undress many times. I thought about myself from every angle, figuratively speaking, and I decided that if I could keep facing people they would not be so apt to notice. I always waited until the corner shower, facing the door, was unoccupied. Then I spent most of my time bending over washing David. It must have worked, for no one guessed.

About this time, for another reason entirely, I didn't have to worry about the shower problem; no one could take showers. We had a typhoon, and what a gruesome mess we were in. By this time dozens of families had obtained passes to sleep outside in their shanties. The central committee and the Japanese were willing for them to do so, for it relieved the critical housing shortage inside the university buildings. Now, suddenly, we had to make room for them in the buildings, for the shanties afforded no semblance of protection from the elements. Not only did we have water waist deep on the campus (it came in the door on the first floor), we had no lights, no gas, and no water that was fit for human consumption without first being boiled. As a result of all this, the commodes didn't work, and with several hundred men, women and children on each floor of the main building we were in a fine fix. Most of the people who had come in from the shanties slept in the halls, and what with mud, people trying to cook, eat, dry clothes, and carry in cans of water to flush the reeking bathroom facilities, it was enough to turn the strongest stomach. David and I were miserably wet. High up in the stairwell above us there was a broken pane of glass, and the water poured in. We managed to keep one corner of the bed fairly dry, and there we huddled at night for the duration of the storm, which lasted for two or three days.

Mabel had a bag of charcoal which we were able to use for cooking purposes, after she had rescued it from under water. Mabel also had a charcoal hibachi, and after drying each piece of charcoal separately, and after hours of fanning and blowing, we got it burning. We did our cooking on the balcony of the museum, among the books.

By this time the far end of the balcony was being used for the safety department. During the flood the safety department made countless coconut-oil lamps, which they posted at various strategic spots in the building. We spent some weird nights watching those ghost processions go up and down the stairs with their coconut-oil lamps, and as a result of being so close to the source of the supply we were allowed to have one of our own. There are always small blessings, and that was certainly one of them, for by this time my kidneys were beginning to act up and I spent much of every night trotting up and down stairs to the bathroom. Not only that, the bed was built up high, and David and I had to climb hand over hand to get into it. For a five-year-old boy it was nothing, but in my unbalanced state it daily became more of a chore. All things came to an end, and finally the storm abated. The water gradually dried up, and the people who had been sleeping in the halls went back to their shanties to try to clean up the shambles they found waiting for them. Life gradually fell back into its old deadly routine . . . get up, do the washing, stand in line . . . over and over, stand in line again. . . .

Hardly a day had passed that I hadn't worried about my brothers. Two of them were old enough to be in the war effort and every day older I got I became more wary of what life has in store for all of us. Nothing serious had ever happened to our family, and I was the oldest child of seven. My father and mother were living, all except one of my grandparents were living, all except one of my cousins were living, and I had many of them. We were a singularly lucky family, and I felt sure that our luck would not hold out forever. I wanted it to, God knows, but I had learned to be afraid. Suddenly, with no warning, I received a note, sent from a Japanese prison camp in Japan, signed "your brother _____." At this late date I have forgotten what the name was, but it was a name I had never heard before, and it was *not* my brother's writing. Handwriting, like faces, I do not forget. It took me only a few seconds to realize that it had been sent by one of our mining camp men, Mr. Johnson, a man about whom we had all wondered. Was he dead, was he alive, what had happened to him? No one knew, for he had no family in the Philippines. I had liked the man immensely, and I was delighted that he had liked me enough to send a note to me. No doubt the Japanese would only allow the prisoners to write to relatives, hence I became his "sister." Several of the Americans who worked at the gate with the Japanese heard that I had received a note, and came up to tell me how pleased they were that I had heard from my brother. Though the note wasn't actually from my brother, it made my brothers seem more near and dear to me than they had for a long time, and I worried more than ever about them. Incidentally, my "brother" in Japan lived to come home and wrote to me a few times before I lost track of him. I love him yet for that note. It was the first inkling I had that there were really people outside of our prison camp life who actually cared whether we lived or died. My garden boy, years before, had described Mr. Johnson to me as "the man with the good face," and it was a most accurate description.

I must tell you about another incident that hasn't too much bearing on the story. Always we are hearing about communism, socialism, democracy, etc. The Japanese wanted us to live according to "the democratic way of life," they said. Their conception of democracy was for each individual to have exactly what each other individual had. As any person with a brain in his head knows, if every person in a certain room were given six apples and told to do with them exactly as he pleased, very shortly some of the people would have no apples, some would have six (saved), some would have twenty-four apples or more. Nothing, or no one, could make all six apples of every individual disappear at the same time. We then have the "haves" and the "have nots." In Santo Tomás most of us had started at the same place, [taking into camp] "food and clothing for three days." Jerry, being the most enterprising soul I have ever known, had a good innerspring mattress (which Don Rudder had willed to him when he was taken to Cabanatuan, and Jerry in turn had willed it to me when he was taken to Los Baños), he had two comfortable chairs, a refrigerator, a gas plate to cook on, and had made (and hidden cunningly) an oven. He got news, not rumors; in short, he lived as nearly a normal American life as it was humanly possible to live. The one thing he could not do too much about was food. Compared to our present standards it wasn't much (after all, he lived on a stairwell) but compared to the standards of the other internees it was Four-0, as he would say. Until Jerry came along, *I* hadn't done at all well, but I had never dreamed of walking into an unknown person's shanty and demanding to be allowed the privileges of their shanty. Quite simply, it had never occurred to me. I had been brought up in the good old American way, what one works for one has, and there is no question about it. I had worked on books till I was blue in the face. The only thing I could hope to acquire was food, and I had done my very best in that regard. As far as I am concerned, if my neighbor makes a million dollars, that's his business, and I certainly have no right whatsoever to it simply because I am his next-door neighbor. I would have made the million if I had thought of it first. If I had brains enough I'd make a million of my own. There were people in Santo Tomás who fitted every category. There were those who had literally nothing except what they wore and slept in, a pair of shorts. And there were people who had very nice shanties and lived, under existing circumstances, fairly normal lives. I don't remember *begrudging* anyone anything.

Granted, I had more than many people had at this time through the efforts of Jerry, but every day that I was on the landing I had to fight for what he had given me. In the early days I wouldn't have fought. I would have felt that it was beneath my dignity as a woman, but I had learned that I *had* to fight if I wanted the little privacy that David and I had. At least we were alone during the night hours. Jerry had always shared his landing privileges with all of his friends and acquaintances. He was glad to do so. I had kept on where he left off. I let his friends, and mine, come up and cook on the hot plate whenever they wanted to. After all, the hot plate belonged to a woman in camp who did not have a landing where she could use it, so she had loaned it to Jerry. No one person could possibly concoct a dish that would require more than ten minutes cooking time. If there were several people who wanted to use it at the same time, we simply took turns. There must have been at least forty people who used the refrigerator regularly. I hate to bring up the Russian people again (though this woman happened to be Russian-Jewish) but they always seem to be making examples of themselves. There is a difference in saying "Come up *any* time and use the hot plate, if I'm not there go ahead and use it anyway"—there is a difference in saying that and in having a woman whom I did not know come barging up the stairway and turn on the hot plate and proceed to cook her meal. She didn't say "May I?" or ask if I minded, she didn't say "Thank you" when she was finished, she didn't say anything, just looked at me with a look that dared me to do anything about it. The first day she did this I was too dumbfounded to do anything. There are such things as good manners, even in an internment camp. The next day she came up the stairs and proceeded to do the same thing. This time, however, I asked her by what right she barged into my "house" without asking, and used my stove? She became furious and told me that "The Japanese said we were all to live exactly alike, and what one person has the other person can have." "What right do *you* have to the stove?" she wanted to know, and I couldn't really answer. I had acquired it through perfectly legitimate means, however, and the Japanese and central committee had neither of them specifically told me that I could not have it. I had just done my best, for six months, to hang on to something that had been given me. It's a long way round Robin Hood's barn, as my grandmother used to say, but I hope I have made my point, and not several other points! This woman had sat on her large Francis for almost two years and had acquired nothing, hadn't even contributed her toilet duty gracefully, but she expected to share all that other people, by devious methods if you will, had acquired. The Japanese were forever criticizing us for not pooling all our resources and every one sharing exactly. I suppose if it were possible, more people would have more, and fewer people would have less, if I make myself clear, but wherever there are human beings, this sort of state is not possible. It's some non-realist's pipe dream.

For almost two years we had heard rumors of comfort kits. During the first year of internment we had received a small parcel of food from the Australian Red Cross. The principal items were cheese and jam, and they were delicious beyond description. For months we had been hearing rumors of comfort kits from the States. So many rumors, in fact, that I had given up even thinking about the possibility. I thought, "So what, if we ever *do* get them they won't amount to anything as far as the overall picture is concerned." A jar of jam is wonderful, but it can't really make much difference when one is beginning to feel the pinch of starvation. However, more and more rumors were coming in. People who had been outside swore that they had seen great stacks of boxes on the piers in Manila. There were boxes and boxes and boxes of cigarettes, so the rumor-mongers said. No one could talk about, or think about, anything except comfort kits and cigarettes. Having become a die-hard, I did not believe it. I finally had to admit that there might be something to the rumor, for someone in camp had actually seen a package of American cigarettes, with a slogan on the package. The slogan was something about "Freedom is our heritage." I can't quote it for sure, for we were never allowed to have a package of cigarettes with that slogan on them. I understand those cigarettes went to other camps, and were distributed to the people without benefit of package.

One dismal grey day, dozens of Japanese trucks, complete with soldiers, came in to Santo Tomás with American Red Cross kits piled high. The boxes were dumped in huge piles, on one side [of] and behind the main building. The sight of a Japanese soldier stabbing his bayonet through a tin of dried milk is with me yet. It was a sickening sight to see it scattered on the dirty road. I would have given my soul for that milk for my baby that was soon to be born, or for David. I still wonder why the soldier did it. Perhaps he thought there was something contraband in it. Who knows what he thought, but it represented a gallon of milk spilled on the ground, and it could have satisfied nothing except a sadist. It was the only time I ever felt it, but there was an ominous feeling among the people who watched that incident.[73] Mostly we were just a cowed, subjugated people.

Eventually a system of distribution was worked out, and each person was given a comfort kit which weighed approximately forty pounds. I wonder if anyone who was not there can realize what that much food meant to us. I am positive, had we not received that comfort kit, many hundreds of us would have been dead long before the Americans returned. In the comfort kits there was every good thing imaginable to eat, or so it seemed to us then. There was chocolate, coffee, cheese, jam, Spam, and

73. "If that man had continued to violate the food packages, there might have been an upsurge of revolt among the internees. There wasn't a one of us who didn't have blood in his eyes. That was unusual for most of the internees, who wouldn't break camp rules" (MS to LB 8/9/87).

a kind of butter that was wonderful. Later we learned that it was fashionable to complain (in the service) about "Spam and axle grease" as some people called the butter. To us, Spam and axle grease was something sent directly from heaven. There were dried prunes, and there was dried milk. To many hundreds of people the most wonderful thing of all were the cigarettes. There were all brands of cigarettes. The cigarettes, as such, meant nothing to me, for I don't smoke, but they offered WONDERFUL bartering possibilities! There were people foolish enough to trade their milk for coffee. Who was I to let a chance for more milk slip through my fingers? After much diligent effort I amassed a great fortune in milk, almost enough milk to take the two children through the next year. Not the quart of milk that children should have each day, but enough to make me feel a little better about the situation. One of the loveliest things in the package was [liver] paté. We mixed it with our rice, or we ate it plain. Any way we ate it, it was wonderfully rich and nourishing and satisfying. In short, there was nothing in the kit that wasn't infinitely superior to anything that we had seen for two long years.

A day or two later after the comfort kits arrived, I finally received Bob's answer to my note about the baby. Years before we had discussed what we thought of women who are not faithful to their husbands, and Bob had made himself quite clear on the subject. I thought I knew exactly what he would say to me in that note, and I had braced myself for it. The only thing I had begged him not to do was to take David away from me. It seemed to me then, and still does, that David was mine and no one in the world (except a wife someday) had a right to take him away from me, no matter what I had done. I hoped, knowing Bob's sense of fair play, that he would let me keep him without my having to fight for him, which I would have done if necessary. I had told Bob, in my note, that I would get a divorce as quietly as possible if and when we were ever liberated. I tried to tell him, but I couldn't have possibly gotten it across to him, how terribly sorry I was to have hurt him. I know that those are the oldest, and the most trite words in the world, and have been used countless times, and I know that people snigger and say bitter things when they are used, but it is still true. I was dreadfully sorry to have hurt him, but I had. No use saying I couldn't help it, for certainly I could have helped it, but I believe if I had a choice I'd do it again, for I still, after several years, can see no man except Jerry.

I repeat, I thought I knew Bob well enough to know what he would say to me. I thought it would be a note full of reproaches, as I'm sure mine would have been, had the situation been reversed. Instead, and I know I did not deserve it, though I appreciated it more than anything I've ever had done for me, I received the most beautiful love letter ever written. It breaks my heart that I let that letter get burned up during the last hectic hour of internment. I would give a great deal to show it to you, David, when the time comes, so that you could know for yourself what a fine man, what a GENTLEMAN, your father was. When he forgave me, and still loved me, in spite of the shame I heaped upon his head, it has never mattered very much since what the rest of the world thinks. That Bob and Jerry both loved me I do not deserve, but I am very proud for having had their love. I could quote things from Bob's letter, even today, but I think I will not. It is not necessary to do so; the point is, he forgave me and proved it in a way that I would never have thought about. Years later I received his will. It came from the War Department. The will had been witnessed by Jack, among others, on the fourth of February, my birthday. He knew that the baby was to have been born about that date. What more, under *any* circumstances, could he have done for me than to give me his all? I was sick for days after the letter came. How vomiting and diarrhea are connected with nerves I do not know, but mine are. That nervous upset was to be the forerunner of many, many more to come. I think my inner workings must be those of an old, old woman—worn out long before the outer body is ready to give up.

Shortly before Christmas the Japanese decided to send two hundred women to Los Baños. They were to be women with-

out children. Since her fiancé was there, Mabel packed her belongings and left, along with the other hundred and ninety-nine
women, early one morning before the sun was up. Mabel had
stayed up all night making a baby sweater from a sweater that
I had brought into camp with me two years before. The sweater
was old and yellow when we were interned, but [the yarn] made
a lovely, soft sweater for the baby. Mabel nearly ruined her eyes
making it, under the dim night light in the bathroom, but I
could not stop her. Though the women were warned not to do
so, Mabel took a note to Jerry, and a pair of string socks which
I had knit for him for Christmas. Mabel was going to the one
place on earth where I wanted to be, and I felt a completely
frustrated woman as I waved good-bye to her. There was nothing
I could do about *anything,* it seemed.

I had two or three world-famous people on my bookbinding
staff. One of them was particularly offensive, for he was a knee-
pincher. I shall not mention his name; he is dead now, poor old
man. There were days when I hated him bitterly for his pinch-
ing. I imagine it was a disease with him, and he probably couldn't
help it, but even realizing this couldn't make me feel less sorry
for myself when this old white-haired fool would sidle up to me
and pinch me. Naturally he did not know that I was pregnant,
though I'm not too sure it would have made any difference to
him. He gave me some cheese once, and it was very good. He
also said something I have never forgotten. One time, long before I became serious about Jerry, he said to me, "Don't ever
let your sins be those of omission." He was a brilliant man in
his field, and had lived a long and eventful life, and I have never
forgotten it.

I finally asked Robert to stick close to my side when this old
man was around, for I couldn't help feeling a little trapped and
unclean when he pinched me. Robert was around most of the
time now, for he had agreed to let me teach him all that I knew
about binding books, in order that the library would not be at
a complete loss when I suddenly departed. I don't mean to imply
that I was invaluable; I simply happened to be the only one who

knew how to make and put covers on books. I felt sure that the head of the library would never look in my direction again after the baby was born—and how right I was!

After Jerry was taken away, Robert supplied me with news of the outside world. Almost every day the library people discussed what rumors they had heard. Uncle Don[74] and his Chinese secretary, Ansi Lee, were members of the bookbinding staff. Uncle Don discussed rumors along with the rest of them. I hadn't worked very long with him until I became very fond of him, and I must admit that I had never even heard of "Donald of China" until some time after I had known him. One day when we happened to be alone he told me who he was. I know that he must have been disappointed when I wasn't more impressed. From the beginning he took a very keen interest in David, and David adored him. For months David made a beeline for his shanty as soon as he was awake in the afternoon, and Uncle Don told him wonderful fairy stories of "Winkie Doodle," with bits of his own true story in China woven into them. In the morning, while Uncle Don pasted pages of books, David played with his small toys on the floor of the balcony of the museum and Uncle Don told him more stories. They never seemed to tire of the arrangement. All the other people near enough to hear him were almost as fascinated with the stories as David was.

When Christmas of the second year of internment came, Uncle Don and Ansi Lee were very kind to David and me. Ansi Lee knit David a sweater from string, and Uncle Don hunted until he found a book of poems for him. They brought them up to the landing the night before Christmas, all done up in ribbons and pretty paper. David was as thrilled as only a five-year-old can be.

I was always concerned about whether or not David took up too much of Uncle Don's time, but he never seemed to mind. As a matter of fact he seemed to like it, and spent hours teaching him to "tell time." He taught David two phrases in Chinese,

74. See n. 55, p. 125.

which dialect I don't remember. One phrase meant "I am well" and the other meant "I am not so well," and I have a vivid picture in my mind of him rubbing his stomach, and half-smiling, saying to David in Chinese, "I am not so well today." Since he died a few months after we were liberated, I assume that the cancer from which he died was even then insidiously eating away at him. I was so grateful to him for taking up so much of his time with David (after all, he had to do his own laundry just as the rest of us did, and he dictated many notes to Ansi Lee during his free time) that I soon began to pass on Robert's news to him. I knew that he would be discreet enough not to endanger Robert by repeating it to the wrong people. He was so discreet, in fact, that it was several weeks before he asked me where I got the news. I merely told him that it wasn't rumor, that I *knew* that it was authentic, and he accepted it as such.

The two things that the Japanese were supposed to have looked for constantly, were W. H. Donald and "the men who had the radio." I enjoyed a vicarious pleasure from knowing where they all were. There were many people in Santo Tomás and Los Baños who knew who Uncle Don was, but I am glad to say that no one ever reported him to the Japanese. Once General Homma, of the Death March fame, came into camp and Uncle Don was nervous for days, for he had known the general before the war. Many times inspection parties toured the shanty area, and he was always afraid that one of the Japanese officials would recognize him. The wonder is that they didn't.

The first year of internment it seemed to me that David went a little mad too, in the room with so many children. The second year, when we were on the landing with Uncle Don's stories to keep him entertained every afternoon, I thought David improved considerably. It could have been that he was five that year, instead of four, but I have always given Uncle Don credit for helping me through a very tough year. As you must realize, I saw him every day at work and I am sure it never entered his mind that I was pregnant.

I did not tell Uncle Don about the baby until the day I was

sent out of camp. That day I made a trip out to his shanty to tell him, for I hated to have him get it as a horrible rumor, and I shall always love him for taking it the way he did. He said "Well upon my word, I never would have known it"—and that was all he ever said at any time about the affair. No questions, no remarks, no nothing; just surprised, but I honestly think he liked me more after that than he had before.

Three or four days after Christmas Mr. Grinnell told Robert to have me come down to the office. I went down immediately and found that preparations had been made for me to go to Hospicio until after the birth of the baby. Mr. Grinnell asked what I wanted to do about David. I told him that I'd do anything to be able to take him with me. In the first place, I thought it would do him a lot of good to go outside. In the second place, I thought it would be wonderful for him to be in a place where there were so few people. Mickie and the two army nurses lived in a room large enough to have accommodated sixteen or eighteen people in Santo Tomás. The three women ate, cooked, and slept in the same room, it's true, but compared with our standards then, there was a wealth of room for two more people. Mr. Grinnell talked fast to the Japanese and finally they gave me permission to take David outside to Hospicio with me. No one had been allowed this privilege before, but my life was full of firsts and I was so very pleased that I didn't question my luck.

The truck that was to take us outside came during siesta hour. Mr. Duggleby, the Japanese driver, David, and I started off on the most hectic trip of my life. I don't know why I didn't have the baby on that trip. The streets of Manila had not been touched for two years as far as repairs were concerned. There were great ruts, holes, and barricades in them, over and around all of which the Japanese driver hurtled with the greatest of unconcern. There were several errands which Mr. Duggleby had to take care of before he left us at Hospicio. After two or three hours of driving we finally arrived at the hospital. Mickie met us coolly but efficiently. The first thing she said was "I'm sorry Margaret, but David can't stay here under any circumstances." I couldn't believe my ears. The Japanese had told me that he could stay, and we had all his credentials in order, but here was Mickie telling me that he *couldn't* stay. Apparently the two American Army nurses (I wish I could remember their names, and I'd give them all due credit) had taken one look at a small boy getting out of the truck with his illegitimately pregnant mother, and had handed Mickie an ultimatum. "If that boy stays here we go back to Santo Tomás in the truck," they said. "We can't be expected to sleep and dress in the same room with a five-year-old boy" said these grown women, these Army nurses, these sisters of mercy. I realized perfectly that I had put Mickie in a nasty spot already, and I could hardly blame her for not wanting to lose her two nurses. On the other hand I couldn't just send David back to Santo Tomás to fend for himself for the next two months. I couldn't understand why or how two women could be that cruel to a child whom they had never seen before. I had never seen the nurses either. Granted, it was their way of show-ing me what they thought of *me* (that I could understand and was prepared for) but *why* take it out on a defenseless child? I still can't understand why Mickie didn't say, as I *think* I would have "Okay, *go* back, there are dozens of nurses who would be happy to come outside to work for awhile." I soon realized that nothing I could say was going to make any difference, any more than David's papers all in order made any difference. Needless to say, I have never been so upset, and God willing, I never shall be again.

After some useless arguing I finally decided that the only thing for me to do was to go back to Santo Tomás and see what ar-rangements I could make for David there. If I couldn't get him properly taken care of, I'd have to stay there myself no matter what happened. On the way back (I was having contractions regu-larly and was terrified that I might have the baby right there in the car), I decided that the thing to do was to ask Robert to take care of him. Before leaving I had willed him my landing, for I knew that I'd never be allowed to use it when I went back into camp. Robert knew David, and what was more important,

David knew and liked Robert. Poor Robert, all the punishment he took in the name of friendship!

After more than an hour of looking frantically for Robert I finally found him, and he nearly fainted when he saw me. He had thought he had gotten me safely and unobtrusively out of Santo Tomás. He had already moved onto the landing, and here I was back asking for more help. I told him the situation at Hospicio, and Robert, [who had become] my staunch friend after Jerry left camp, wanted to go over and strangle the nurses first. Then he said he would be glad to take care of David. Gretchen promised to help out. She had no children of her own, but she loved David and I knew that she would be good to him. God rest her, she's dead now, of cancer which developed in Santo Tomás. David and I bade each other a tearful farewell, and the Japanese driver, Mr. Duggleby, and I started off again. By this time I was so sick, and so tired, and in such a mental turmoil that I came very nearly being a fishwife when I got back to Hospicio and had to face those despicable nurses across the dinner table. It was fortunate that, during my months of sleepless nights, I had steeled myself for just the treatment I received from the nurses; surprisingly enough, the ill treatment hurt very little. I comforted myself by thinking that I, obviously a bad woman, could never have been as unkind to *anything*—let alone a defenseless child. Probably, if I weren't also human, I'd eliminate this story (my brother assures me that no one in his right mind would publish such a story), but it was the beginning of many more such incidents, and has stuck in my mind much too clearly to forget yet awhile. No doubt I deserved just that sort of treatment ([in earlier times] they would have made me walk around with a scarlet letter on my chest), but it was the first time in my life that anyone had openly shown [negatively] what they thought of me. There must have been dozens, over the course of my twenty-seven years, who had not liked me. There were plenty of people I hadn't liked, but it was the first time that anyone had had public opinion on their side, and could show exactly what they felt.

Mickie realized that she was going to have to put up with me for the time being, whether she liked it or not, so she made the best of a bad bargain. I learned quite a lot about her during my stay and thought, had she ever given me a chance, I could have loved her. She had a keen sense of humor and was fun to be around.[75]

Buster, the younger man at Hospicio (whose Spanish wife was on the outside), was wonderful to me.[76] From the very first moment he was trying to help me, and he continued to be good to me until the last time I saw him, in San Francisco after we were liberated. I send and get a Christmas card from him each year even yet.

I wonder why it is that men, generally speaking, are a great deal more kind than women are. Is it because men face facts, and women bury their heads in the sand? I don't mean to say that there are no kind women, for there are, but I found that most of the women who were kind to me had had experiences of their own. Not necessarily similar to my own. In some cases they had been married twice, or had been in love with a man other than their husband, or *something* unusual had happened

75. "Mickie was never very friendly toward me, right from the moment of my arrival in the Philippines in 1936. I wanted to wait for a couple of days to get married, so we could get reacquainted after a year apart. But she convinced Bob, her brother-in-law, to marry me the night I got there. We were both interned in Santo Tomás at the beginning of the war, but she didn't look me up. I searched for her, and when I finally found her she lay on her bed indifferently. Her first husband died on a Japanese troop ship [at the end of the war]. After the war she returned to the States and married a policeman who lived in southern California. They had no children. She died a few years ago; I never saw her after Gerry Ann was born" (MS to LB 8/10/87).

76. Merrill Ralph ("Buster") Keaton, an American interned in Santo Tomás, worked at Hospicio de San José, ostensibly to help Mickie, but actually to be near his Spanish wife, who lived outside camp. Located on a small island in the Pasig River, this institution was originally an orphanage operated by the Sisters of Charity, but during the war it was expanded to care for 130 old men. After the war Keaton returned to his home in Oakland, California (MS to LB 8/10/87 and Stevens 206; Keaton letter to Margaret Sams, 1/28/46).

to them, so that they realized that everything in the world is not either black or white. There are dozens of shadings, and through their own experiences, these women had been given insight enough to know that just because the world considers women such as I "women of ill repute," (a perfectly strange man walked up to me and called me that one day) there are, by virtue of circumstances, other ways of looking at [character]. It may be that men are more understanding because on the whole they've had more experiences which have made them have to look at things from a broader viewpoint. I don't know what it is, but I do know that I am now much less ready to jump to conclusions and to condemn other people than I once was. There are two sides to everything; what the world thinks is merely a matter of what part of the world one lives in anyway. Customs in every country vary, customs in every locality vary, and though I realize that having a child by a man other than one's husband is more than a custom, still it was merely by chance that I wasn't able to get a divorce first and have the baby under conditions that are considered perfectly normal nowadays. Divorce hasn't always been the accepted custom but I believe, in the States at least, it is more or less accepted even though we all agree that it is a custom that has many bad points. Suffice it to say that in my experience there are more considerate men than women, and that the English people in Santo Tomás were nicer (or should I say more broadminded?) than the Americans were. I have always wondered if the English people would have been so considerate of one of their own English women if she had "thrown her hat over the barn."

New Year's Eve Buster and I really became acquainted, for Mickie and the two Army nurses put on their red armbands and went to the home of some Spanish people for a party. We expected them home early, ten or eleven, for it wasn't at all safe for them to be out after dark (there were very strict rules about it), but they didn't come until well after midnight. Buster and I sat and worried and fretted about them as if they were children. (Much as one may dislike a badly behaved child, one would not will-

ingly see the child hurt!) Buster told me his story and I recip-
rocated. As I have said before, we all have a story—some better,
some worse, and every one is interesting to me. Watching and
listening to people has intrigued me always, [learning] what has
happened to each one of us to make us the individuals we are.

Not long ago I saw a picture that I can't forget. It was someone's interpretation of the wrong turn in the road of life. The
wrong turn led straight down, not a curve in sight. The right
one was curved and tortuous, but always up. I don't believe it
for a minute. The wrong one does *not* necessarily go straight down.
There were many people who unhesitatingly said that I had made
a wrong turn, in other words had "made a mess" of my life. It's
not so, and there must be millions of others who have made
a wrong turn and have come back up the hard way. Who is to
judge whether or not it's a wrong turn anyway? I am sure there
are as many turns in the road down as there are in the road up.
One's conscience is always to be dealt with and it is always prodding one.

As soon as I was established at Hospicio, the young Spanish
doctor who looked after the old men at the hospital checked me
over and found nothing wrong. Thereafter I went into full-scale
production on baby clothes. I sewed from morning until night
and I loved every minute of it. I had been concentrating on collecting material for months. I had scraps of handkerchief linen,
and I had batiste which had come in the Red Cross shipment.
From many sources I had gotten small amounts of various kinds
of lace. After she recovered from the shock of my story, Louise's
mother (whom Louise did not tell until after I left Santo Tomás)
started making hairpin lace for me.[77] Mrs. Larkin is a sweet little
white-haired woman, a lady of the old school. While I was at
Hospicio she sent a pound can of dried milk "For *you* to drink,
Margaret," she said, and though I felt like a criminal doing it
I drank it for the baby's sake.

Diapers were the biggest problem. Mabel had given me some

77. See n. 70, p. 142.

new birdseye material before she went to Los Baños. I cut the diapers in oblong lengths; they were as narrow as I dared make them, but they were still large enough to squeeze the baby into when we were liberated. Mabel had also given me my quota of "kotex" material. It was Mabel's duty to distribute this material among the women in Santo Tomás and her discretion was never questioned. This material was heavy and made lovely small "camisas." Somewhere I had bought or traded for some pink and blue embroidery thread and some blue yarn which had once been someone's sweater. The fact that the yarn had been used before did not detract in the least from the beauty of the booties and sweater that I knit from it.

A friend of Mickie's, a man whom I never did know, loaned me his baby's bassinet. It had been a lovely thing in its day. It sat on a framework and had wheels which made it possible to push, almost like a buggy. The bassinet hadn't been used for a long time, so it needed painting badly. Lacking paint I decided to line it with the piña which I had grabbed along with the cotton materials the day we were evacuated from Suyoc more than two years before. To my eyes, unused to anything beautiful, it was out of this world.

Before I left Santo Tomás I had used part of my hoard of money to buy a small wooden box. Every day I finished some baby garment and carefully laid it away for the great event. I had enough work cut out for two months and thought I'd just about be finished by the time the baby came. I sewed from the moment I had my bed made, and my corner of the room scrubbed and tidy, until lunch time. After siesta I sewed again. Sometimes I sewed at night, even with the nurses watching me with an evil light in their eyes. Most of the time, however, I went outside and sat under the trees to do my sewing and left the nurses to their own devices.

Aside from being a good and sympathetic listener, occasionally inviting someone to eat with me when I managed to get some extra food, and doing a few physical things for people I was never able to help other people very much in Santo Tomás.[78] I felt that I always carried my share of the load, but I could do very little more than that. Having been born with an insatiable desire to cook (or is it to eat?) I was soon persuaded to cook for the nurses, Mickie, and myself at night. I provided my share of the food, and somehow it always tasted better if there were a sizeable quantity cooked. We each got our own breakfasts, and each washed our own cup and bowl and spoon. One of the old men in the hospital had a garden, for he was strong enough to go outside part of every day. He told me that I might use his greens any time I wanted to do so, for he had more than he could ever eat. Usually, then, I had a dish of raw greens for my lunch. For dinner we almost always had a can of something or other from our kits and a bowl of soup which was served on the line. It seemed a little like heaven to have so much to eat, but I couldn't help worrying about David in Santo Tomás.

During the time I was outside things in general began to tighten up. We celebrated our second anniversary of internment while I was at Hospicio. It was about this time that things began to go our way in the war effort. We had been told months before that when the tide turned we could expect things to get tough. We had thought they were tough before, but we didn't yet know the meaning of the word.

Every day while I was in Hospicio, Buster, who was in contact with all the old men upstairs at the hospital, tried to make deals for me with my canned goods. At that time one could buy a

78. "It seemed as if I should do more than my share when there were old people in camp who couldn't do anything. Nevertheless, except for making curtains for the newsman [see p. 98], I seemed to have all I could do to work in the library, perform the required chores, and take care of David. It was much more time consuming when you were a single parent because you had to wait in endlessly long lines for meals, for instance; teaming up with a man cut down on the waiting. It did not increase the amount of our food, but the food tasted better if we could put our three portions together and add to it whatever else we could scrounge" (MS to LB 8/10/87, 11/10/87).

pound of powdered milk for the reasonable sum of fifty pesos, twenty-five good American dollars. Through Buster I bought four cans, I traded my cigarettes and coffee for more, and David and I between us had eight in our kits. How I loved the thought of that milk. No miser ever loved his gold as much as I loved the thought of the cans of milk under my bed. I finally acquired twenty cans, I believe it was. In a note from Jerry (my last one, by the way) he said that I could count on three of his cans of milk, if he could get them to me. Occasionally Buster went outside and he managed to buy several cans of Quaker Oats for me. With oats and milk I felt that nothing could faze me.

When I had been at Hospicio three weeks the doctor examined me again. He said that he was sure I must be mistaken about when the baby was due, for I just wasn't "large enough to have the baby yet." He said "I've watched you from an upstairs window and I wouldn't know you are pregnant if I hadn't heard the baby's heart beat myself." This was frightening. I was sure there must be something wrong with the baby, for I knew exactly (to the hour) when she had been conceived. The morning after the doctor examined me I felt a little more on the sickish side than usual and that afternoon, as I bent over the bassinet scrubbing it for dear life, I definitely felt downright awful. I had a terrific backache, and headache, and every once in awhile I'd have a contraction. The contractions I was more or less used to, for I'd been having them for weeks. I didn't mention how I felt, naturally, for I would rather have died than show any sign of pain before the nurses.

That night I cooked dinner for all of us as usual. By gritting my teeth and holding my breath I managed to keep from howling every time a pain hit me. I had not had a normal delivery with David, and I did not know how it felt to be having normal labor pains. I thought I was having a particularly lousy day, but thought I'd probably be all right the next day. After dinner I started to go to the bathroom. As I was leaving the room I had such a violent contraction that I couldn't help gasping. I felt dizzy and held on to the door for support, and when it was over went on to the bathroom. I still didn't say anything, and neither did Mickie or the nurses. However, when I came back to the room Mickie asked me how long I'd been feeling badly. I told her, and she looked funny and said, "I think we'd better see how close together the pains are coming." I laughed and told her not to worry, she'd have to put up with me another six weeks yet. I'd no more than said it when another violent pain had me in its grip and I felt definitely unwell, and proceeded to lose my dinner. At this Mickie really did look serious and told Buster to go upstairs and call the doctor. And here I can quote again, even after nine years, for one of the army nurses who had gone to bed by this time said, "Mickie, for God's sake get her out of here; she's going to have that brat right here." I swore, if it killed me, I'd not make another sound—and I almost didn't. I couldn't help gasping a little once in awhile, but I didn't scream, or groan, or do any of the things that women are permitted to do at childbirth.

The doctor finally came and after we'd gone upstairs and I had been examined he said, "Yes, you're going to have the baby, but it will be hours yet." I was horrified, for I'd heard old-wives tales all my life about eight-month babies. I told him I *couldn't* have the baby yet, and he just patted me on the foot and said, "I'm afraid you're *going* to have the baby anyway."

After the examination we went back downstairs, Buster helping me; I haven't forgotten the comfort I got from his good strong right arm helping me down the stairs. Twice he had to stop while I held on and gritted my teeth and great drops of perspiration trickled down me, but he could not have been sweeter if I'd been his wife.

And then an all-night session began for Buster, for Mickie, and for me. Mickie stayed with me most of the time, and counted the minutes between pains. Buster started out on foot to scout up a car to take me to another hospital where the arrangements had previously been made for me to have the baby. It was miles from the Hospicio, and out of the question for me to walk. I couldn't. Buster would come back every once in awhile and stick his head under the mosquito net, grip my hand tight, and say that he was still trying to find a car. The army nurses didn't once get out of their beds, of course, but they snorted and fumed and muttered under their breath every time I made a sound. Mickie didn't turn on the lights, so they weren't disturbed too much, but I suppose they couldn't sleep quite as well as they were accustomed to. I was sorry to put Mickie on the spot again, but it was out of my hands by then.

Just before the sun came up Buster came proudly into the driveway with a laundry truck which he had talked the Filipino driver into letting us use. We got to the hospital where a sweet-faced nun gave me breakfast of egg, "puto" (a sticky, sweetish native rice bread), and a small, weak cup of coffee. It was all the hospital ever had to offer for breakfast, and was more than I'd had for many breakfasts, but the sister apologized for it and said that she was so sorry that she had no more to offer a "mother-to-be for breakfast." The coffee even had sugar in it, and she apologized!

About eight, after I'd been made ready for delivery and was in the delivery room, they wheeled an old man (a Spanish doctor) into the room to deliver the baby. I was too sick to open my eyes when he came in, and I was sicker when they wheeled him out, so I never did see him. About the time the pains were what we call "unbearable" (though we always bear them) they decided to give me, for lack of any other anesthetic, a little chloroform to help out. Instead of helping out, it completely stopped the pains, and I had it all to do over again after I regained consciousness. I came to, gripping Mickie's hand until it was almost broken, but she let me hang onto her, and it was a comfort, for there was no one or nothing else to hang onto.

Buster was outside pacing the floor in agitation, as an expectant father might have done. For days the little Filipino nurses thought that he was my husband, he'd done such a good job of pacing. Strange, wasn't it, that on such short acquaintance a man could take such a tremendous interest and be so very kind to a woman whom he had never seen before. To me, Buster will always be a hero, and no doubt I will never see him again as long as I live; in my heart he has a very special place.

About the middle of that morning, January 23, 1944, Gerry Ann was born. I couldn't open my eyes to look at her then, and so I did not see her until the following day. Buster came that afternoon with a huge basket of gladiolus. Where he got them in that hunger-ridden, war-torn city I will never know, but it touched me so that I cried great weeping bucketfuls of tears. Mickie came to the hospital once during the two weeks I was there, and brought a Spanish friend of hers with some baby clothes for Gerry Ann. Christening clothes they were, and most beautiful. I spent the next days in bed shortening them. Two or three times after that I saw Mickie, by accident, and that almost ends our story as sisters-in-law.

There are so many things that I shall never forget, but one of the most poignant is my first sight of Gerry Ann. She was so very tiny and thin and sort of cold feeling, dressed in the Filipino version of hospital baby clothes. She looked exactly like a starved baby bird to me, and I have never felt so sorry for anything in my life. What had I done to her? I promised her faithfully that I'd spend my life trying to make it up to her; her lack of a name, her lack of a good start, everything. I adored her! The first thing I did was to go over her thoroughly, as all mothers do, to see whether or not she had all the prescribed parts. She was perfect in every respect except one. At birth one of her eyelids had been damaged a little and was very red. I felt badly that she had a birthmark (as I thought it was) and that it had to be in such a prominent place. The nurses assured me that it would go away within a few weeks, and it did. To my great delight I discovered that she had fingernails and toenails exactly like Jerry's. She had the bluest eyes I have ever seen and I was terrified every time I looked at her for fear she was blind. They simply didn't look as if they *could* see. A new baby is the most wonderful of all works of art. Just watching her could tear me apart. Every breath she took I analyzed. Is her heart all right? Can she see? Can she hear? A fleeting baby smile, done in sleep, could set my heart to trembling.

We had to teach her to nurse, and how I managed to have milk for her is one of the unpredictable things in this world, for I had only been able to nurse David for three months. But nurse her I did until the day we were liberated when she was thirteen months old. And then I nursed her some more, for she would not touch that strange American food, and thereby hangs another tale. I had prayed and starved and cried and prayed some more for food for her to eat, and then when we got it she would not eat it!

After a week in bed I was frantic to get back to Santo Tomás and David, for every visitor in the hospital (I was in a ward full of Filipino women) had woeful tales of what was going on *inside*. When I finally got back I found that things weren't as bad as they had been pictured, but they had tightened up considerably. Everyone tried to talk me into staying outside for two or three months, said a pass could very easily be arranged with a heart condition as the excuse. They had decided that I really did have something wrong with me when the chloroform had had such an instant reaction. Nevertheless, I had one great urge and that was to get back to David. I also wanted to introduce Gerry Ann to Santo Tomás and get that next hurdle behind me. Now that she was born I didn't care who knew it, and I was so proud of her that it almost physically hurt me to look at her. I was aching to show her to Louise and Robert and Gretchen, for nothing is ever complete unless one can share it with loved ones. Granted, the Filipino nurses were very sweet to us and never tired of bragging about Gerry Ann; how much smarter and cuter and better behaved she was than the little Filipino babies were, but I needed my three staunch friends' approval of her also.

The day the birth record papers were brought to me, to be filled out, was a horror. I gave her name as Gerry Ann Sherk (months before I had decided on her first two names) and prayed that they, in the hospital at least, would not find out the difference before I left. I felt sure that Bob would understand, and forgive me yet again.

I celebrated my twenty-seventh birthday in the hospital with Gerry Ann by my side. I kept hoping that Mickie might come over to see me, but she didn't. The nurses had discovered it was my birthday, as a result of Gerry Ann's birth records, and were extraordinarily good to us. The night nurse brought a small gift for me, before she went off duty at six, and all day small gifts kept arriving for me or for Gerry Ann. I was pleased with all the gifts, but I couldn't help feeling badly, for they didn't know that I wasn't a respectable woman and I doubted if they would have been so thoughtful had they known the true circumstances.

For another reason entirely I shall not forget that birthday. It was the day that the famous Rice Cake story hit the papers. Until that day I had not realized quite how stupid the Japanese propaganda could be. I was awakened early in the morning by the laughter of the Filipinos. Everywhere they were laughing. The gardeners outside my window were laughing and chattering away in their native dialects. The cooks, the cleaning women, the nurses, everyone seemed very gay and I couldn't understand why. The paper that morning had had quite a tale to tell. A Japanese fighter pilot, so the paper said, had flown into a group of American fighter planes and through his superior tactics had succeeded in shooting all of them down except one before he ran out of ammunition. He was about to return to his base and let the American get away, when he suddenly thought of his lunch which contained rice cakes. Immediately he returned to the attack, and flying close to him threw the rice cakes at the American plane. Seeing the rice cakes hurtling toward him so confused the American pilot that he flew into the sea and destroyed himself. This story was so completely ridiculous that it kept us all, Americans and Filipinos alike, in belly laughs for days.

The day Gerry Ann was two weeks old, despite the doctors' and nurses' well-intentioned advice, I went back to Santo Tomás. I had not been allowed out of bed until that day, so I was weak and wobbly and jittery. Buster came over from Hospicio to go to camp with me. He had notes and money which he was taking in to Mr. Grinnell anyway, it being his turn to go to Santo Tomás, so I did not cause him an extra trip, but I know that it must have taken a great deal of courage for him to walk in the gate with me that day. For all they knew in Santo Tomás *he* might have been Gerry Ann's father, although I had never seen him in my life until five weeks before. Buster was worried that day about the things he was carrying, for the last few people who had gone through the gate had been very thoroughly searched and some of them had been slapped. Mickie had been slapped shortly before and he wasn't at all anxious, as you can imagine, to be found with incriminating evidence on his person.[79] I had a bright idea, and we spent the last few blocks before we got to the main gate stuffing the papers and money inside Gerry Ann's diaper (and she didn't let us down!), and though the Japanese asked me to let them look at her at the gate, ap-

79. The Japanese slapped the internees hard, on the cheeks, to humiliate them for committing various minor infractions of the rules, such as not bowing —or not bowing properly—in their presence. Internees tried to evade their captors by looking elsewhere when they passed, or pretending to be preoccupied. Sometimes they got away with it and sometimes they didn't; "if all else failed, the prisoner who met a guard and was forced to bow would drop an object on the ground so that he would have to bend over to retrieve it—thus saving his face while satisfying the demands of the enemy." The mildest punishment for not bowing was for the internee to be called back and made to bow. Slapping was next in severity; the Japanese slapped the Filipinos around a great deal, "presumably just to show they were powerful," says Jerry. "No one ever fought back." Beating was the third most severe punishment in this escalating scale, and shooting or bayoneting was the ultimate reprisal. "Contraband was a shooting offense, and I had lots of contraband," said Jerry, "a camera, a radio, scissors, a long glass, and knives. I periodically rebuilt my radio so people wouldn't know what it looked like. Once I left it inside a canteen— the screw cap tuned it." Part of a building in Santo Tomás was on columns on which the building could roll during an earthquake; Margaret and Bob Merriam put Jerry's contraband down into one of the columns just before she was transferred to Los Baños (JS and MS to LB 8/10/87; MS to LB 11/10/87; Arthur 30).

parently it never occurred to them to unwrap her and look her over. I was concerned, as we were putting the things in Gerry Ann's diaper, for the Filipino driver of the caratella saw everything we were doing and could have gotten himself a nice fat reward for that bit of information, but he was another good Filipino.

My insides were tied into knots as I walked across the campus toward the main building. There is no way of describing the feelings I had that day. Walking into a den of wild lions would have created almost the same effect, I imagine. There was a comparative (though false) sense of security, once I managed to get to the main building and found Louise's shanty in the patio. I had only one thought, always foremost in my mind. "Dear God, don't let them know how I'm feeling. Please let me keep smiling if it kills me." Louise and Gretchen took care of Gerry Ann while I tried to find a room that would accept the baby and me. Robert insisted that he didn't want me to take David right away, for he knew that I would have all I could handle for a little while. He had gotten along famously with David while I was away. I finally found a room in the annex with space in it, and the room monitor, an Australian woman, was kind enough to let us in. The sensation we caused that day!

One of the things that had worried me constantly about the baby coming was the fact that I did not dare prepare David for the arrival. David was almost six by this time, and had had my undivided attention all of his life. I felt sure, if I could have prepared him, he would have thought it wonderful, but as it turned out that was one worry I met and needn't have. Under no circumstances could David have been more proud of the baby. For weeks he went around asking all and sundry "Have you seen my Mommy's new baby?" He was so proud that it hurt. David had been wanting a "baby brother" for years, and he decided immediately that a baby sister was just as good, maybe a little better.

While I was getting things arranged at the office and the annex, Louise and Gretchen fell in love with Gerry Ann. She had gained a few ounces and had lost her redness and she was, without any doubt, the most beautiful baby I have ever seen. (I never meet an ex-internee, even now, who doesn't mention how beautiful Gerry Ann was.) It was the first time she had gotten to wear any of her own clothes, and she was darling. Everyone, even my most bitter critics, admitted that she was lovely, and she was healthy, and that she had beautiful clothes, and that I certainly did not "deserve such luck." I knew that I didn't deserve it, but I was thankful for it.

I was so tired and weak and shaky by the time I had all the arrangements made for Gerry Ann and me, that first day, that I could hardly walk, let alone carry the bassinet with the baby. Robert and a friend of Louise's were delighted to do the little chore for me. They were human enough to get a tremendous kick out of people staring and pointing and gasping and generally making fools out of themselves over one tiny, sweet baby. For several days thereafter Robert carried Gerry Ann in the bassinet for me. He paraded her, I think, just for the sake of the sensation it caused. Apparently there was much doubt about her being mine, at first, for people realized that I had been in camp until three weeks before she was born and they could not believe that they had overlooked such a juicy bit of scandal. It was rumored that I had gone outside and adopted her. Later they were forced to admit that she must be mine, for I made no bones about it. She *was* mine, and I was terribly proud of her.

Gerry Ann and I finally got settled in our new room in the annex, a couple doors down the hall from David's and my original room, and I felt like a woman with a "new identity," as David says. Two years had made me a different woman, in a different room, with a different child. I wondered if all this could have happened to just anyone, or could it have happened only to me? Perhaps I was blind, but I could see nothing in my background which could have pointed in this direction.

After I had gotten Gerry Ann settled for the night I washed her day's supply of clothing (and a baby in internment soils as many clothes as a baby out of internment). As I hung them up in the dark I was proud of those tiny, pretty little garments.

There weren't any other women washing at that time of night, so I decided then and there that I would do as much of my laundry at night as I possibly could. I would know that Gerry Ann was all right, and I'd have plenty of room at the wash troughs. Later it became quite the thing to wash one's clothes at night.

I went to bed after Gerry Ann's ten o'clock feeding and almost immediately I became aware of the children coughing on all sides of us. Any night in the annex was noisy. With so many children crammed into such a small space it was inevitable. However, as a rule it was an occasional cough or cry. This night the coughing was almost continuous. The child on the other side of Gerry Ann coughed all night, and though I had not heard whooping cough for many years, a cold sweat broke out all over me. I thought I would go mad before morning came, and I could find out whether or not it really was whooping cough that I was hearing. After Gerry Ann's two o'clock feeding she cried and cried and there seemed to be nothing I could do for her. For awhile I walked the floor, and then I decided to put her down and try to keep calm and get some rest, for I knew that I'd have no milk for the six o'clock feeding if I didn't. Of course the women in the annex, who hadn't heard a tiny baby cry for two years, were livid about the whole situation. I could hear them muttering on all sides of me, and it helped immensely toward making milk.

Morning finally did come, and as I had suspected there was whooping cough in every room in the annex. Why no one had mentioned it to me when I moved into the room the afternoon before, will always be one of the mysteries of life. I felt that I could never possibly live with myself if I let Gerry Ann get whooping cough. As it was, I had enough on my conscience about her to almost break my heart. I camped on the doctor's door step until he arrived. He said, "Probably she won't get whooping cough since she's so young, and you are nursing her, but just in case (since she has slept all night next to a child who was coughing in her face), we'll give her the last of the serum. We'll give it to her in very small quantities." He said, "It probably isn't any good, since it's two years old," but it relieved my mind a little. I felt worse than a murderer when they stuck the needle into her. Either the serum or the fact that she was two weeks old and I was nursing her prevented her from taking whooping cough.

From the contagious disease angle we had been most fortunate for the two previous years. This measles–whooping cough epidemic among the children was the first of its kind. The doctors had expected an outbreak of some sort almost constantly, for the first year, but we had all begun to breathe more easily the second year. During the time I was outside the Japanese began to crack down, as I have said before. The children's diseases that ran rampant for awhile were traced directly to the Italian children who were brought in to camp at that time. Diseases had a wonderful field to work in, for there was no place that one child could be isolated from another. Why we never had more serious epidemics was an act of Providence. The constant fight against dirt, garbage, flies, bedbugs, and lice no doubt contributed to our lack of serious epidemics. One man had died of polio within a few days after he became ill. A child had acquired the same disease but, as a result, had been repatriated on the last ship. I think we all felt a touch of terror for awhile after those two cases were forced upon our attention.

There are no words to describe the emotional upheaval I went through that day and the days that followed. I ran the gamut of emotion. Almost without exception, the people whom I had expected to be nice were hateful and vice versa. The ones that I wouldn't have bet a dime on came to see whether or not there was anything they could do for me. The ones who were hateful I could look right in the eye and not see any more than I saw the wall, the nice ones nearly killed me. I cried buckets and buckets of tears. There seemed to be no end to my tears, and I had little or no control over them. "To hell with the hateful ones," I felt, but I couldn't cope with the nice ones. I hadn't really expected to find *any* nice ones. Several people brought small gifts for Gerry Ann. A woman whom I had never spoken to before (a woman who had no children and spent much time on her appearance and always looked immaculate) brought a small bottle of Johnson's baby oil. She said, "I've been saving it to use on my face, but I wanted you to have it for the baby." An incident of this kind could put me in the clouds. An hour later I might be walking with Gerry Ann, giving her a sun bath, and anything could happen. Once an old woman stopped me and said "What is your baby's name?" I told her, and she said "Yes, I know, but what is her *last* name?" Another one stopped me and said, "Where did you get the baby? I did not see her in your stooomak." Bob told me another story. After Gerry Ann was born a group of men whom I did not know were discussing the situation and one of the men said something about a bastard. One man in the group (and who the man was I do not know, but I here and now thank him) spoke up and said, "Let's call her a love child, shall we?" and I can never be grateful enough to that man. For some reason or other that term had never impressed itself upon me before, but it was so apt, so well put, that she will never be anything to me except my "love child."

Uncle Don and Ansi Lee thought the baby was wonderful. It thrilled me that they were so sweet about her. They seemed not to notice the reaction of most of the rest of the internees. Uncle Don said "She looks just like Churchill"—but of course she didn't! Two of Jerry's good friends came around to see me and offered to do anything they could. They were nice, but naturally there was nothing any one could do for me except *not* to make an issue of me, at least not in front of me.

Why it should have surprised me I don't know, but I found that many people who were nice to me had never in their lives done a questionable thing. Many other people whose moral standards (as far as *I* was concerned) were certainly not above reproach could not see me for dirt. Let me explain that last statement more fully. There were literally hundreds of people who could understand the fact that I might have had an affair with Jerry. When I became pregnant, if I had had an abortion and after the war had gone back to my husband, there would have been very little criticism of me. (I happen to know for a fact that it works this way.) Many people seemed to understand and accept this as normal procedure in such cases. That I had no intention of working out my problem in this way seemed to throw people off their balance. They seemed to think that there was no question about the fact that my mental processes were not what they should have been. If I had had any intention of going back to my husband after the war there would have been no question about my becoming pregnant. Some people even went so far as to blame Jerry for "letting such a thing happen." How can people be so lacking in understanding? Later a man said to Jerry, "You should prosecute someone for not letting Margaret have an abortion."

On the whole I believe the feeling in the camp was more sympathetic than I might have expected. At first I did not realize the cause. Later I understood. It seems to be the nature of people to get more of a thrill from a story if it isn't working out well. Jerry was in another camp. If he had been at Santo Tomás, I think public feeling might have been much more severe. As it was, people seemed to think I was a woman who had been "done wrong" and they were a little lenient. Later, in Los Baños, where I might have expected more understanding, I got none. It seems to be much more fun for people to cluck their tongues and say, "Can you *imagine?*—poor thing," than to say, "They *are* doing well?—Well, I'm so glad!"

One night three weeks or so after Gerry Ann and I got back to Santo Tomás I got up in the night to nurse her. Since we were not allowed to have a light everything was done by the touch system—a good system, but not quite as satisfactory as a light. As I changed her diaper she seemed to be fretting more than usual and suddenly I felt something crawling on my hands. I couldn't imagine what it was, for I kept her and her bed as clean as it was humanly possible to keep them. Bundling her up, I rushed down to the bathroom to examine her under the dim night light. I found her covered with tiny ants. I was simply horrified when I discovered them all over her head. They had already eaten a raw spot in the top of her head, right over the soft spot. She had been sleeping in her bassinet and apparently the ants had crawled up its legs and into her bed. I couldn't sleep the rest of the night, and after I nursed her I kept her in bed with me until morning. The legs of the bassinet set in cans of water solved the problem the next day, but I was always afraid the bassinet might accidentally get pushed against the wall (our spot in the room was behind a door this time) and that the ants might try it again, more successfully.

As soon as she began to grow I realized that the bassinet could be nothing more than a temporary bed. Mrs. Chamberlin[80] (she's dead now too) discovered a crib that wasn't being used and brought it to me one day. The only problem was a mattress. After days and days of sneezing and coughing and sewing I finally managed to make a mattress from kapok and a coarse grade of pinapok, a native material made from pineapple fibre. As a mattress maker I am not very good, but Gerry Ann didn't complain and it served the purpose very nicely. I bought a large patati ([a sleeping mat] woven from palm fronds) and cut it into squares to be used in lieu of a rubber sheet.

The days dragged into weeks and Gerry Ann acquired a tan from her daily sun baths, became chubby in a delicate way, and by the time she was three months old weighed ten pounds. Every day she had two baths and was dressed in clean clothes from the skin out. She was so beautiful that I couldn't help strutting when I took her for her walk. I kept her on the same four-hour schedule that David had been brought up on and we were getting along fairly well. David still slept with Robert, but he came to the annex several times a day. We ate together and I bathed him and saw to it that he was kept clean and out of trouble. He began to grow up as a result of the new baby, and I was pleased to see the new independence. He lacked only a few days of being six years old and I was planning a birthday party for him.

80. Edith Russell Chamberlin and her husband were "an older couple who helped out at the annex. He made small repairs. She was very kind to me" (MS to LB 11/10/87).

The birthday came and went and we had the party. Uncle Don and Ansi Lee again, Robert and Gretchen, and Louise and her son Bobby. It was a lovely party, as parties in those days went. I even managed a kind of cake. As I recall it only cost about $20 by the time I finally got enough ingredients together to make it. David loved it, and that was satisfaction enough for me. He even received two small gifts, and Uncle Don gave him a slip of paper on which he had written "I. O. U. a bicycle if and when we ever get out of the internment camp." Uncle Don kept his promise and even added one for Gerry Ann for good measure. We saw him once in New York, after we were liberated, and shortly after that his check arrived for the bicycles. Good Uncle Don, we did love him so much.

The first letter I had from my family came a few days after David's birthday. It was from my grandmother and, necessarily, said nothing. It really didn't need to say anything. It was enough to know that she still loved me and cared enough about me to write. A day or two later the second letter arrived, this one from my mother. For more than two years I had heard no word from them and then suddenly there were two letters within a few days of each other. My mother's letter filled me with foreboding. My father had been seriously hurt in an accident, his back broken. The letter had been written almost two years before, and I felt sure that what ever was to happen would already have happened. I couldn't quite get over the shock of that letter, for I had never thought of my father as crippled or dead. I had always felt that there was nothing that could stop him. He was such an alive sort of person, so active, that I knew it would kill him to be a cripple and helpless. To think of him as dead was even worse. What would my mother do, what would become of my brothers and sisters? How could they get along without my father? Not from a financial standpoint alone, but from every standpoint?[81] That way lay madness and I dared not think about it.

81. "For a time, my mother supported four children on the proceeds from my father's life insurance. After I returned from internment, she took com-

Apparently packages came on the same ship that brought the letters from the States, for a few days later there were dozens of rumors about personal packages. I can still remember that day and the excitement that filled the air. I was washing at the wash trough when the news started flying that they were broadcasting on the loudspeaker in front of the main building names of people who had packages. People dropped their dishes, their clothes, anything they were working on, right where they were and ran like sheep for the front of the main building. I felt a little as I remembered feeling when I was young—during the Depression. Hoping that I'd get a thing, knowing very well that I wouldn't get it, for we couldn't afford it. Not even envy for those who were getting packages, but a sort of contempt for myself for even wishing that my name would be called when I knew very well that it wouldn't be. And that horrible pride of mine, which I seemed to be able to do nothing about; it simply would not let me go along with the mob and take a chance on my name *not* being called. For at least half an hour I must have kept on washing at the trough, completely alone. Then someone came back and picked up her laundry and said, "Hey, have you gotten your package already?" I went along with the gag and grinned and said, "Sure, three or four of them." The woman stopped and looked at me and said, "No fooling, I'm *sure* I heard them call your name." I still didn't believe her and kept on washing, though my insides were gradually turing to water.[82] Minutes later Robert came galloping around the corner looking for me and said, "For Christ's sake, go get your packages—you've got two

munity college courses and excelled, but was considered too old for most jobs. Later she became a real estate broker and had her own office and made a comfortable living. Throughout her long life (she died at 87) she supported Jane, her youngest child, born retarded in 1938. Jane now lives happily with our sister Ann, mother of ten children, in Collinsville, Illinois" (MS to LB 8/10/87).

82. "I hadn't heard from anyone throughout the whole war, so I couldn't believe I had a package then. Moreover, my mother got only one card from me during wartime, a card after I returned to the United States saying that I was interned" (MS to LB 8/10/87).

of 'em." I knew he wouldn't kid me about anything as serious as that, so I too hurried off to the main building.

The most wonderful package I have ever received in my life came from my mother. If I had been able to write to her and tell her the things I needed most there would have been no single change in the package. Needles, pins, thread, soap, vitamins, dried fruit, chocolate, shorts, a pair of sturdy shoes, clothes, and shoes for David, and several yards of mosquito netting. A ten-pound package, I believe it was, and it was ten pounds of gold to me. It may have been then that I discovered that few moments are completely happy. There were many people who did not receive packages that day and I could not help feeling sorry for them, perhaps because I knew so well how one feels when one is left out. I couldn't be totally happy with my package because, having been left out for so long, I knew just how those other people felt. Unfortunately, there was only enough to share with my very few friends, and not the others.

I was worried sick about Jerry. I had not been able to let him know about the birth of the baby. My last note from him had been very terse and to the point. When Bob's note had come, I sent it to Jerry so that he would know our status exactly. Bob did not want to divorce me and I felt as if the world were closing in on me when Jerry sent Bob's note back to me (as I'd asked him to do) and had enclosed his own few lines, which said nothing.[83] That had been before Gerry Ann was born. For all I knew he might have decided that he was sick of the whole bargain. I wouldn't have blamed him too much, but I was going slowly mad wondering. The last of March, rumors had begun to circulate to the effect that another shipment of people were to be sent to Los Baños. This time women and children were to go, we heard. I stewed and I worried and I wondered what

83. "I guess I didn't know what to say. I thought Margaret knew the answers to everything because we had discussed them before I was transferred to Los Baños and had made our commitments at that time" (JS to LB 8/10/87). See n. 10, p. 15.

I should do about it. Every day and every night I wondered what I should do. Should I go and find out whether Jerry and I really had made a mess of our lives, or whether we really did love each other as devotedly as we had thought. I suppose you wonder how anyone can be doubtful about a thing like that? I knew that I loved him, but I also knew that if there were the slightest doubt on his part, *I* wanted no part of the bargain. It was no bargain unless we both felt the same way.

There were notices on all the bulletin boards asking those who wished to go to Los Baños to sign up by the deadline. I went around in a trance for days. I asked Jerry's two friends what they thought I should do. Being diplomats they said, "If you think Jerry will be expecting you, you'd better go." The year before Jerry had said, "If you ever get a chance to come I'll be waiting for you." This year, however, the picture was considerably changed. I was no longer a respectable women with one child; I was now a "bad" woman with two children. The truck was no longer running between the two camps so there was no possibility of a note. All night, the night before the deadline, I lay awake going over all the possibilities, just as if I hadn't done it a thousand times before. I made up my mind that I wouldn't go, I simply could not take the chance. Five minutes before they took the notice down I went over to the main building and signed up, against the combined advice of Robert, Gretchen, and Louise.[84]

We waited for days then to find out who would be chosen to go, and I felt confident that they would not let the children and me go. After all, Gerry Ann was not quite three months old. I felt that, even if Jerry had changed his mind, we would at least be better off in Los Baños when liberation came, for I was confident that there would be fighting. I thought that we'd have a better chance in the country than in the city, especially as far

84. "They were all afraid that Jerry wouldn't honor his commitment, but they didn't say so to me" (MS to LB 8/10/87).

as food was concerned. As it turned out, I couldn't have been more wrong.

The list of people to go was finally published, and down among the S's I found our three names. And then began the business of packing our belongings for the trip. Every suitcase and box and bottle and bed had to be marked and tied a certain way or the Japanese might do anything unpredictable. We still use the suitcase we had then, and it still bears the mark the Japanese demanded on each bag and bundle.[85]

Those last few days before leaving Santo Tomás I felt more desperate than I have ever felt in my life. Louise and Gretchen were sure that I should not go and Robert was definitely upset with me. I felt that I was hurting my most staunch friends, the only people in the world whom I could depend upon, but at the same time I knew that I could not stand the insecurity, the uncertainty of my position very much longer. I'd go mad. I knew that I'd much rather know exactly where I stood and start working toward a new life from there, than to be constantly wondering what the future held for me. I knew, beyond the shadow of a doubt, that I could not go back to Bob no matter what his note had said about taking Gerry Ann and treating her as his own. Human nature is not made that way, in the first place, and in the second place there is never any going back. I was no longer the same woman I had once been, and there was no way of going back even if I had wanted to. One can only go forward. If Jerry no longer loved me I wanted to know.[86] Poor little Gerry Ann, how I managed to nurse her I don't know and it's no won-

85. The suitcase, battered but unbowed, labeled "Sherk, M.," is a small overnight bag of a tweed-patterned fiberboard popular at the time. It reposes in the guest bedroom closet at the Sams's California ranch, along with the worn wooden box that housed the contraband radio in Los Baños.

86. "I felt desperate because my friends had unsettled me. I had had no notes from Jerry because the truck wasn't running between Santo Tomás and Los Baños and he couldn't send any. But I went because I *had* to know where I stood with Jerry. I couldn't stand not knowing; even bad news would have been better than no news" (MS to LB 8/10/87).

der she cried after every feeding. I tried desperately to keep calm for her sake, but it wasn't in the cards.

Jerry had left several things with me which he did not want to take to Los Baños, for fear of a Japanese search. His passport, his Cavite pass, several odds and ends. Before I left Santo Tomás I had to get rid of these things, too, for I too did not want to have a searching party find them. Robert and I very carefully concealed them in the overhead of the museum, where they remained safely until Jerry collected them after the war.

A few days before Gerry Ann was three months old we were piled into trucks and we rolled out the gate of Santo Tomás. Whether the Japanese did it, or the Americans did it, I don't know, but they put the children and me in the one truck with a tarp over the top and it was a blessing. The sun was unmercifully hot and the dust was so thick it nearly choked us. We were in the truck with a woman and her son who had been bombed in Baguio the first day of the war. The woman had lost her leg, and her son (a baby of a few months at the time it happened) had been wounded in the leg. At first they thought the leg would be all right, but as he grew older it became more and more apparent that some serious damage had been done to his leg, for it was not growing as the other one was. He was the prettiest little boy I have ever seen, and by far the best behaved.

I had very carefully put Gerry Ann's best blue camisa in the bottom of her bassinet to be put on her just before we arrived. The camisa was the color of her eyes, and had been made from a scrap of one of the three dresses that I had worn into Santo Tomás. We were filthy when we arrived, so it was a good thing that Gerry Ann, at least, was prepared for the emergency.

David had impetigo so badly that I was very worried about him. He had great sores all over his body and had been going every day for weeks to the clinic to have them painted. They did nothing but thrive on the gentian violet which the nurses put on them. It was no uncommon sight, the impetigo and tropical ulcers which came next, but I was ashamed that I had let David get it. How I could have prevented it I don't know, but

I felt guilty about it. He was a fierce-looking sight for he had several of the spots on his face and they were all painted a bright purple.

The ride to Los Baños in the caravan of trucks was hectic, but it was nothing compared to my mental state. I had decided that I would do absolutely nothing if Jerry weren't at the truck to meet me. That would answer all the questions I wanted to know. After several hours of riding we drove in the main gate at Los Baños. The surrounding country was beautiful. There were fewer people here, and it seemed even less after the congestion of Santo Tomás. As the truck stopped and I looked out I could see a few faces that I recognized—but no Jerry. I thought I'd wait until the other people disembarked and their friends took them away, and then I'd slip quietly away and find a place for the children and me. I had already made up my mind that Jerry wasn't coming, when suddenly I looked down and there he was at the side of the truck, grinning and holding up his arms. Mabel [Carlisle] wasn't far behind him. Such pure joy cannot be written about. I handed him Gerry Ann, and most of my problems! He took them all, willingly and gladly, and Gerry Ann looked at him and he swears that she stuck her tongue out at him. And I was ashamed that I had doubted.

Jerry Sams in the Santo Tomás camp, taken with a camera he had managed to conceal from the Japanese

Shanties constructed by some of the internees to give themselves a sense of privacy

A camp work detail, cleaning talinum

Jerry's room, number 40 in Santo Tomás, before he moved to the landing

Meals were eaten outdoors at the back of the main building, Santo
Tomás

Typically crowded conditions in the men's dormitory (the gym),
Santo Tomás

Los Baños

Before the war Los Baños had been used as an experimental farm in connection with the University of the Philippines. As far as I know, it had the only cows in the Philippines which actually gave milk. The Philippines have a tiny bug, a parasite, which prevents grazing cows from giving milk. Naturally the Japanese were anxious to have at their disposal all of this life-giving substance that they could find.

Los Baños was beautifully situated. On three sides of the compound, as far as the eye could see, there was nothing except the unending brilliant green of coconut and banana trees. Though I did not know it until later, the fourth side lay close to Laguna de Bay. We were inside a barbed-wire fence, of course, and the inevitable guards patrolled constantly, but there was enough acreage here and the terrain was such that we could see beyond the fence to the blue mountains in the distance. There was a feeling of space here which we never had in Santo Tomás and I for one, having grown up in the west, where a feeling of space is one's heritage, got a lift every time I got far enough away from the barracks to see out. As I look back, the wonderfully blue sky with its lazily drifting white clouds, the green-blue mountains in the distance, the brilliant flowered hibiscus close at hand, and the glistening green groves just over the fence, did a great deal to make the next year bearable.[1]

Immediately upon our arrival in Los Baños Jerry took us to his small room (the communications room it was called, since it had a record player and microphone) where he, with the help of a navy nurse, had prepared a delicious meal for us. The most outstanding thing about the meal was the "applesauce." There are no apples grown in the Philippines, so it was a real treat to eat anything that resembled them. They had cooked and mashed a green papaya, seasoned it with brown sugar, cinnamon bark, and calamanci juice, and after not having tasted the original fruit for two years, it could very easily have passed as the real McCoy.

When I had finally decided to go to Los Baños, it hadn't occurred to me that we might live under quite such primitive conditions as we found there. At least in Santo Tomás we had been allowed to take a shower [nearly] every day, there were lavatories with modern plumbing facilities, there were some sidewalks, and some of the roads within the camp were paved. In Santo Tomás we had cement floors which were easily scrubbed.

David had just had his sixth birthday and had never in his life seen anything except the conventional flushing article in the bathroom. I don't suppose he knew that there was any other kind. During the evening, when we were trying to unscramble our

1. Before the war, the town of Los Baños had been a resort, located on the shore of a large, freshwater lake, Laguna de Bay, with a backdrop of Mount Makiling and rice-terraced, emerald green hillsides. Named after its hot springs, "the baths," Los Baños was also the site of an agricultural college where experimental groves of coconut palms, bananas, and mangos produced abundant crops throughout the war—which the internees were forbidden to eat. Twenty-six barracks were eventually built on the grounds of Los Baños Agricultural College, beginning in the spring of 1943, to relieve the crowded conditions in Santo Tomás. Each housed 75–100 internees. The Japanese initially planned the facility for 7,000, but had to scale down their plans because of an inadequate water supply and the unavailability of materials to store or transport water. The internee population, second largest in the Philippines after Santo Tomás, eventually ranged between 2,100–2,400 (MS to LB 8/10/87, JJH to LB 11/21/87, Stevens 48–51, Flanagan 25).

boxes and bundles and beds and get them to our new "home,"
David received nature's call. (The Japanese had dumped all baggage in a huge pile beside the road, so it was one grand shambles.) Each barracks was separated from the next one by a combination bathroom-laundryroom. Along the inside wall, rough
planking had been nailed over a galvanized iron trough through
which, at certain times of the day, designated men poured water
for flushing purposes. At intervals the planks had holes cut in
them. This, then, was our new bathroom. I had not been in
it yet when David had found it necessary to go. I sent him by
himself, naturally, and he was back in a few minutes saying, "There
isn't one, Mommy." Twice this happened and each time I was
a little more exasperated with the poor child for I *knew* it was
the bathroom; it said so on the door. The third time he came
back crying. I gave up and went back with him. I was appalled.
The odor, the flies, the heat, the general dirtiness of human beings was a constant cross to bear. Never any privacy, with a queue
usually standing looking down one's throat, each person jealously
guarding his place in the line. I told him to go ahead and use
it, and I am still amused when I recall with what utter horror
he said "You mean on the *floor,* Mommy?"

I think I might as well "take off" here about the necessity, the
joy, of the simple thing called toilet tissue. I wonder if you've
ever stopped to think what a blessing is the simple roll of toilet
tissue that one can buy at any corner grocery. That last year we
used books. We were delighted with Shakespeare, for his pages
were thin. Jerry and I had not more than a dozen books between us and I could never help feeling a little sacrilegious when
we'd tear a few more pages from our dwindling supply. In a queer
sort of way it amused us to see how very rudimentary is this
[phenomenon] called civilization, and at the same time it hurt
to have to know the things we were learning.

The first night we were in Los Baños Jerry played the same
records for the camp that he had been playing for months and
we sat on the steps of his "house" and tried vainly, it seemed,
to get reacquainted and catch up on the events of the last year.

I learned that night that having a child under the circumstances we'd had ours can be hard on the father too.[2] We found that our only real problem, however, was *me*. I had developed through necessity a hard, thick, protective coating of ice in all my thinking and feeling and it took months of work on both our parts to begin to thaw me out and make a decent human being out of me again.

That night will remain with me forever, for there was no love-making, as one might expect, there was only a feeling of amazement that here I was at last with the father of my child, my love, and we were strangers trying desperately to get acquainted. In our own eyes we were a man and a wife trying, so very hard, to bridge a terrible gap. To others we were Jerry Sams and Margaret Sherk, victims of a chance opportunity, he to live in his barracks, I in mine. The things that go through one's mind at a time like that. Here I was with Jerry's child asleep in the room behind us, and yet I did not know an intimate thing about him. Was he happy before breakfast? Did he sing in the shower? Did he hang up his clothes at night? How did he like his eggs cooked? I was two people, one sitting off at a distance watching this farce, the other struggling to get a little of it into words that might begin to make him understand the hell that I had been through, the reason I wasn't (and never could be again) the woman whom he had loved the year before. At the same time I wanted him to know how very much I still loved him, would always love him, but he *must* understand that it had to be a two-way deal. I wanted no charity. If he didn't feel exactly as he had the year before, I would have no part of it.

Uncle Don and Ansi Lee came to Los Baños at the same time the children and I came. Jerry had not met Uncle Don when he was in Santo Tomás. Our first afternoon I asked Jerry if he'd be good enough to tell him the news occasionally. Jerry took

2. Jerry Sams recalled, "You don't consider the consequences of passion at the time but you worry a lot about how to feed the baby once it's there and food is so scarce. Furthermore, as Gerry Ann's father I was considered a criminal in camp" (JS to LB 8/10/87).

my word for Uncle Don's trustworthiness, and after he had walked the children and me home to our barracks, he went back and found Uncle Don, introduced himself, and they went to Jerry's room where they lay on the floor in the darkness and listened to "the man," as we soon decided to call Jerry's radio.

My first introduction to the camp doctor, Dana Nance,[3] who was to play an interesting and important part in our radio ac-

3. Dana Wilson Nance was born on October 7, 1904 in Nashville, Tennessee, but raised in Soochow, China by his missionary parents. His mother tutored him at home until he returned to America to attend college. He earned two degrees from Vanderbilt University, a B.A. in 1925, and an M.D. in 1929. In the early 1930s he spent two years as a U.S. Public Health Service doctor in Manila, and practiced medicine for the rest of the decade with his brother in Shanghai. In January 1941, concerned with the worsening situation in China, he sent his wife Anna and their three children back to the States, and later that year became medical director of both Benguet Consolidated Mining Company and Notre Dame Hospital in Baguio. Interned in Baguio at the outbreak of the war, Nance set up the camp hospital and persuaded the Japanese to let him stock it with some of the equipment and supplies he had providentially scooped up after a Japanese attack forced American troops to desert Camp John Hay. His bold, impetuous, but concerned approach won him the chairmanship of the camp executive committee, and some criticism from internees such as Natalie Crouter, whose democratic orientation disapproved of his imperiousness. In 1943 the Japanese commanding general of northern Luzon politely asked, considering that the Baguio internees had enough doctors, whether Nance would accept a transfer to Los Baños, whose medical director had been repatriated on an exchange ship. Unlike other internees, who were transported by charcoal-fueled truck and train, Nance was escorted by a chauffeur in a confiscated Cadillac.

In May, 1945 Nance returned to his children in New Orleans with Anna, who had gone to the liberated Philippines to meet him, and the family moved to Oak Ridge, Tennessee, a "wartime boomtown with wooden sidewalks traversing hip-deep mud" because of the presence of a large Atomic Energy Commission plant. There Nance was director of medical services for the AEC until 1970; and he and Anna became, as the local paper said, "the center of social consciousness." Dana was a founder of the Bank of Oak Ridge, Anna was for a time executive director of the Chamber of Commerce. Their protests against racial discrimination helped to integrate the town well in advance of Civil Rights legislation. As Dick Smyser, the *Oak Ridger*'s editor said, "They were involved with cleaning up elections, establishing the city's . . . model mental health pro-

Los Baños • 195

tivities for the next year, was most inauspicious. The morning
after we arrived in Los Baños, Gerry Ann started sneezing. She
sneezed almost continuously for three or four hours. I was frantic and blamed myself for having been selfish and brought her
on such a long, hot, dusty trip. We went to see the doctor and
he stopped the sneezing almost immediately with a little boric
acid solution in each nostril, but I felt that the doctor was giving me a much more thorough going-over than he was Gerry
Ann. Naturally he was curious about my status. He had known
Jerry for several months and he wanted to know what sort of
woman would do the thing that I had done. Had Jerry been
"taken" or did I just "play for keeps," as one woman accused
me of doing? All nice people, I don't care who they are, think
the same thing. "No decent woman would do such a thing" and
it takes a tremendous bit of doing for people to readjust their
mental picture of a "bad woman." It's disconcerting to find the
bad woman is just an ordinary woman, a little on the large side,
and not even pretty. I know the doctor finally did come to like
me and realized that circumstances sometimes do make the bad
woman, and not vice versa.

As I said earlier, David was covered with impetigo when we
arrived in Los Baños. As we got off the truck, Jerry took one
look at him and said "My God, David, you look as if you'd fallen
in a garbage can." The next day he started to work on him. Somewhere he had gotten one half of a large oil drum, which he was
using for his laundry tub. He heated water in the tub, traded
someone for some blue soap, and then scrubbed David for dear
life. This procedure went on for days. Almost immediately we
could see a change for the better. No doubt it was the hot water,
as well as the blue soap, which started to work on him, for of

---

gram, pushing for property ownership and self-government. [They believed]
you just might 'do some good.' You would surely have some fun." After obliga-
tory retirement from Oak Ridge in 1969, Nance went into private practice in
Atlanta, and retired again a decade later to Guadalajara, Mexico, where he died
in May, 1987 (JJH to LB 11/21/87, 12/15/87; Dick Smyser, "A Name for Oak Ridge
to Remember," Editorial, *Oak Ridger* [Tennessee] 19 June 1987:4).

course he hadn't had a hot bath for two years. For weeks David had been going to the clinic. Nothing had happened except that the impetigo had spread like wildfire. As if by magic Jerry was curing him. Again I bowed my head to the master of my fate. When we had left Santo Tomás the children were still in the throes of the measles–whooping cough epidemic. Shortly after we arrived David came down with an extra-specially good case of measles. Before I had time to draw a good breath they had him in an isolation ward. There were fewer children here, and apparently they wanted no epidemics in Los Baños if they could be prevented.

A few days after we arrived I received the third and last letter I was to receive during internment. The letter from my mother was more than a year old, telling me that my father was dead. In a way it was a comfort to know that it wasn't a recent thing, that he'd been gone a year, and that my mother would already have begun to make the awful readjustments that followed. What can one ever say at the death of one's beloved father? A part of one's life is finished.

The children and I had been in Los Baños only a short while when Jerry was given to understand that he had held a position of respect and importance in the camp, and since he had violated that trust (!) it would be just as well for him to find another camp detail. He continued to teach his electronics class for some time after that (after all, that was to the camp's advantage), but he had to give up his "communications detail" which had allowed Tommy and him to live alone in the communications room. This was a privilege from the camp, so this must be taken away from him. From communications he went to a woodcutting detail. I was dreadfully sorry for Jerry but he took it as he always takes things, in his stride, and it made us closer than we might have been otherwise.[4] This way we were two against the world,

4. Jerry explained, "During this time I was teaching advanced electronics and communications in camp for two hours a day and chopping wood for another two hours, until the school system went to pot because as the food rations were cut people grew too hungry to study.

and we were young and learning to be tough-minded. Nuts to them!

In Los Baños we were allowed a space four feet by twelve feet per person, which was almost twice as many feet as we'd had in Santo Tomás. The barracks were very long, with a hall down the center of each one, dividing them. What each barracks looked like more than anything else was a tremendous barn two hundred feet long, made of native grasses for the roof,[5] and sawali matting for the sides, with stalls on either side of the long hard-packed (except when it rained) dirt hall. Each barracks held approximately one hundred people. The stalls, or cubicles as we called them, had very rough planks, with large cracks between them, for flooring. I was duly grateful for the planks, splintery or otherwise. Each partition was six feet high, made of sawali, so that if one got very close to the sawali, one could see through it. One could hear everything that was said in the adjoining cubicle, but at least one did not have to dress in front of the world. Not only that, each cubicle had a door, the swinging barroom type door, to be sure, but at least it gave one an opportunity to see whether it was a barefooted or booted, sabre-dragging caller.

For a change we had a good spot in the barracks. Our cubicle was the next but one from the end. The end cubicles had plywood partitions, instead of sawali. It was a break to be near the end of the barracks, for it meant that not so many people would

---

"The woodpile was out of bounds. I passed out one day after I had been chopping wood for about an hour on a nearly empty stomach. When I came to I realized I was all alone—a real problem in an out-of-bounds area. Fortunately, when I came back into camp a friendly Japanese guard, called 'St. Looey' because he had lived in St. Louis and knew English well, let me in without reporting me. The same guard twice gave us contraband eggs and milk, hiding them in his blouse as he brought them to our cubicle" (JS to LB 8/10/87).

5. "The sharply-sloped roof was composed of meter-square nipa sections—thin bamboo strips folded over pencil-thin bamboo pole frames and laced through (like weaving) with rattan to hold the nipa fronds together. Not only do these roofs shed water during rainstorms; during hurricanes the nipa panels open up and the wind sails right through, instead of tearing the panels off" (JS to LB 8/10/87).

hear and complain when they heard Gerry Ann cry at night. Whether she had colic or whether she was just plain hungry I don't know, but she never missed crying after a feeding and there were times when I thought it would be the final straw. No child ever cried in Los Baños that adults on all sides didn't hiss, "shhhhhhhh!" I came as close to hating people there as I have ever come to it in my life. What in heaven's name did they think we did to our children? Pinch them so they'd *have* to wake up and cry in the night? I have yet to talk to a woman who was interned with her children who does not feel the same way I do in this regard. At the same time I have heard people say how kindly the children in internment were treated. Without exception, the people who say this had no children.

I had not guessed, even yet, how cruel and selfish is the human animal; particularly the adult ones, and most particularly the supposed-to-be intelligent ones. Always I've heard about the cruelty of children, but it is as nothing compared to that of their elders. This seems as good as any other time to bring up a thing that I should forget, but I am most certainly going to write about it first, before I forget about it. Months later, when the question came up as to whether or not children should be given half or whole rations, through a decision of the men's barracks the children were cut to one-half ration.[6] In many, many cases these men had wives and children of their own, at home in the States. The Japanese had never allowed children a whole ration, but until things became really tough, we, the internees, had all shared equal portions per person, adult and child alike. This meant that each person got a slightly smaller amount of food than if adults

6. Margaret observes that "The Los Baños and Santo Tomás leaders were largely American businessmen who couldn't appreciate a woman's point of view. Growing children needed full rations. These men were privileged; they had money and outside contacts. It never occurred to them that there were 'peasants' in the camps—single women with children, but with no money and no contacts. Power and access made these men relatively comfortable. The Japanese could have evened things out but they didn't" (MS to LB 8/10/87).

had gotten whole rations and children half rations. The quantity of food that we were allowed remained the same; it only differed as to how we decided to divide it. Growing children, in many cases, eat more than an adult and no doubt need more. As long as people were rational they agreed with this, in principle anyway. People with children voted to give them whole rations, but we were far outnumbered by the number of single people. We could do as we pleased after we got our soup and rice from the line. In our cubicle the food was always religiously divided into equal parts.

Both Jerry's radios were built before my arrival in Los Baños and they were built the hard way. The first one, which he lost, came the hardest, since he made it with charcoal resistors, paper and tinfoil condensers, and coils wound from magnet wire taken from the nurses' call-bell system in the hospital. When this radio was completed, one of the fellows who had collaborated in its construction announced that he had "just the place to keep it," and that was the last Jerry ever saw of it. Since building a radio was a two-man job (one to work and one to watch for the Japanese and the internees alike), Jerry got together with Tommy Obst, whom he had known before the war. Tommy was a physicist. Together they had a vast amount of knowledge and although the Japanese didn't know it, they presented an almost unbeatable combination. They started the construction of another radio, using the camp record player as the power supply and Jerry's work detail in the "communications department" as his cover-up. The small radio which I got for Jerry in Santo Tomás arrived at this time, and many of its parts subsequently found their way into the radio he was then building. From that time on the radio was built into many different forms, not only to keep it from the Japanese, but to keep the internees from knowing what it looked like.[7] Jerry rightly thought that any man can be made to talk, and the fewer who knew what it looked like the better his chances would be.

7. See n. 79, p. 172.

Some time before I arrived, authentic news was getting around camp.[8] Since Jerry was confident that the few people whom he told were not the source of the "good rumors," Tommy and he decided to build a jammer in order to keep Jerry's first radio from getting the news, and its possessor passing it on indiscriminately. They tuned the jammer on KGEI. When they were certain that the other fellow was not near his radio they turned on their own radio and got the news. Afterward they turned the jammer back on. The fellow was greatly disturbed about the fact that he could no longer get KGEI, but apparently never suspected the reason for it. The Japanese were also aware of the jammer, but presumably thought that some of their own boys were doing it. When the internees were forced to abandon that part of the camp, much later, Jerry and Tommy decided to put the jammer on Tokyo instead of San Francisco, and just let it run. They coupled the jammer into the power line, which made it difficult to locate, for the power line ran all over that part of the country. The Japanese realized that the interference came from the power line and kept themselves busy for weeks changing pole transformers and insulators. It is assumed that they never did find the jammer.

Every night during the music hour Jerry got his daily news bulletin. People were outside listening to the records and apparently never gave Jerry a thought, or if they did, considered that he was busy with the records. What made this dangerous was the fact that often a Japanese guard would decide to visit the communications shack to see what made the music. One night

8. Authentic news was news verified from an actual short-wave broadcast on an Allied radio station (received on a clandestine radio)–KGEI San Francisco, and some stations in the USSR and Western Europe. Arthur claims that the Japanese "planted stories that President Roosevelt had died from syphilis, that General MacArthur had not in fact escaped by PT boat from Corregidor but had been captured and shamefully hanged in Tokyo, [and] that the war was expected to last until 1952" (127). Jim Halsema, a professional reporter-in-the-making who listened continually to Dana Nance's clandestine radio in Baguio, says he never heard such items; they may have been internees' rumors (JJH to LB 11/21/87).

after the news went off Jerry listened for a few minutes to some of the latest popular music from home. He was getting such perfect reception that he decided on the spur of the moment to let the rest of the internees have a bit of it too. He says he simply couldn't resist letting them hear "I Don't Get Around Much Any More." His eager listeners hounded him for weeks to "play that record again." Tommy, I am told, died the death of a rag doll during this performance, but no one of the internees or the Japanese, who frequently came out and listened to the music, ever realized why he couldn't "play that record again."

When I started this, I had no idea that it was a book about Jerry. I had thought it would be a book about my own reactions to the war, and why. As Jerry likes to kid me by saying, "If it hadn't been for me you wouldn't have a story," which is quite true. Jerry's wonderful ability to look death and destruction in the face and laugh at it all is one of his most fascinating characteristics. Jerry does all the things people dream about doing but never do. Sometimes he terrifies me, and sometimes he makes me very proud, and sometimes he embarrasses me, but he always *does* the things that I want to do or say but haven't the nerve to do or say. There is no other man like him, and I feel sure that there is no other man in the world who would have taken our new relationship as Jerry did. To him, I was his wife and my place was by his side. Nothing anyone could say or do could alter that fact.

An incident that occurred a few nights after the children's and my arrival [characterizes] Jerry. Without any warning the Japanese put on a search. We weren't sure what they were looking for, but having a pair of guilty consciences, we weren't taking too many chances. At the moment the Japanese were searching the gym, where the unattached men lived, Jerry put the incriminating part of the record player in his pocket,[9] and we started out. We went directly to the gym to see what was going on. I was new at the game then and was scared silly to go walking

9. Which at the time contained the radio receiver (MS to LB 8/10/87).

right down where all the guards were, but Jerry seemed not to give it a thought. I clung to his arm like a leech, and I have known no other strength like it. It can stiffen my spine every time, just to be near him. Strength of will is his dominant characteristic. We got as close as we could and saw all that we could without making ourselves too obvious, and then walked away again with the incriminating evidence still in Jerry's pants pocket. I'm quite certain that it would have burned a hole in my pocket. Jerry just seemed to be amused that the Japanese were so far off base. Gym indeed!

Almost nothing was funny the last year of internment, but Jerry's shoe story comes close. Jerry had done some work on the telephone system at the request of the central committee and had established a reputation for walking along looking up at the telephone lines, tracing the line. One day he decided to test an idea. He wanted to see whether or not he could walk right out the gate. He walked up the road, gazing up at the telephone lines as he went. He bowed to the guard and kept right on walking—right out the gate. (Of course he was still inside the main fence, but nevertheless we were not supposed to go out that gate.) He kept walking and followed the telephone lines to the Japanese barracks—about a block away.

It was obvious that a big party was in progress upstairs. There were dozens of pairs of Japanese shoes at the bottom of the stairway. Jerry checked in every direction. Absolutely no one was watching him. He quickly threw at least one shoe from each pair of shoes as far as he could throw them down the canyon and went right on walking—back inside the camp fence, where he bowed to the Japanese guard and kept walking—gazing up at the telephone lines. He managed to stay around in that part of the camp for about an hour, when "all hell broke loose." . . . Jerry thinks they were blaming someone in their own group for the loss of the shoes. He came back to our cubicle absolutely delighted with himself. A part of me could not help being pleased with him, too, but it was just one more time I was scared silly—just thinking about the repercussions that could have ensued.

Jerry is a born nest-builder and almost immediately started to demonstrate his ability in that direction. The housing people had not allowed for Gerry Ann when they assigned my space, but after Jerry made them realize that she also was a person, and therefore entitled to a certain number of feet, they allowed Jerry to move our partition over the given number of feet. Every inch of wood in the barracks was terribly rough and splintery. When Jerry moved the partition—everyone was moving partitions during those first few weeks—he decided to plane all the rough surfaces. He worked and perspired and planed until the wood was beautiful to see and feel. The next thing he did was to make shelves in one corner, and then he cut a door on the outside of the barracks. With a door on the outside we could get to the bath-laundry room by a much shorter route, and increasingly often these days a quick trip was necessary.

After partitions were moved and doors cut (about which the Japanese screamed long and loud), the next thing, in order of importance was to make a media agua,[10] and a drainage ditch outside the barracks. It is almost always warm in the Philippine Islands in the lowlands (which is the reason we are still alive), and it rains constantly, for days on end, during a typhoon. When there are no typhoons it just rains every afternoon during rainy season. Rainy season, where we were, started in April and ended in September or October. Therefore, the importance of drainage ditches and media aguas cannot be exaggerated. A media agua is a piece of sawali (in this case) which can be raised or lowered at will, and protrudes ten feet beyond the roof to shed water. At the same time it will allow the window to remain open in order that one will not suffocate with the damp, sticky, steamy heat. The media aguas were a community affair, and were uniform in size and extended the entire length of the barracks. Ditches were a community affair also. It wasn't fair for Jerry to

10. "Media agua" is Spanish for an awning or lower extension of a roof. Vito C. Santos's *Vicassan's Filipino-English Dictionary* (Manila: National Book Store, 1986), spells the Tagalog adaptation *medya-agwa*.

have to help at my barracks, and then go back and help at his. At best Jerry and I don't have a great deal of community spirit; at worst, and those days were worst, we didn't have any.

During rainy season, mud was inches deep all over the camp; sticky, gluey, muddy, mud. There was mud even in the hall, for the roof leaked. Almost without exception everyone either wore bakia [clogs] or went barefooted in Los Baños, and we battled constantly with mud, inside and out. Our family adopted the Japanese custom of taking off our bakia before entering our cubicle. This eliminated much backbreaking scrubbing. Outside there seemed no easy way to outwit it. Since the soles of bakia were made of wood, and they were held on by a piece of innertube across the instep, bakia were extremely unreliable footwear when one's feet were wet. I despise mud and it was a horrible sensation to be trying to get to the bathroom in a hurry and have one's bakia stick. When a bakia stuck in the mud, one groped wildly behind one for the missing "shoe" while one tried frantically to keep one's balance. In most cases both feet were in the mud up to the ankles before a trip to the bathroom was completed. I was much too old to enjoy the sensation of the dark brown stuff oozing between my toes. You may think it silly to devote a paragraph to mud, but it was a constant source of irritation. Nowhere could we escape it during rainy season.

It took several months for the barracks to be gotten into livable condition. During the first month the Japanese organized what they called a "working party." These people were allowed to go outside to an abandoned part of the camp and bring back specified materials which were needed to fix the occupied barracks. The enterprise was to be purely individual. What one could find was to be one's own, *if* the Japanese guards agreed to it. Jerry is an individualist and this suited him perfectly. He has an instinctive ability for figuring out ways and means of getting more done with less effort than anyone I have ever known. For example, someone had given me four small wheels with which they thought Jerry could make some sort of buggy for Gerry Ann. When Jerry was getting ready to go with the working party he decided to take the wheels. He took bejuco as well, which could be used in lieu of rope, and I'm sure he dragged at least half of one of those abandoned barracks back on those wheels. Not only that, he made three trips while the rest of the internees were making one. I have never been so frightfully sorry for and proud of anyone in my life. He nearly killed himself that afternoon, and I knew that it was all for me, for *us,* for our first "home." After the job was completed, our good, kind, sweet internees decided that everything that had been brought back should be divided equally among the entire camp. Dozens of people hadn't even gone, I among them, and many had sat back and snickered at the fools who went out in the noonday sun and tried to kill themselves. "For what? We'll be out of here in a couple more weeks, didn't you hear the rumor about _____?" With my own ears I heard some of the men in my barracks while they were sitting in the shade taking a siesta, laugh at how hard Jerry was working, and they were the very first ones who thought that it would be an excellent idea for the "loot" to be divided equally. As a matter of fact, Jerry's pile of goodies seemed to tantalize the people in our barracks who had not gone on the looting trip. Jim Tullock came to see us several times to tell us that people were really insisting that we divide our pile. Jerry finally told Jim to "cool it"—and told him he'd "kill any SOB who laid a hand on" his stuff. After that the haggling over our pile of loot gradually quieted down and we kept it all.

Dozens of pictures are seared into my brain. One of them is of Jerry, squatting in the burning, blistering sun, dressed in a native straw hat and a ragged pair of shorts, "sewing" a nipa roof on a bamboo frame for a combination cook shanty and playpen. Also, there was to be a workbench at one end of the playpen so that Jerry could keep an eye on Gerry Ann while I was doing the daily laundry. Jerry had lost a great deal of weight during the last year, and as he squatted, swearing and perspiring, he looked like a little gnome, but I was very proud of him, for *he* at least was doing a job instead of sitting and bickering and wanting people to share their loot with him. He wasn't asking anyone for anything except to let us alone and let us make a home for ourselves. It was to be our first home, and the one of which I have been the most proud. It was all blood, sweat, and tears which went into it (to borrow a phrase) and nothing else in camp compared with it. We loved it. We thought we would probably not live until the Americans came, for the advance across the Pacific sounded so terribly slow as we listened to it day by day, but at least we'd have the best and the most we could possibly get out of life while we had it.

A cook shanty was a must for everyone, for we had to get in out of the rain a great deal of the time. We were not allowed to cook in the barracks, for they would have gone up in flame at the drop of a match, if there had been a match. I always wondered about the Vestal Virgins who kept the coals glowing. No one had seen a match for years, and yet there was always a light somewhere for a cigarette or a fire.

When the children and I went to Los Baños we took the innerspring mattress which Jerry had willed to me the year before. Our cubicle was too small for a double bed, so we decided to cut it in two and make a bed and a couch. All Jerry's friends assured him that an innerspring mattress could not be cut in two with a pair of pliers, but they didn't know Jerry as I knew him. I covered the couch with an old bedspread for which Jerry had made a deal a year or so before. Jerry had made a table before we arrived out of some hardwood which he had retrieved from an old bunk bed. After he had planed, sanded, and waxed the wood with a melted candle, it was perfectly beautiful. Definitely it called for a tablecloth. Having none, I made use of the material that I had inadvertently cut too small for the news correspondent's shanty windows two years before. I made mats and napkins, hemstitched with their own drawn threads. A lovely table with pretty mats and napkins made us all sit up straighter and remember that there were such things as table manners. When David saw his napkin he said, "What's that? What's it for?" When I told him he said "Well, I don't need it. Besides I never spill anything."

Jerry even made a closet in one corner of the cubicle, and it gave us a heady sense of well-being not to have to stoop over and pull out everything we owned from under the bed. The closet actually had shelves in one end and we made a few hangers for our worn out, beaten up, moth-eaten "best" clothes, the clothes we were trying to save to be worn when we were liberated.[11]

Bolts of material had come with the Red Cross packages. The central committee decided that each woman should be given enough material to make a dress. Since my mother had included two pairs of shorts in her package I felt that I could squander my material on our house. My practical nature is always at war with my impractical side. I made a curtain for the closet door, and a curtain for the window, against the good advice of everyone I knew. Very often I am glad that my impractical side wins. Certainly I was never sorry in that case. When everyone is barefooted and in rags it doesn't matter too much whether one has one dress or not. I had two pairs of shorts, and what's more, I had a pair of shoes. What more could I want?

In a corner opposite the closet we placed a portable radio cabinet on the shelf that Jerry had built first. The radio was completely bare of its inner workings, but was a pretty little cabinet and it gave our cubicle a wonderfully homey touch, we thought. Every time the Japanese searched our barracks they had a fit when they saw that radio cabinet. I couldn't help getting a great big bang out of it. They'd suck in their breath and practically leap across the room and grab the cabinet and all hell would break loose for a little while. Finally they would calm down. Jerry, of course, was always in his own barracks when we were having

11. Many internees in the various camps in the Philippines saved "best" clothes from before the war to wear home upon liberation, almost as talismans to ensure that inevitability. Often these clothes, such as heavy woollens, were inappropriate to the climate in which the internees were currently living, and occupied valuable space in their luggage and in their cramped living quarters, but were preserved nevertheless, and were routinely aired and laundered. Margaret says her mother swears "I was wearing a candy box ribbon in my hair when I disembarked" (MS to LB 8/10/87).

a search. I always felt the Japanese couldn't give me, a mere woman, credit for doing anything that was really dangerous. Especially a woman alone with two children. They did remark about the cubicle, though: "Who has done all the work on your cubicle?" "What, no husband, who then?" Finally they'd give in, "So it's a *friend* who has done all this work. Amazing people, these Americans."

In the fourth corner Jerry built shelves for dishes and made a built-in electric hot plate beneath them. Sounds highfalutin and it was. He had the ceramic from a regular hot plate which had burned out. He took the steel strand of a piece of army telephone wire and wound it around a dowel until he had the required length for the hot plate. The electricity he got from the ground! There were a few scattered bare electric bulbs in the barracks. At this time we were allowed to have them on during certain hours in the evening. In the daytime the electricity was turned off. It was our luck to have one of these bulbs hanging over our cubicle. Jerry discovered that when the Japanese turned off the electricity, the switch had been in only one [wire] of a 220 v circuit, so that a 110 v existed between the other wire and the ground. All he needed was a good ground system. This he obtained by laying about forty feet of copper wire in the bottom of the drainage ditch which was just outside our back door. Knowing nothing of the rudiments of electricity, it seemed like magic to me. In this way we had electricity for the radio and for the hot plate. If we were discovered with the hot plate we wouldn't be shot, but it would be reasonable for the Japanese to assume that it was our only reason for wanting the electricity.

Our "stove" brought us an additional problem. Not only did we have to guard it from the Japanese, we also had to guard it from the internees. There seemed to be nothing that could infuriate an internee like another internee having something that he did not have. Until the power line was bombed at a much later date by the Americans, we had our electricity. We had one near catastrophe. Once when the drainage ditch was being cleaned by a group of internees, they dug up our copper wire. Fortunately for us, one of the members of the cleaning crew was a friend of Jerry's. Jerry persuaded him to put the wire back and say nothing about it. Suffice it to say that we are here to tell the story. If the Japanese had discovered the wire and had really investigated us, we would not be here, for our cubicle, our cook shanty, the drainage ditch, the roof over our part of the barracks, and the floor under us were simply alive with contraband of every description.

Jerry decided that we should have a porch added onto the outside of our cubicle. The problem was lumber. We could use the media agua for the roof, but we needed a floor and three sides. Our cook shanty was completed and was a combination cook shanty, workbench, and playpen for Gerry Ann, who was growing in spite of the inadequate food. She wasn't fat, but at least she wasn't too awfully thin and she was pretty and well tanned. Jerry thought we could use the porch for sleeping quarters. At one end of the porch he would build a bench upon which I could prepare what food we had. The cubicle then, could be a real living room.

The Japanese had a large pile of lumber outside the fence which they were going to use when more people came to Los Baños. Jerry decided that this lumber was fair game. The Japanese kept a guard there constantly, but guards were simply something to be outwitted. For several afternoons, until he had as much lumber as he needed, he put on his Filipino hat, took a long piece of bejuco and went off to play with death. He went during siesta which, as usual, was the best time to do anything that one didn't want too well scrutinized. Between our barracks and the next camp was a barbed-wire fence. This camp was later opened for the missionaries when they were brought in a few months before liberation. The guards patrolled the fence, of course, but Jerry would wait for the right moment and lie down and slip under the wires. The ground on the other side of the fence was covered with tall weeds. Jerry would slip cautiously through the weeds, a few feet at a time. Eventually he'd make his way to the pile of lumber, where he'd tie a couple or three pieces of lumber together with the bejuco. Then he'd crawl back to the fence. Gradually he'd pull the lumber toward him, wait for the opportune moment and slip through the fence. A terribly dangerous game, and I was sick every day before he got back, but I think he rather enjoyed it. Eventually he had quite a stockpile which we cached under the floor of our cubicle. Gradually we'd take the lumber out and say, "Look what we found under the floor of the cubicle." For days on end people spent their spare time tearing up the floors of their cubicles! Surprisingly enough, many of them did find pieces of lumber and what-have-you which the Filipinos had hidden there when they were constructing the barracks.

How many times one thing leads to another. We now had the material for the floor and a board walk out to the cook shanty, which helped immensely in the mud, but we needed sawali for the sides and a door. The Japanese had two or three barracks out of bounds, in which they had piles of sawali, doors, lumber, [and other supplies] which they told our committee we might use if we didn't touch other specified articles in the barracks. Our committee let it be known that they didn't want us to bother the barracks. They were dickering with the Japanese in the hope that they could get the whole barracks to be used for further construction purposes. In the meantime Jerry wanted a door. One afternoon he went up to see the two internees who were working there on construction, their camp detail. There were only the two Americans in the whole building, and there were no Japanese. Jerry tried to talk them out of a door, but couldn't. While they weren't looking he simply picked up a sawali door and took it home with him for his own personal construction purposes. No one saw him take the door, but the Americans missed it immediately. Since Jerry had been the only internee seen in the area during the afternoon, word was sent out that Jerry was to be sent up before the court to stand trial for stealing said door. The Japanese didn't know anything about it, nor care. They had already said we could have the things. It was our own American men who insisted that Jerry stand trial for stealing a miserable sawali door from the Japanese, or from the Americans, however one chooses to look at it. The internees hadn't seen him take the door, but they were sure that he had done so. On those grounds they were going to bring him to trial and put him in jail if they could. Fortunately Mabel came to the rescue with a good friend, the best-known criminal lawyer in the Far East. Jerry went to see him, and the lawyer told him exactly what to do and say. No one in their right minds cared about a cursed door, but people were getting queer, and the most trivial things took on an exaggerated importance. There was no understanding or compassion or kindliness left in the average internee. Dog eat dog seemed to be our motto. The jury did acquit Jerry, but it was a most uncomfortable time and it was pointed out to us again that there are few men that one can call friend. The incident naturally drew Jerry and me even closer together. The payoff came a year or two later after we were in the States and Jerry was working in Washington, D.C. One of the two men who had insisted that Jerry be brought to trial for his "horrible offense" was in Washington. He called Jerry and asked if he might come out to our house that night and bring a mutual friend to see us. To me it was pure unadulterated crust, and I have no use for the man and never will have. He came out, and we were nice to him, and gave him a drink, and I hope I never see him again.

Before I get too far ahead of myself I must mention a story in which even the worst of the worrywarts participated. The Japanese brought a large group of Filipinos into the camp to wire our barracks for electricity, and to secure the nipa on the roofs so that it would not blow away in a storm. The partitions between each cubicle were only six feet high, but the peak of the roof was at least thirty feet above us. Hence the Filipinos scrambled around aloft among the rafters, and enjoyed themselves tremendously. Whenever a guard was looking the other way nails by the handfuls were dropped on the various beds, in the various cubicles. Not only nails, but wire, and bejuco, and electric insulators by the score. Everyone participated in this game, and we were all sorry when the job was finished. Poor Japs, everyone trying to outwit them, and we did on so many occasions.

Not too long after we arrived in Los Baños, the part of the camp in which Jerry had been living was made out of bounds. We felt lucky when he drew the barracks directly across the road from mine. In this way he could be at my barracks most of the day and not have to leave until the first warning for the night roll call. In moving, the internees were forced to abandon the large camp garden which had been put in at the expense of much back-breaking labor. (During the last months of internment our entire vegetable supply came from our own garden.) The internees moved as much of the garden as they could and left the rest for the Japanese. Everyone felt that the Japanese had probably moved the internees from that part of the camp in order that they might have a ready-made garden. Who knows? Jerry brought home one small red-pepper plant from the abandoned camp garden and we planted it outside our door. After it started to bear we pulled one tiny pepper each day to put in our rice. Once in awhile when we wanted to do something especially nice for someone we'd give them one or two of these tiny hot peppers. That lovely little pepper plant lasted until the very day of liberation. We had one pepper for the day of liberation, and one for the next, and then we would have been finished for there weren't even any new flowers on it. We walked right off and left both of those peppers on that plant!

Jerry was always on the lookout for food. At the time we abandoned the camp garden there was a lot of confusion. People were moving their entire household effects, clothing, beds, cooking facilities, and garden plants. More than anything else we looked like a large army of giant ants on the move. Back and forth, back and forth, everyone ragged, some beginning to get beri-beri and tropical ulcers. Tempers short, always. During the confusion Jerry took advantage of the situation and slipped up through the back part of the camp, through the fence, and into a banana grove. A banana tree is rather difficult to climb. Jerry did it, however, and started hacking on a large bunch of bananas with his bolo.

Each tree has a large trunk and leaves and one bunch of bananas. No branches. New shoots come up around the bottom of the tree as soon as the parent tree sprouts a bunch of bananas. Hence a banana grove is hard to see through. The tree, being almost entirely made up of water and fibre, snapped under the strain and dropped Jerry to the ground with a loud noise. The sound brought the Japanese guards to a dead halt. They put their guns on the ready and waited. Jerry simply out-waited them. He had fallen into the young shoots, weeds, and ferns which were growing under the banana tree, so the guards did not see him. Eventually he sneaked back through the fence and home to our barracks. Then a new problem arose. How to hide so much food?

And that brings up a point I had almost forgotten. There were several men in camp who had a thriving business. They bought internees' Red Cross food and then sold it to other internees at exorbitant prices. At that time a can of Spam brought fifty pesos ($25.00). I now buy it at the grocers for forty-nine cents. That is what is known as inflation, I believe. It seems there are always problems. These people had so much food in their cubicles that they were forced either to stay with it, or to have someone whom they trusted stay with it at all times. Day and night. Hell to be rich, eh?

As food became more scarce, so did wood with which to cook it. Our predicament was brought to the attention of the Japanese. They were willing to do nothing about the food situation, but they were willing to help out with firewood. Again they allowed a working detail to go outside the fence to collect firewood in a certain designated area. Naturally, Japanese guards accompanied the working party. I thought then, and still am inclined to think, that the Japanese have a perverted sense of humor. They could as easily have let us collect coconuts, or bananas, or casavas, or any number of other fruits that were there for the taking.[12] But no, we could have wood with which we could cook

12. In the college's experimental groves. "We were in the middle of hundreds of acres of banana and coconut groves. I saw them when my friend from

our miserable handful of rice, if we weren't too tired to walk after the wood, that is. Jerry went, though our own need for fuel was not as desperate as most people's, for in case of emergency we always had our built-in hot plate. We did need food urgently however, for when the children and I had arrived in Los Baños we had decided that we'd pool all our Red Cross kits and use one can a day to supplement the rice and soup that we were given on the line. We thought that the cans might last the duration, but before too many weeks had passed it could easily be seen that they would be a thing of the dim, dark past long before we were liberated. We decided to save a can of salmon for Thanksgiving, and a can of Spam for Christmas. We set aside a can of Gerry Ann's precious powdered milk to cover all eventualities.

Jerry went with the wood-gathering detail for one purpose only, and that was to see how much food he could scrounge while the guards were not looking. A luxuriant patch of ginger was growing in a spot very close to the wood gatherers. Ginger, to the great majority of the American public, means a brownish powder which comes out of a can, used almost exclusively for pumpkin pies at Thanksgiving. To us, in the Philippines, it meant a lovely green plant with white, orchid-like, fragrant blossoms. The roots of the plant are the edible part, and they grow in clumps just under the ground. Jerry had taken his jacket and his tropical hat when he set off on a hot day, so I was prepared for anything when he returned.

Jerry had gotten a little friendly with two of the Japanese guards for many reasons. Since we had so much potential dynamite under the floor of my cubicle, it seemed to us that it would be a wise precaution to have some of the guards know us. Where we lived, how we lived, that we had a baby (our own particular, questionable relations they need not know, and I don't believe they did), that we were to all outward appearances the most

---

Beaumont flew us over Los Baños after we were liberated" (MS to LB 11/10/87). See n. 1, p. 191.

innocent of internees. Then, when they looked for the radio they certainly would not think of looking in our cubicle first, for they would already have seen it. One of the guards, with whom we had become acquainted, had been quite friendly. As a matter of fact, he had gone out of his way to be nice to us. He brought us a dozen duck eggs, and a quart of fresh milk (Gerry Ann's first and last taste until she was fifteen months old), an act for which he could have been shot had his superior officer known about it, an act for which our own internees would have gladly shot us if *they* had known about it. This business of everyone hiding from everyone else seems to me the most hateful of all ways to live. That Japanese guard was just as afraid that one of his brother guards would see him taking a parcel of food to an American as we were afraid that our own internees would see him doing it. At the same time we needed food desperately and we almost liked that Japanese guard, as an individual. He was delighted with Gerry Ann and showed us pictures of his own baby at home. We even learned a little from him. He had no hope of going home to Japan for many years (he probably never got there), and yet he was reconciled to it in a way that Americans could never be. It's a long way round Robin Hood's barn to tell you that this guard was one of the guards on the wood-inspecting detail. He let Jerry back in the gate with his jacket absolutely bursting its seams with ginger, and the prize of prizes, a handful of tiny native tomatoes. Jerry had tied the arms of his jacket together and had stuck twigs into the open ends to prevent the guards from seeing the ginger. That he was lucky enough to draw the right guard was in the lap of the gods. The week before this same guard had brought the dozen duck eggs, of which there were several left; we had a feast that night. Scrambled eggs with tomatoes and ginger in them. To palates that were starved for anything with or without seasoning, it was delectable.

With the dishpan full of ginger Jerry brought home we were able to negotiate terrific trade agreements. A handful of it could bring us the greatest luxury obtainable—sugar, a whole cupful of it. For weeks we drank hot ginger tea every night before we went to bed, and though I doubt if there was any food value in it it helped fill the ugly, empty void a little, that horrible void that was always present, but more so at bedtime.

Jerry and I never became intimate with any of our neighbors for several reasons. The primary reason, of course, was the radio. Every evening at six we listened to KGEI San Francisco. I should say, Jerry listened with earphones and I kept watch. Jerry's hearing isn't as good as it might be. He could never hear the high notes that his receiver made, even when they were most audible to me. It terrified me for fear other people's hearing was as keen as my own. It took a lot of work to keep the receiver in perfect receiving condition, and as a result Jerry spent many, many hours working it over. Those hours were a perfect torment to me, yet I was delighted with him for doing it. Those working hours of his meant that I had to be constantly on the alert for our neighbors, friends, David and his pals, and always the Japanese.

It seemed to me then that I would never get over the nervous shakes and the resulting diarrhea that accompanied them. Sometimes I'd have seizures as often as a dozen times a day. It depended entirely upon how many times a day I was frightened or made nervous about something; the situation was disconcerting, to say the least. It always amazed me that there was milk for Gerry Ann to nurse every four hours, though there wasn't much doubt as to the quantity or quality. I tried desperately to keep calm, for her sake, but it simply was not possible.

The constant threat of a Japanese searching party was ever with us in Los Baños. At all times we had to have Jerry's radio gear in a position to be gotten out of sight at a moment's notice. If you've ever been around a radio in the process of being built, or worked over, you know that it is almost impossible to keep from spreading the equipment over an entire room. Sometimes it would get a little out of hand, and a knock on the door could send me into the shakes and off I'd have to trot to the bathroom. Then Jerry would have to come out of his trance and keep guard himself, and so our days went.

The first really vigorous search I well remember, for I have another picture of Jerry burned into my brain. He had to be in his own barracks during the inspection, as I have said. The unattached men's barracks were usually searched first. However, there was supposed to be no movement between buildings during a search and I confess that I felt like a pretty weak-kneed sister as he left me to go to his own barracks. The party of Japanese finally worked their way down the hall to my cubicle, and it was hard for me to wait when I knew that I had everything they were looking for, right under my feet. They came in, in their heavy-booted, sword-swinging way, and started systematically combing my cubicle. We were always terrified that we'd forget some tiny little gadget, or piece of wire, or screw, or bit of solder which would put them on the scent. (Even yet, ten thousand miles and almost nine years away, I get cold hands and begin to shake inside when I really try to remember exactly how we felt at that time.) They finally finished the search, with much sucking in of breath about how nicely the cubicle was fixed, and they had the usual fit about the empty radio cabinet. They always wanted to know where my husband was, but since there were only three people listed in my cubicle they never pursued the question. As they went out the back door I saw Jerry sitting on the steps of the end cubicle though he should have been in his own barracks. His back was turned to us and he had his hat pulled low over his face, but the hunched over, starved look of him tore at my heart. When he turned around to look at me I could see a thousand years of worry right there on his face. It was so real to me that I could hardly see how the Japanese missed the look, the worry, and the tension. We didn't speak to each other, of course, and he sat there until the Japanese were out of sight, but it is a picture that has warmed me when I've heard the rumor-mongers hashing and re-hashing our story.[13]

13. I (the editor) asked Margaret whether this was actually true—after all, how much mileage can even experienced gossips get out of old scandal—or whether it was only her sensitive and perhaps exaggerated perception of an antagonistic situation. She replied, "I know that our story was repeatedly re-hashed because other people told me what they said" (MS to LB 8/10/87).

Along with the terrific strain of hiding the radio went the strain of always being a public spectacle wherever I went. When Jerry was with me it was fun, in a way, to hold his hand and walk proudly with our baby, but when I had chores that necessitated my going alone it wasn't so much fun. I didn't *really* mind, and yet I did. In a strange sort of way I was proud of myself for having had courage enough to do something that few of them would have dared do. I felt that in my case it wasn't lack of character that had let me do a thing that the whole world considers wrong. I had known what I was doing and in a way that is hard to understand I was proving to myself, and to Jerry that I *really* loved. There was never the slightest question in my mind about the fact that I had never loved *enough* before to do what I had done. Funny to be able to see two sides of a situation so clearly. Makes it hard to decide what really is black and what is white. Much easier to be a good girl and sit back and condemn all those who aren't.

Once when I was walking down the dirt road to my barracks I met a man who, when we had been in Santo Tomás, had paid me quite a lot of compliments in his spare time. I was almost always in the library, and it was easy for him to stop by the desk and pass the time of day. He had once asked me to meet him at his shanty and "see the sun rise." I was very pleased that I hadn't fallen for the line when, some time later, I discovered by accident that he was married and had a wife right there in camp! A sunrise is always beautiful and it was before I had met Jerry, and I remember that I was slightly tempted, though I felt sure he meant a great deal more than "see the sun rise." This man had a degree from one of the best schools in the United States, he had a very good position with one of the companies in the Far East, he was nice-looking and was a highly respected member of society. This same man then, I met in Los Baños. I was carrying Gerry Ann. He stopped me to admire her and, so help me, he asked if he and his wife might adopt her. I was never more surprised and taken aback. How can people be so dumb? Would I have a baby under circumstances like those and then give her away? The mental process, or lack of one, that went on there was beyond my comprehension and still is. And how can anyone have gall enough to walk up to someone and say "We'd love to adopt your baby, we'd make a good home for her, how about it?" Words fail me.

That man merely insulted my intelligence. It remained for another man to really insult me. In Santo Tomás I had been in a room full of women, some of whom were Manila's elite. For weeks one of the women in our room kept kidding me about the man in camp who was anxious to meet me. He was Manila's no. 1 bachelor, so she said. Finally, out of sheer boredom and, I confess, a bit of curiosity as to what constituted a city's no. 1 bachelor, I consented to go for a walk with him one evening. As far as I was concerned there are millions like him, and it was simply boring to have to ward off his hands in the dark places while we promenaded with the other hundreds in front of the university building. I had thought that sort of kid stuff stopped when one became an adult, particularly since I had done nothing to invite it. I didn't know the man really, and I wasn't about to get acquainted in that way. This same man wouldn't even speak to me when I arrived in Los Baños with Gerry Ann. Deliberately turned his back, in fact, so he wouldn't have to. Friends who were disappointed in me I could understand. People who were really conscientious in their objections to me I could understand, but that I could never forgive, though I understood it well enough. Here I could go into a long-winded and completely unprofitable dissertation about men. Suffice it to say that there are some wonderful men and, fortunately, several of them were fond of me for no good reason that I could ever see. I realize perfectly that these two stories may put me in an ugly light and I could (probably *should* have skipped them) but I am determined to put it down exactly as it happened.

Reading this over I am reminded of the woman who said to Mabel, "But what are they going to *do* with the baby after we are liberated?" As if, surely, we could just pretend that the whole thing had never happened as soon as we were back in civilization.

She was a good-looking woman, but too dumb to have a baby under any circumstances, I think, even though she had a job with the State Department. Later on we saw this same woman when we lived in Washington and she came to call on us, not because she was a friend of ours, but strictly from curiosity. Obviously I am a wicked woman, though I pride myself on being a good housekeeper and I try to be a good mother. I cleaned and polished our house until it shone, and I scrubbed the children for dear life, in order that I might dissatisfy her curiosity. She seemed utterly amazed that we could have a beautiful home, a nice family, and apparently Jerry and I were congenially and happily married. I am sure she is still talking about it and still wondering how long it can last "for surely no life begun as theirs was can last."

When Gerry Ann was six months old the camp had a siege of dysentery, some amoebic and some bacillary. Amoebic dysentery is supposed to be more dangerous for it is more insidious. The [parasitic] amoeba can be in the colon for a long time, getting a stranglehold on the victim without the "owner" being aware of it. Bacillary is much quicker. If one catches the bug, one knows about it very soon. It either kills one in short order, or one gets over it soon with proper attention and medicine. Sulfa drugs, according to my encyclopedia, are the only drugs that are effective in its cure. Our Red Cross shipment had been loaded with sulfa drugs, so we were lucky in that respect.

Our sanitary facilities, as I pointed out earlier, were practically non-existent. Our not-so-modern conveniences were flushed twice a day, and in the meantime there were millions of flies. Flies are the principal carriers of dysentery. The epidemic, which people had more or less expected for months, suddenly spread like wildfire. I tried to be as careful of our food and our cooking equipment as I could be. In spite of it I suddenly began having severe stomach cramps. Within twenty-four hours I was too weak to walk to the hospital. Dysentery, which I had dreaded all the years I had lived in the Philippine Islands, was upon me. The epidemic started during the rainy season, at a time when our bathroom was out of order and we were having to use ordinary Chick Sales, minus floors and roofs. I remember staggering through the mud, with the rain beating down, slipping and sliding and wishing I could die, I hurt so, and knowing that I didn't *dare* have dysentery for I had to take care of Gerry Ann—not only take care of her, *nurse* her, or else *she* would die. The second day after I got sick I had to have help to get back to my cubicle. A woman whom I had noticed often, who lived in the same cubicle in the opposite barracks, came out to help me home. Jerry saw us sloshing along in the mud and came running to help. Shortly after that the doctor arrived, with the laboratory verdict. I had bacillary dysentery.

The doctor gave Jerry orders to scrub everything that I might have touched in the past day or two, and boil all the clothing, Gerry Ann's, David's, Jerry's, and mine. In the meantime he had to care for the two children, cook for them, bathe them, and somehow manage to get the clothes dry. It was a man-sized order.[14] Not only that, he was to bring Gerry Ann to the hospital every four hours for her feedings. Bear in mind that this was the rainy season, which meant rain, rain, and more rain. Jerry won a lot of staunch admirers, particularly among the women, for his excellent performance. He had his trials and tribulations too. As soon as the water began to boil the oil oozed out of all the seams of his tub. Not only that, the clothesline broke after he got them all clean and hung up. Also, he had me to contend with, for the first time he brought Gerry Ann to the hospital, four hours after I had left her, she had all the skin off of her poor little nose. Jerry had asked a friend of his to watch Gerry Ann while he got started on the clothes. They set her on the couch which Jerry had made, and naturally she tumbled off onto the splintery floor. It was her first skinned nose, and it looked like sheer negligence to me. Just four hours after I had trusted

---

14. Margaret's irony here is unintentional. In doing this "man-sized order" of domestic labor, Jerry was performing the tasks that women (including Margaret herself) routinely had to do.

him to take care of her! It's funny now, but at the time I felt
that it was just one more tragic blow.

To show the rapidity with which we were being hit with "the
bug," the first person I saw when they carried me into the dysentery ward was the woman who had helped me to my cubicle
the day before. A story goes with Marguerite Lee.[15] She did more
for my self-confidence than anyone else could have at that time.
We were in the same ward several days, and we were alone the
last night before we were sent home. That night we got acquainted.
I don't know of a better place to get acquainted with a person
than a hospital ward. There are all kinds of people and internment (and hospital wards) don't change the spots a bit. The spots
just show up a little more plainly. To my way of thinking this
woman had proven herself, and I liked her. I also liked the looks
of her two small sons and her husband, James. They made a nice
family picture. For the months that we had lived opposite each
other I had thought they were probably mining people, for I
knew they had come up from the southern islands several months
after we were interned with some other mining people. I honestly hadn't thought a great about them one way or the other.
Almost all the mining people had turned a cold shoulder after
Gerry Ann was born, so who was I to get snubbed again? While
we were in the ward together I learned that they were Adventist
missionaries. They'd been in Korea for years, then were sent to
the southern islands for safety, and later by the Japanese to Manila. That night Mrs. Lee told me that she had asked to see
Gerry Ann, once when we were in Santo Tomás, and I had been
unnecessarily brusque. Perhaps I had been, for there were so many
curiosity seekers that I could not distinguish between friend and
foe. She talked to me that night like no one else has ever talked
to me. She was so kind, so understanding, so considerate, so
charitable. She quoted passages from the Bible that I hadn't
thought of for years, and certainly would not have dared apply

15. Mrs. Marguerite Lee's "husband made the sewing box in which we kept
the clandestine radio" (MS to LB 8/11/87).

to my own case. She wasn't in the least sanctimonious. She gave me new confidence in myself, and new pride. Her husband had brought cocoa for her to drink at bedtime and she shared it with me. To me that proved that she was practicing what she preached. I thought then, and still think, that if all missionaries were as good examples of their faith [as she was] there would be a lot more converts to the Christian religion. Unfortunately, there aren't. We had other missionaries who made me ashamed that they were out spreading the word of God, in the name of Christianity and America. To most of them it was words; they had no idea what it was *really* all about. Fortunately, it is not for me to judge, for I might not be as charitable as Mrs. Lee was with me.

Every four hours during the days I spent in the hospital Jerry brought Gerry Ann to be nursed. I was constantly afraid that I'd contaminate her, even though the doctor, the nurses, and I took all the precautions that we could while she was with me. She got through without contracting the bug. I was amused at Jerry. He was ingenious as usual. On rainy days, having no umbrella, he put Gerry Ann in a bayong (a kind of native shopping bag), set his native hat on top of that, and carried her over snug as a bug. He, of course, would arrive soaked to the skin.

In any of its phases dysentery is ugly. Getting rid of it is one of the ugliest experiences I've had. To be awakened every morning and told to drink a glass of castor oil is just so much purgatory. Of all medicine that is nauseating, castor oil heads the list. As I understood it, the sulfa killed the bugs, and the castor oil got rid of them. I finally went back to my cubicle ten pounds lighter, to the same routine of diaper washing, trying to scare up enough food for a noon meal, keeping watch while Jerry either listened to or worked on his radio, and always and ever being a little more hungry with every passing day, and a little more worried because David was beginning to lose weight and Gerry Ann was just holding her own.

Hunger and nerves must be coordinated somehow, for as each day passed and we became a little more hungry, with the terrible gnawing hunger that comes with malnutrition and gradual starvation, our nerves became just a little more ragged. The Japanese, with their clever sense of timing, decided that it was a good time to cut our salt ration.[16] For a week we were not allowed any salt, and they might as well have cut off our toes one by one. Eventually the lack of salt would have killed us, but for some inexplicable reason, known only to the Japanese, they just as suddenly decided that we could have a certain small amount again. We had not seen table salt for two years. The kind we used was the large-grained variety that one uses when turning an ice cream freezer. It was wonderful to be allowed to have it again. There is always a black market when people are refused the necessities of life, and on the market salt sold for twenty-five dollars a pound.

Our pride was shattered when we broke all our dishes; this was almost worse than having no salt. Almost every one in camp used the common soup bowl variety of enamelware. A soup bowl apiece and a large spoon were our everyday equipment, whether or not one fancied oneself an epicurean. Jerry had acquired some pink glass dishes, the dime store variety, but nevertheless they were dishes, and not enamel, and we cherished them above almost anything we had. With the table Jerry had made, and the mats and napkins I had made and hemstitched, and our glass dishes, we always felt proud of the table we could set, whether we had any food on it or not. Somehow the rice and the soup tasted a little less watery and the worms that we came across in the rice didn't leave quite the same taste in our mouths. We were undoubtedly too proud of the table we could set, "for pride goeth before a fall."

It was my job to wash the dishes at night while Jerry stayed in the cubicle with the children. Often Jerry told David bedtime

16. The excuse given was that "the salt was needed in Japan for making munitions" (Arthur 109). "*I* never heard that excuse," says Margaret, nor did Jim Halsema, prewar Baguio resident and wartime internee in Baguio camp. Halsema's historical research on World War II in the Philippines has led him to read a vast array of primary and secondary sources (MS to LB 11/10/87; JJH to LB 11/21/87).

stories, altered to fit the circumstances. It was always dark by the
time I had the dishes finished. The dishes were done at a long
community trough, its cold water always dirty and floating with
refuse from our many tables. It was built onto the end of the
bathroom. Why we didn't all die of dysentery is still a mystery,
for the food was served on one side of the bathroom. Sometimes
the smell was overpowering, and the flies were always with us.
The working detail who flushed the toilets twice a day had some
large portable steps. When they were ready to go to work they
moved the steps up close to the wall and let down a window
through which they poured water, bucketful after bucketful, until the all-clear signal was given. Dozens of people had tripped
over the steps in the dark, and everyone in camp had cursed them
as a hazard. It remained for Jerry to do something about them.
As usual, I washed the dinner dishes in the dark and started back
to our cubicle. Somehow I either misjudged my distance or the
steps had not been put back exactly where they were usually put;
at any rate, I ran smack into the steps with my dishpan full of
clean pink glass dishes, fell, and broke every single one of them.
The fact that I carried bruises and skinned legs around with me
for days, or that I cut my hands (slightly, to be sure) was trivial
compared to the loss of our beloved dishes. We were crushed!
Jerry felt as badly about their loss as I did. He went out and
borrowed a saw, went straight to the bathroom, found the steps
in the dark and sawed them in two! And all hell broke loose!
All the people in the barracks were delighted, and gave Jerry a
cheery pat on the shoulder for getting rid of a menace, but the
flushing-toilet detail and the carpentry detail were furious. So
furious, in fact, that they went to the central committee about
that so-and-so Sams, who had "*deliberately* destroyed camp property." The central committee decided that Jerry either had to build
more steps or, at the very least, supply lumber to build more
of them. If neither was done they threatened to have him in
court again. I was a little stunned that Jerry would do such a
thing, but he said he was taking no more chances on my breaking a leg. He just laughed at the committee members when they

came with their long faces to try to persuade him to do something about the steps. So we stuck out our chins once more and held out for days, but eventually the pressure got too much for me, and I persuaded Jerry to give them some of our lumber to build more steps—lumber from our carefully guarded hoard under the floor, too!

It was about [this time] that we had no water for two days. After standing in line for several hours we were allowed a dribble to drink, but that was the size of it. Jerry, always to the rescue, dug the drainage ditch a great deal deeper in front of our cubicle, and enough water seeped in so that we could wash Gerry Ann's diapers and the dishes. I was worried about that water, but luck was with us and we suffered no ill effects. It was just one more example of the Japanese kindness, which we were becoming used to. It didn't even surprise us too much, as I recall, for we always had a water shortage in Los Baños[17] and we were always expecting even worse things to happen, so we rather took it in our stride.

Jerry came in worried one day. The fact that *he* was worried was enough to make me practically frantic with worry. If Jerry was concerned enough about anything to show it, the situation was desperate. During his woodchopping detail that morning he had heard a rather accurate description of his radio, as it looked

17. Given the abundant but variable annual rainfall, at nearby Canlubang ranging from .78 inches in February to 15.6 inches in August 1943, it is difficult to understand why there was a chronic water shortage at Los Baños. One explanation is that the water came from a "monkey pond" on a nearby hillside, which held abundant water when it rained but almost dried up during the dry season. "We were always supposed to boil the water, because it was contaminated," says Margaret. This problem notwithstanding, a sufficient water supply could have been provided but by 1943 lack of imported materials, such as steel pipe, prevented the construction of a new waterworks or additional barracks. "I've heard that the lack of abundant water was the real reason that Los Baños was not developed to receive all of Santo Tomás," Margaret adds (MS to LB 11/10/87; General Headquarters U.S. Army 7th Fleet, 5th and 11th Airborne, Allied Geographic Section Southwest Pacific Area, *Terrain Handbook 44* [Brisbane, Australia: Lucena, Nov. 30, 1944], p. 67).

at that time. The internee didn't know that Jerry was the man with the radio, but it let us know that it was past time to change the shape of our pride and joy. Jerry got his pencil and a board (there being no paper) and set to work. He had a given set of rules to follow. The radio had to be a certain size, for his parts were a certain size. The problem appeared complicated. How to change it so that it would not look like a radio and yet keep it within easy reach? It was hard work, to say nothing of being noisy, to tear up the floor every time he wanted to get at the radio. Besides, well-handled boards in the floor might become pretty obvious to inspection parties.

We had a brainstorn. It would be risky, but we decided to take a chance on it. I was always having to mend and patch our meager store of clothes. We decided that the thing to do was to make a sewing box for these clothes, establish the fact that it was a sewing box, and then turn it into a radio cabinet. The box we could leave out at all times then, and it would be equally easy to get at to listen to the news or to try to hide in case of emergency.

Shortly after I recovered from dysentery I persuaded Jerry that my missionary friend and her husband, James and Marguerite Lee, across the way, should hear the news occasionally. I felt as sure of their loyalty and integrity as I have ever felt about anything in my life, and they lived up to my expectation. After talking it over we decided to bring James into our closed corporation, if he wanted to join. Finally one day we told him exactly how we knew what was going on; instead of backing out quickly, he was an eager beaver and anxious to help out in any way that he could. We loved him for it. He was a little worried about letting his wife know what he was getting himself tangled up in, for he didn't want to worry her, but eventually he told her the story. James was an excellent carpenter and had a lot of tools. He said that he would be glad to make the sewing box for us, which he did, a few days before another typhoon began. We left it out in the cubicle at all times, conspicuously open, with all the mending equipment inside.

Jerry started making his radio over to fit the sewing box. During a typhoon, we thought it a good time to start, for we were not likely to be subject to too many inspections or casual visitors, we hoped. It was a real typhoon, and we were wet and cold and generally miserable for several days. We put everything we could spare against the outside wall, to keep the rain and cold wind out, and more or less huddled against the two inside corners of the cubicle.

In spite of the weather we had several visits from Japanese guards during the typhoon, but there were no inspection parties. Jerry always went to great pains to point out his wonderful little sewing box "which I have made for my wife." The Japanese were always appreciative. They sucked in their breath, rattled their bayonets, bowed, and I almost felt ashamed to be putting it over so well. Every guard who ever came to our cubicle wanted to play with Gerry Ann. Without exception she screamed every time one came near her. At that time we were having almost nightly visits from the guards. Since David went to school in the morning and took a nap in the afternoon,[18] (James and I took turns standing guard for Jerry during this remodeling job), Jerry was fairly uninterrupted during the day time. When Jerry finally got to the testing stage on his receiver, and he was making it squeal in that terribly high pitch (which he couldn't hear at all), I felt as if the whole barracks, to say nothing of the Japanese, would descend upon us at any moment. The smell of solder never fails to bring back those faraway days. I could never understand why the people in the barracks didn't smell it and question it.

Eventually the receiver was in perfect working order and we

18. The internees provided schooling that included college-level courses, under conditions reminiscent of Mark Hopkins on one end of the log bench and the student on the other. For instance, Bob Kleinpell taught a twenty-week course in historical geology, followed by another in Cenozoic geology. Dr. O. A. Griffith, an Anglican priest, taught literature and philosophy; "Uncle Don" (Bill Donald) taught economics; van Slooten, a Dutch priest, taught ancient and medieval world history; and Tommy Worthen, a radio announcer, taught Tagalog, the Philippine language of the area (see Arthur 79–80).

were back on the gold standard. Immediately we began to catch up on the news that we'd lost for a few days. Now it was routine for Jerry to tell James what was going on every day, and once in awhile he would come over and listen on the earphones. It's surprising how loud they can sound in a quiet cubicle, and again I was on edge constantly. There was never any way of knowing when a Japanese guard would walk down the hall while Jerry had the earphones on. [Because] the door was just a partial door, Jerry always sat in the corner facing the door, so that he could see the legs go down the hall. Personally, I preferred to have Jerry listen and let me keep watch. He could tell me the news later. I must admit that I felt a bit trapped in the phones. Jerry had worn them for too many years, apparently, to have that feeling. However, I did occasionally listen to something that Jerry thought I should hear.

We had a wonderful time putting the earphones on Gerry Ann, for there was no way on earth the Japanese could make *her* talk. She couldn't talk. Her face was delightful to watch as she listened. It pleased us to be quite positive that there was no other baby in the world listening to a radio under quite the same circumstances. From such things we derived great pleasure and it made life worth living. In order to avoid any questions on David's part about why Jerry spent so much of his time on the floor in a corner fooling with a pile of junk, Jerry sometimes put the earphones on him. However, he would turn the controls so that David heard nothing but an occasional squeak. If David had been a little older it would have been an impossible situation for he would have remembered what a radio was. As it was, we had very little fear from the source, for we never mentioned the word radio, or receiver. We called it by many names, none of which meant anything to him. David was a rather dreamy child, and was used to seeing Jerry sitting with his head down fooling with a bunch of wires, so he did not question it.[19] It's the unusual

19. "David was dreamy, always in his own world. He didn't pay any attention to Jerry's radio in internment. After we got home, David was mad about

that sticks in a child's mind.[20] The routine makes little or no impression on a child. We think that is the reason that David remembers very little about internment. It was the only world he knew, why should he remember it? I am convinced of this when I realize that almost the only things he does remember have to do with a boil being lanced and some ice cream he got once when he was in the hospital.

One night shortly after Jerry had the new radio in working order, I came back from washing the dishes, chipped enamel ones, now, to find a Japanese guard in the cubicle talking to Jerry. They were standing up. The radio was across the room, leaning against the wall, as we had decided to leave it. The guard's rifle and bayonet were planted firmly on top of [the closed sewing box in which it rested]. For a second I thought I'd faint, for I was sure our time had come. At that point I suddenly realized that the conversation was amiable and nothing unusual was in progress. I didn't walk over and grab the radio and make a dash for it as I felt like doing. Instead I smiled, didn't look at the radio again, and the evening went off without a hitch.

At this point I must go back and tell another story of Jerry and his radio. It was two or three weeks before Jerry got things

---

comic books and read them over and over. On cross country trips, he either read comic books or was asleep during the whole three thousand miles; he never noticed the scenery we drove through.

"One day David came downstairs dressed as Superman. A little while later he came in and said, 'I'm going to change my identity'—and he came down dressed as the Lone Ranger. These 'changes of identity' were a daily occurrence for two or three years after we came home" (MS to LB 8/11/87, 11/10/87).

20. Autobiographies by distinguished writers that focus exclusively on childhood exhibit a myriad of very precise reminiscences of the daily routine, as volumes by Russell Baker (*Growing Up*), Maya Angelou (*I Know Why the Caged Bird Sings*), Richard Wright (*Black Boy*) indicate. However, it is not by accident that autobiography is far closer in technique and manner to fiction than to biography; autobiographies bear out Mark Twain's contention in his *Autobiography* that "When I was younger I could remember anything, whether it had happened or not; but my faculties are decaying now, and soon I shall be so I cannot remember any but the things that never happened."

organized at my barracks, after he had been forced to leave the communications shack where he had been living until I appeared on the scene. During this time he used the doctor's room at the hospital for his extracurricular activities. The doctor, Dana Nance, was very willing for the radio to be there. In fact, he would have been happy to have the thing there all the time. At that particular time, a Japanese guard with a broken leg was in the hospital, in the room that adjoined the doctor's room. A thin sheet of galvanized iron was all that separated the two rooms. With Jerry's faulty hearing, I was worried about the situation, so one night at news time I went over with him. It didn't bother me nearly as much to have him in danger if I could see him. It was the waiting that killed me. There were three of us in the doctor's office. Doc, Jerry, and I were back in a corner on his bed. Jerry had the earphones on when someone knocked on the door. Doc went to the door and there stood a Japanese guard. Between the bed where Jerry sat and the door there was a thin cloth screen, such as hospitals use around the bed of very ill patients. By this time I was farther out of the corner and could see all parts of the room, Jerry in the corner, not bothering to take his earphones off, Doc at the door in the other corner of the room (same wall) talking to the guard. The only thing that separated Jerry from death was a thin cloth screen. Sometimes I have thought we must all have more of the actor in us than we realize, for I was smiling my sickly best at that guard, Doc was talking in his most engaging manner, and there sat Jerry not bothering to faint, or crawl under the bed, or *anything*. My admiration was unbounded, but at the same time I wanted to shake him for not trying to conceal the situation while Doc was holding the Japanese in conversation. When I brought up the subject later all he said was, "Good God, I couldn't quit then, it was at a crucial point in the news. Figures of our damage, and theirs!" His time hadn't come yet, for the guard was satisfied with whatever Doc told him and went his way without walking on into the room.

As the food situation became more critical the black market

(for lack of a better name I shall call it that) flourished. Eventually the black market was to eat itself up, as it were. There was only so much food to be cornered on the market and eventually the hoard was gone. As the black market trade fell off, trading with the guards became rampant. The central committee frowned upon it. Japanese guards caught in a "swapi-changi" deal with the internees were severely punished. They weren't punished because they had violated the law, but because they had helped the enemy.

Where there is money involved almost nothing is too dangerous. Where starving is involved nothing is too dangerous. Since we had been warned by our committee not to have dealings with the guards, many law-abiding citizens did not wish to blacken their otherwise good names by openly disobeying the rules. However, they were quite willing for Jerry and me to be the middleman in their deals. Jerry's and my names were already beyond recall, so it didn't matter too much to us what more was said about us. Especially so, when our children were hungry and there was a chance to get food for them simply by disobeying the rules. For each trade that was negotiated we were given a percentage of food—beans, rice, or sugar being almost the only commodities that could be bought, borrowed, begged, stolen, or traded. Watches, pens, rings were brought to us. Jerry would let it be known that he had a good watch for trading purposes and that night a guard would appear from nowhere to examine said watch, and to haggle over the amount of mongo beans, or rice, or sugar that he would give for a watch. The guards preferred 21-jewel watches, of course, though they could be persuaded to take a less expensive watch. It was nothing to see a guard proudly display three or four good watches on each arm. How they got around it with their superiors I don't even pretend to know.

This was a dangerous game, considering our radio activities, but an interesting one nevertheless. The important thing was that it put food in our mouths. There were times when I hated the whole rotten situation, for I guess I must have one of those split personalities that I'm always reading about. Part of me enjoyed the danger, and part of me despised having to have any dealings with the enemy. And they were our enemies, and they never quite let us forget it. I always fully expected to run into a guard who would make us give him a watch for nothing, for they so easily could have, but it never happened to us. I was *really* frightened only once. It was a situation that got a little out of hand, and threatened to get completely out of hand, but I'm getting ahead of my story.

During the last few months of internment any number of people were trading with the Japanese. Nerves were at the breaking point. To make matters no better, the girl across the hall went out of her mind. For two days and nights they left her in her cubicle before they took her away to a room where she could be alone, and I felt as if perhaps I'd go crazy too, but quick. She talked and talked and talked, and then cried and pleaded for mercy and forgiveness, and then talked some more. Everyone in our end of the cubicle nearly went crazy in sympathy. We all liked the girl. She'd been especially nice to the children and me. We all felt terribly sorry for her, but there was very little that could be done for her. She seemed in such mental torment that going out of her mind hadn't helped the situation at all.[21] She did eventually get better, and I understand is completely well now.

For weeks Jerry and I had looked forward to Thanksgiving. We were going to pool our resources with three friends and have a wonderful Thanksgiving dinner. We had saved a can of salmon for the great day, and Red and Page were to bring the dessert. Every day of internment I had felt a little bit more tired than I had the day before, just as everyone else had. What with trying to nurse Gerry Ann, the siege with dysentery, a few tropical ulcers thrown in for good measure, and the first signs of beriberi, I wasn't too surprised when, on Wednesday before Thanks-

21. "The doctors left her there for two days. I don't know why. It was shattering to hear her because we listeners weren't sure but that we might be joining her pretty soon" (MS to LB 8/11/87).

giving, I really felt unwell. However, I had looked forward to that can of salmon for too many weeks to afford to get sick and miss it. I managed to keep on my feet most of Wednesday, and felt sure I could hold out until after dinner the next day. Thursday morning I couldn't raise my head without vomiting. I didn't let Jerry know how really ill I was, but when he volunteered to get the Thanksgiving dinner, I was only too glad to accept his offer. I will never forget what it did to me each time he walked across the floor. I thought I couldn't stand it, but I did. As a matter of fact, I held out until dinner time and I even got as far as the dinner table, but so help me I couldn't have eaten a bite of that salmon if my life had depended upon it. I didn't have the faintest idea what was the matter with me. I think the doctor didn't either, but the next afternoon they gave me one of the last spinals and operated on me. I understand that I received one of their very last intravenous injections, too. I had had my appendix taken out years before, but Doc was convinced that I had been fooled. All my symptoms, the blood count, everything apparently pointed to acute appendicitis. However, I hadn't paid my good money for nothing years before, my appendix was definitely gone when they looked inside. I did have something peculiar looking, he said, "probably T. B. of the lower bowel," though the doctor had no paraphernalia for making sure. At any rate, they poured me full of sulfa something-or-other, clamped me shut, and prepared for me to die—or get well. Apparently I have the constitution of an ox.

For a while it looked serious, and I certainly have never felt like that before or since. I didn't care at all if I did die; I was simply too tired to care about anything, and when they brought poor little starved Gerry Ann to me to be nursed, every four hours, it seemed like the final straw. It seemed more than I could stand, and yet I didn't have the heart to tear her away from the pathetically dried-up breast because it gave her satisfaction to have it in her mouth. I let her nurse long after she had gotten the little milk that was in it, and each pull of her hungry little mouth seemed to pull my very nerves out. At this point it is hard for

me to realize the way I felt each time I saw my two Jerrys at
the door. There was nothing on earth I wanted to do like turn
over and never have to open my eyes again, or never hear another
baby cry.

The following Thursday I still wasn't caring about anything.
Jerry brought some food that he had prepared for me. God knows
where he had gotten the ingredients, for we were having nothing but lugao on the line at that time.[22] I made the most tremendous effort I have ever made in my life and I ate a teaspoon
of the food, as he held it for me. I won't say that it tasted good
to me, but at least it wasn't lugao. The very smell of the lugao
had been making me sick at my stomach. I had to make a la-
borious effort and turn myself over so that I wouldn't have to
look at it when they brought it to me to eat at meal times.
When Jerry came to the hospital I gave it to him, though I had
to fight everyone to keep it from being carried back to the kitchen
and devoured by the first person who saw it. I can still want
to be sick when I think about lugao. It is nothing but a very
thin rice gruel, about the consistency of thin paste. Occasionally
they threw in a handful of ground corn. (Lugao, a few green
vegetables, a very watery soup made of weeds, and occasionally
a piece of pork was our diet for the last two or three months
of internment.)

Jerry always visited me at night during visiting hours. One
night he stayed after visiting hours were over. I was afraid that
he'd get picked up by the guards on the way back to the barracks, but he stayed on and on and I have never heard him talk
so ugly to me. He was giving me what-for, and told me, "It was
a damn dirty trick for you to leave Gerry Ann and me to shift
for ourselves." I don't know whose idea it was, but apparently

22. "Lugao is a revolting glue they made in camp out of cracked rice, corn,
a few worms, and other debris. It made good library paste but it was disgust-
ing to have to eat it. I had given up. I wanted to die. But Jerry had spread
out the lugao and toasted it until it resembled cornflakes; it tasted good compared to anything we'd had for a long time" (MS to LB 8/11/87). *Vicassan's* merely
defines *lugaw* as "rice pudding or gruel."

he had decided that I had to take a little interest in the situation or I'd be just one more internee who didn't make it. I had no idea that Jerry was deliberately taunting me, for a purpose, but it certainly had the desired effect, for I decided that very night that I'd get out of that bed and show Jerry Sams a thing or two if I never did another thing in my life. Within a day or two I was sitting up in bed starting to make Christmas presents for the children. And I've been showing Jerry Sams a thing or two ever since.

The remaining time I was in the hospital Jerry brought my meals, and though they were, in quantity, about what an undersized canary would want, they were wonderfully good. Somewhere he found two tiny tomatoes. He scrounged an egg. He saved the lugao that had ground corn in it, spread in in a pan and dried it, and then browned it over the fire. All in all, his culinary efforts far surpassed my own.

Again, it was Jerry's lot to take care of the children while I was in the hospital, and again he stayed at my barracks. He had a most disconcerting experience one night. Gerry Ann usually nursed in the night. When I was gone she could not, for no one was allowed out of his or her barracks after nine o'clock at night. When she awakened she cried, when she cried the whole barrack rose up in holy wrath and as usual Jerry was on the spot. He tried walking in the cubicle with her, but without much success, so he decided to walk down the road with her, rules or no rules. He ran squarely into a Japanese guard with fixed bayonet, and we will never know who was the most surprised and frightened, the guard, at seeing an internee out walking with a baby, against every rule in the book, or Jerry at running into a scared guard with an itchy finger. And with all this, Jerry never missed a night of getting KGEI, though he had to get up in the middle of the night to be safe from the guards and the internees.

The day I tottered home from the hospital was quite a day. We stopped and weighed on the gym scales and I was down to a scant hundred pounds [from 140], and Jerry was down to 120 pounds from his original 187. We were not looking our fittest.

That day we made a momentous decision. Jerry was furious with me for not staying in the hospital another few days until I felt a little more human, but once I'm on the road to recovery I cannot stand a bed, let alone a hospital. I still couldn't navigate more than a few steps under my own power, so we decided that we would stay together in my barracks until I was able to take care of the children at night. We had known all along that it was pure foolishness for him to stay in one barracks and I in another, but we had thought it best not to bring down too much condemnation on our heads. By this time people had more or less decided, I suppose, that we weren't just victims of a chance opportunity, and all the people in my barracks, anyway, seemed to think it only natural for him to be there taking care of us. And how he took care of us. If I hadn't already loved him I would have loved him then. What proved his love for me beyond the shadow of a doubt was the fact that he got a can for me and made me use it, instead of going to the bathroom, and then he emptied it. That, my friends, is love. The fact that I had to lean against the wall in order to make it all the way to the bathroom did not enter into it, for I would never have mentioned such a thing under any circumstances. I still had some pride. It was his idea, and he insisted on my cooperation. There will be people who will say, "How *can* she tell such things?" For them, a wave of my hand! They simply don't understand that it all has to be told.

From the day I staggered home from the hospital, our every spare moment was concentrated on having a good Christmas for the children. For all we knew it might be their last one and we were determined that it should be a good one. Almost immediately Jerry started rounding up food, and after we were able to buy a pound of rice for fifty pesos, we decided that we would have a party. We invited Bob Kleinpell and Uncle Don.[23] Both

23. "Ansi Lee didn't come because she had another invitation, but she knitted David a sweater. That Christmas was truly one of the best days of my life, with those two darling men. They felt the same way about it. Bob always mentioned it every time we got together" (MS to LB 8/11/87).

238 • The Wartime Memoir of Margaret Sams

of them were intelligent, good talkers, good company, good men, and as hungry as we were. Bob had a can of dried fruit which he contributed, and I started collecting enough other ingredients to make a fruitcake. Jerry managed to buy a pound of mongo beans, and we made a grave decision and had part of the beans ground into a coarse flour, which cost us something like a fourth of the entire stock of beans. This flour, mixed with a scraping of casava flour and rice flour (which we had had ground from our rice at the same rate of exchange) made the cake have an unusual nutty flavor and texture. The hardest thing to find for that cake was the coconut oil to make it stick together. We paid a fantastic price for some very rancid oil. We finally managed to work enough of the horrible copra smell out of it so that it didn't entirely ruin the cake. All the oil that we were able to buy the last several months of internment was so rancid that it almost took the skin off of our mouths. It looked like something drained out of a crankcase, and we often wondered if it hadn't been. It smelled like wharves where copra is stored, and it tasted more like lye soap than anything else I can think of.

In making out our menu for the Christmas dinner (truly a work of art) we decided to sprout part of the remaining beans for a salad. Part of the can of Klim, which we had saved for so long, we would make into cottage cheese to go with the bean sprouts. Camotes (a native sweet potato) were to be served on the line Christmas day so, with our can of Spam, we all lived for the great day.

The children were to have a party Christmas afternoon, but Christmas morning there must be presents, too. I spent long hours knitting David some string socks, and Jerry made him a wooden toy. For Gerry Ann I made a small book of animal pictures which I embroidered on pieces of white, heavy material. Red, a navy nurse, had given me some starch to make the pages stiff. She had been carefully saving the starch for a liberation day uniform. I knitted little white shoes for Gerry Ann, since she was learning to walk, and I made her a little pink pinafore.

For our table decoration we had been saving a tiny red paper

Christmas tree which I had bought in Santo Tomás the year before. David had made some paper chains and various small decorations. From another nurse we had gotten a small piece of cotton, which was to help out wherever I needed it. We had saved tinfoil for three years and had carefully hoarded it from year to year. Christmas Eve afternoon I was tired out, but excited, and more happy than I had any right to be, for I felt that we had really accomplished the impossible against insurmountable odds. I even had a Christmas present for Jerry, donated by Red and Page.[24] It was a beautiful leather tobacco pouch filled with picadura, a very strong, rank, native tobacco. Along with the table decorations we had a candle, and when the whole picture was completed I was beautifully happy. Jerry thought it was lovely too. In order to get the proper effect he decided to light the candle. And that was our undoing! I have never seen anything go up in flame as quickly as that paper and tinsel and cotton decoration. But for Jerry's quick-wittedness the whole bloody barracks would have gone up as quickly. He grabbed the flaming mess and threw it out into the yard, and with it he threw away my happy Christmas spirit. I don't suppose I have ever been as sunk about anything so inconsequential, or so upset with Jerry, but my great grandparents hadn't crossed the prairie for nothing, and before night we had another table decoration, a paper tree David made at school with some greenery. It was even pretty, but nothing could have compared with our first creation.

Christmas Eve brought our good friend Mabel, with a present for each of us. Each present was beautifully wrapped with scraps of long-saved paper and ribbons. Christmas Eve brought us something else, too, that touched me more than I would have thought possible. During the first days of Santo Tomás the Japanese were using every propaganda means at their disposal for breaking down our morale. I mentioned earlier the memorial service we had

24. "Red" was Mary Harrington, a Navy nurse who had lived in Cancao, an area of Cavite, across the street from Jerry before the war. T. Page Nelson worked in the High Commissioner's Office as a representative of the Treasury Department.

had for Deanna Durbin when she had "died giving birth to a child." The Japanese papers had told us this, you remember. After Mabel and Johnnie had left,[25] Jerry decided to get in a little extra time on his receiver. He was sitting on the floor in the corner as usual, when all at once he sat bolt upright and hissed at me, "Come here!" Without saying another word he took the earphones off and put them on me, and I was absolutely electrified to hear a woman's voice saying, "Good evening ladies and gentlemen, this is Deanna Durbin speaking to you. I am dedicating this evening's music to the women of the Philippine Islands." And then she began to sing. I still cry when I think of that night and what that music did to me. It isn't that I've ever seen her in my life. I don't know her, and don't even particularly want to know her, but we had thought her dead for almost three years. Suddenly, to hear her talking to "the women of the Philippine Islands"—to *me*—I could hardly keep from shouting it from the housetops, and I dared not tell a soul. At that particular moment I don't believe I'd have cared a fig if the whole Japanese army had walked in and caught us listening.

Christmas morning finally came and Jerry and I were as impatient as children for its arrival. We had a marvelous breakfast of hotcakes and butter. The small tin of butter ("axle grease") was Mabel's gift to Jerry, and Gerry Ann and David simply could not get enough of the wonderful hotcakes, made from rice, casava, and bean flour. The bit of soda which had gone into them I had saved for more than a year. The doctor had given me two or three tablespoonfuls before Gerry Ann was born. The children were beside themselves with their Christmas presents, the breakfast, and anticipation of the dinner that was to come. Not only that, Santa was to be at the Church in the afternoon. All the children in the barracks visited each other's cubicles to see what Santa had brought, and to see how each cubicle was decorated. I have never before, or since, known the wonderful Christ-

25. Johnnie O'Toole, a mining machine salesman, was Mabel Carlisle's fiance. They were married shortly after the war (MS to LB 8/11/87).

mas spirit that the people in Los Baños showed that Christmas. So what if it was for the day only?

Christmas afternoon arrived and one of the loveliest pictures I have is the one I have in my mind of tiny, elfish, blond Gerry Ann in her little pink pinafore and white "shoes" receiving her present from Santa Claus. David had new shorts, made by Mabel, and a sleeveless sweater knit by Ansi Lee.

Christmas evening arrived and brought Uncle Don and Bob Kleinpell. After he took stock of the mouths that were to eat one can of Spam and the trimmings, Bob was afraid that there wouldn't be enough, so he slipped back to his barracks and brought a can of corned beef which he had been saving for the last rainy day. That dinner and the good fellowship which we shared completed one of the most wonderful days of my life. Uncle Don was in rare good form that evening. I had never before heard him talk so well, or so much. Among many, many other stories he told us of his part in the liberation of Chiang Kai-shek when he had been kidnapped several years before by the Manchurian warlord, Chang Hsueh-liang. Uncle Don told us of his early life in Hong Kong, and how as a young reporter fresh from Australia he had been chosen from many others because he did not drink or smoke. Uncle Don never did learn to drink or to smoke and having been selected was one of the proudest achievements of his life.[26] For the time and the place, the day couldn't have been more perfect. Unfortunately, I had to have an anticlimax. Our stomachs had shrunk a great deal more than we realized, and I was deathly ill for the following week. I vomited practically continuously for several days. I think I almost burst my stomach. I still feel a little apologetic for being such a pig, though I consume twice that amount of food at each meal now, and feel no qualms about my appetite; nor do I suffer any aftereffects.

With Christmas behind us, our last can of food gone (with the exception of three small cans of strained baby food and part of a can of powdered milk), with nothing to look forward to

26. See n. 55, p. 125.

except more long, dreary months, or years of the everyday hell we were living, our morale hit a new low. Almost every day now American planes flew high overhead, but they made no attempt to give us help of any description. At first the mere sight of them had given us new courage. Now they began to make Jerry and me feel just a little belligerent. We loved [the pilots] dearly, for they were American, but at the same time we couldn't help feeling resentful that they seemed completely unconcerned about the fact that we were sitting there starving to death, while they were leisurely flying around the sky, going about the business of winning a war! From listening to "the man" we knew that they were getting closer, for in October they had landed in the southern islands. The day they landed, Jerry was as excited as a child, and it was all I could do to restrain him from telling every soul in the camp. By that time I was skeptical that they'd ever liberate us, and felt sure that they'd bypass us and go on to China, or Japan, or somewhere else.

The morning of the day the Americans landed in Leyte[27] I had gotten Jerry to promise that he would help me scrub the floor, but after he heard the news of the landing I couldn't have persuaded him to scrub a floor for love or money. "So the damned floor *is* dirty. Who cares? They've landed!" he said. I think he could not understand my apathetic attitude, and I knew I couldn't understand his being so excited about a landing that was hundreds of miles away, and doubtless wouldn't affect us for months yet, perhaps years. Suffice it to say that I shall always remember the day the Americans landed, for it was the first time Jerry had ever refused, point-blank, to do something that I really wanted him to do. As the months went by I think even Jerry was a little ashamed that he had gotten so excited about the initial landing.

The lower in spirit I became, the more I worried about my mother and my six brothers and sisters. I knew that my mother must be having a hard time trying to take care of them, and I

27. October 21, 1944.

knew that Edward and Tommy were more than likely in the war and I felt in my bones that one of them, at least, would not come through it. I felt that it would probably be Tommy, the wonderfully sweet-dispositioned third one of the children, the one who had always done what Edward did, but who had never had the cocksure way about him that Edward had been born with. Tommy forced himself to do the things that Edward did without a thought. I felt sure it would-be Tommy, following Edward's lead again, who would not come home. And the lower my morale became, the more I wondered how on earth Jerry and I could ever work out our own problems.[28] Could we, against so many odds, make things work out the way we wanted them to? I had not heard from Bob for a year, not since the letter I had received in answer to mine about the coming of the baby. We had heard that many of the men in Cabanatuan had been shipped out to Japan. The year 1945 started with a most unpropitious beginning. I could not force myself to make the new calendar for more than the first two months of the new year. The whole thing began to seem foolish. Why count the days? Who cared?

Some enterprising committee made a thorough examination of all the weeds in camp and thereafter we all collected, every day, all the "edible weeds" that we could find within the confines of the camp. Pig-weed, we discovered, is really delicious, but most of the so-called edible weeds are tough and stringy and most unappetizing. Camote tops are good, and we could never get enough of them. They make one's teeth black, but we didn't mind a little thing like that in those days. Banana trees are edible, and so are papaya trees. Neither of them is good, but they let one go through the motions of eating, anyway. Green bananas, about the size of one's thumb, have a puckery taste, but when sliced very thin (skin and all) and fried in rancid coconut oil they reminded us of potato chips. Fried banana skins are also edible, though not good.

28. "Vis à vis our respective spouses" (MS to LB 8/11/87).

Jerry had a banana plant in his garden which he had grown from a tiny shoot. We were very excited when it started to flower. We could hardly wait for the slow weeks to pass, so that we could actually have a whole stalk of bananas for our very own. One day when the chow situation was a little more critical than usual, Jerry came trudging in with that whole stock of tiny, horribly green bananas. I was positively aghast. The bananas weren't more than three or four inches long, and would never get ripe under any circumstances now. After Jerry had finished talking horse sense into me I realized that it was for the best, for the garden was quite a distance from our barracks and it would have been senseless for us to expect people to leave the bananas alone until they were ripe. Even if they got to the picking stage, someone else would have harvested them. One of the most disheartening things that happened to us was to go to the garden at night and count the number of beans or the tiny little eggplant or the one tiny, scrawny ear of corn (which we ate, husk, silk, cob and all) and then go back in the morning and find every semblance of anything edible—gone!

Someone gave us a "sword-bean" which we planted in our garden. We had four or five good meals from the one plant; one bean pod for each meal. They were wonderful beans, each pod about a foot long; they are similar to lima beans, except that they are outsized.

People were beginning to eat slugs, which I do not believe I could ever have eaten under any circumstances. The stray dogs and cats had long since disappeared. Dog, which I ate but did not recognize, was quite good. Very good, in fact. Hungry as I have been, and I mean literally starving to death, I can never understand the books I read which tell of eating human flesh. As long as there is a shred of mind left, I do not see how this can be done. If people have become insane, I suppose it is possible. I don't believe I could become that insane.

One day shortly after Christmas the Japanese called a surprise search. As usual, I was allowed to stay in the barracks. All the women who had small babies were allowed to remain in their cubicles with the babies. I know of no more eerie feeling than to be shut up alone in a cubicle with almost everything that is being searched for under one's feet. After a continuous noise, the silence was almost shattering. There is a constant hum where there are many hundreds of people confined in a small space, and when they suddenly leave, it's like a powerful, quietly running motor being shut off. The silence actually hurts.

This particular day the search lasted a great deal longer than usual. With the exception of the half-dozen women with tiny babies who were scattered throughout the barracks, everyone was down on the road while the Japanese systematically went through the barracks. Suddenly they started on the police barracks, which was next to ours. Apparently they thought they would find what they were looking for, for they immediately started tearing up the floor boards, and I immediately felt like a rat in a trap! At almost the same time they started searching the barracks on the other side of me, and my heart almost stopped beating, for I felt sure that my life was practically over.

To say that I was afraid is putting it entirely too mildly, but in the meantime something had to be done, and done quickly, and I was the only person on earth who could do it. I thought frantically of every conceivable hiding place. Not only did I have to think of the present, I had to think of retrieving the things later, in case I managed to keep them from the Japanese. We were not supposed to leave our cubicles while a search was in progress, but I had to take a chance on the guards seeing me. I gathered everything that I could carry, radio, tubes, wires, condensers, junk of every conceivable shape and size, wrapped them in a bundle of clothes, and started for the bathroom. My first thought was to put the things down inside one of the johns, as the most unlikely place the Japanese might search, but then I realized I couldn't do that, for the bathroom was the very first place everyone went the minute a search was over. The pounding, tearing, breaking, stomping noise was getting closer by the second, and I positively had to think of something. Suddenly it came to me.

Soap was a thing of the past, so everyone soaked their clothes in containers to facilitate the scrubbing. Buckets, pans, barrels, dishpans, every conceivable shape of container was set in a long line outside the wash trough at the end of the bathroom, with the laundry soaking in readiness for tomorrow's washing. I felt sure that the Japanese weren't going to come along and search each bucket of dirty, wet, smelly clothes. I quickly grabbed our sawed-off barrel, emptied it, shoved the radio and spare parts into it, and covered it with dirty dry clothes. I rushed back to my cubicle and arrived just in time to greet the little yellow boys with a smile. I thanked God that Gerry Ann couldn't talk. Another search had been met and conquered.

As a rule we were allowed to stay in our cubicles while a search was made. This time the Japanese had lined everyone up in the road, down in front of the barracks, with guards to make sure that no one left the group, and then they had systematically gone to work. This particular search was more violent than they usually were because, with no premeditation (as far as I know), the men in the bachelor barracks suddenly marched over to the searching party and said, "Look here, you can't search our barracks unless we are in the barracks with you." This flouting of authority upset the Japanese, and they decided to show us who controlled the situation. Immediately the guards who were going through the barracks next to mine were sent to the bachelor barracks and they went at it with a vengeance. Apparently the guards felt sure that what they were looking for *must* be in the bachelor barracks, since the bachelors had insisted on being present while it was being searched. The guards found nothing of any interest to them in that barracks except an empty gun shell. I don't suppose a gun would have caused any more excitement. Night coming on was the only thing that prevented the Japanese from demolishing more barracks, we presume—who knows?

I feel sure that each time one is called upon to meet a crisis, one is a little less capable of meeting the next crisis adequately.[29]

29. When I asked Margaret why she didn't think coping with one crisis made

That statement isn't entirely true, of course, for one has more confidence with the successful passing of each crisis, but it also takes something out of one that cannot be put back. Probably I should say that it takes something out of *me*. Perhaps other people aren't like me. I only know that each time the Japanese were deceived one more time, I felt a little more shaky after they were gone and a little more sure that sooner or later (there *is* a law of averages) we'd be caught. I look at Gerry Ann yet and wonder why she isn't a nervous wreck, simply from having nursed from such a shaky bag of bones for so long.

The next search proved to me, beyond the shadow of a doubt, that our time had not yet come. This time Jerry and I thought we'd play it smart. The Japanese had never looked in our cupboards or bothered with our food, probably because there was no food worth mentioning. However, we had empty milk cans, left over from our Red Cross kits, and we decided that the thing to do was to fill several of the empty cans with small extra radio parts and put them back in the cupboard. Some of the parts were being saved for the day when Jerry was going to build a transmitter. Several times he had broached the subject to members of the central committee, but they had talked him out of it.[30] However, we felt certain that the time would come when a transmitter would be our salvation.

We had been warned that a search was to begin at any time. We hastily filled the cans with spare parts and "secured" everything else. Jerry made a last-minute run to the bathroom. When he came back he was running and out of breath, and said to help him empty the cans quickly. We raised the board and simply dumped the contents under the floor, without trying to push the things back out of sight. We had no more than gotten the

one *more* rather than *less* able to cope with the next, she replied, "I could no more have talked to you about the war right after the war than I could have flown. I didn't get over one shaky thing before the next one came along and made it harder and harder to cope" (MS to LB 8/11/87).

30. Because they felt it was too dangerous for him to build one (MS to LB 8/11/87).

board back in place when the guards were in the cubicle. The very *first* place they looked was the cupboard. They took the lid off of every can! Less than five minutes before every can had been full of radio parts. Why did they look there? God knows! They had never looked in our cupboard before, and they never did again. Why, at the very last minute before they arrived had Jerry suddenly decided that it wasn't a good place for the junk? Again, God knows. Jerry didn't even know, except that "Something told me to get it out of the cans." Strange are the ways of Providence.

A mining engineer, Pat Hell, whom I had known before the war, was the head gardener in Los Baños. I had lost track of him after the first year or two in the Philippines. We had been in Santo Tomás for several months when the Japanese brought in a man whom they had captured in the hills. Everyone heard about it, but no one seemed to know his name. I was surprised a few days after that to meet Pat, who had grown a long beard, and to discover that it was he whom they had brought in. Seeing Pat that day demonstrated more clearly to me than anything else could have, what fear can do to a human being. Pat had always been very cocky and self-assured. He had been a big, good-looking, American male-creature, and he was no longer any of those things. He had been hiding in the mountains for so long, had lived on such a meager diet, that he was terribly thin. He had let his beard grow, and he constantly looked behind him. Fear was written all over him, and apparently he could not help himself, and could not realize that he no longer had to defend himself from the elements, from the natives, and from the Japanese. I decided right then that there were advantages to being inside a fence, much as I despised it and wanted to get outside it. This same man, then, had gone to Los Baños and had found new confidence, of a sort, in working hard at our camp garden. When the children and I went to Los Baños he made it a point to look us up. He met Jerry, liked him, and apparently wanted to help us, for many times after that he came by our cubicle and brought us vegetables. To be sure, they were always damaged, and there were never more than a few pods of okra, or a tomato, or a pepper, for the entire camp would have had a fit if he had given us "camp property." Damaged or otherwise, there was nothing in life that was more acceptable to us than food.

During the last few months of camp a few of the more daring souls, all unattached males, began to play a very dangerous game. It was a game that required several people, outside contacts, inside contacts, good timing, and most of all—*good luck*. The game was to slip through the fence, buy food from the Filipinos, slip back through the fence, and sell the food to the internees. For a mestizo (half Filipino and half something else, in this case usually American) it was not quite so dangerous, for he could always pretend that he was a Filipino. For an American, there was no pretending. There was no way on earth for him to hide his white skin, or blue eyes, the reason a great many more people did not hide out in the mountains for the duration. If an American was caught there was nothing he could do about it except get shot. Every sound, those last weeks of internment, took on an exaggerated meaning. Every nerve in me was tuned to sound. The hours I have spent listening for a heavy-footed step, or the soft pad-pad of a barefooted internee! For all my listening I never knew when I might miss a footstep, or when we might give ourselves away by an accidental squeal from the radio.

One particularly hot, sultry afternoon Jerry was not in the cubicle and neither was David. Any time we were not all together I was a little worried. It was a still afternoon when the shots rang out, and I knew deep inside me that they were shots that meant business. I am ashamed to say it was with a sense of relief that I learned within the hour that Pat had been shot and killed by the guards. He wasn't leaving camp, he was coming back into camp. I was ashamed of my feelings then, and I still am today, but I was so relieved when Jerry and David got back to the cubicle that I was almost sick. It still does not seem fair to me that Pat should have lived right up to the [war's] end, and then have been killed.[31]

31. Arthur discusses this, 139–43.

Speaking of sounds reminds me of the most gruesome sound I have ever heard, and every morning while we were in Los Baños we heard it. I had heard it first in Manila, when David and I stayed outside in the apartments that were taken over by the Japanese who took Corregidor. Two and a half years later it made a great deal more of an impression on me. In Manila I had thought, "animals." In Los Baños I still thought "animals," but now I knew that they were dangerous, wild animals. Early every morning, the Japanese who were on duty turned out for a nondescript, saber-dancing ritual that was terrifying to hear. The guttural, inhuman, unearthly bellowing that accompanied this setting-up exercise was something I hope never to hear again. I understand that they make these same noises in the thick of battle, and I dare say this practice session early every morning helps to contribute to its quality. For my money they were *all* good, and I give them all due credit for producing the desired effect, terror.

Jerry's receiver had been acting up a little and he needed to work on it. I finished the dishes earlier than usual, got the children into bed and to sleep, and Jerry decided that it would be a good time to get out the soldering iron and get to work. We hadn't had a Japanese visitor for a day or two so we felt a misplaced sense of security. Our table was by the door, so I sat down, got out the never-ending mending, and set to work, mending and guarding. Jerry started to work in the corner by the closet on the small bath table that we had for Gerry Ann. Just at the last moment he decided that perhaps he should have an alibi for the soldering iron being out, in case we did have a visitor. We had a leaky cup which he worked on first. Usually when I heard a Japanese coming there was time enough to warn Jerry, and he could secure operations; this night the guard came striding quickly down the walk and into the cubicle before I could make more than a tiny squeak. My nervous reaction is to smile (it hasn't a thing to do with the way I feel), so I smiled broadly at the guard and kept his eyes on me for just the second that it took for Jerry to slip the receiver off of the table and behind the curtain to the closet. It was dim in the cubicle. No doubt the guard's eyes had to become adjusted to even that much light, or he may have been a little nervous too, for I saw every move Jerry made. The Japanese missed it completely. Jerry immediately took up his part of the act. He showed him the cup he was soldering, smiled at him, and so another narrow escape was behind us, or at least under control. My hands shook so that I couldn't sew unless I braced my elbows on the table. I can only think that the Japanese aren't as good students of human nature as they might be, for certainly Jerry and I are neither of us actors. Could be that when one's life depends on it, one is a better actor than one thinks. Then, too, a conqueror has a role to play. The guard may have had an exaggerated sense of his ability to make the conquered bow and tremble before him.

A couple or three days after Pat was killed, more shots rang out. By this time everyone was so jittery that we weren't even trusting our own shadows. This time we were all in the cubicle, but the shots still had an ominous ring. Almost immediately we learned that another internee had been shot, in much the same way Pat had been shot. The boy was young, and he was coming back through the fence with food. They didn't kill him, but they crippled him, and then they let him lie in that terrible, tropical sun for two hours before they decided to drag him away and kill him. For two hours the whole camp hoped and prayed, the central committee begged them to save his life, and Doc pleaded with them to let him go out and administer aid of some sort, but to all overtures the answer was "No, he shall be an example to all of you." And so they killed him, and we buried him, and none of it would have happened if the boy had had just a little food, food that was abundant on the other side of the fence.[32]

The guards at our camp were changed periodically. At our

32. Arthur characterizes George Lewis as a "hard-luck guy" who had gone to the Philippines to work as a mechanic for Pan Am at Cavite (see pp. 145–46).

camp duty was more or less a rest cure for the soldiers. After they had guarded for us for a few months a new contingent was sent in for a rest, and the rested ones were sent to the front. After Christmas we got new guards. This time they were young Formosans, and with their arrival trading between guards and Americans became a much more intense game. Formosans, for the most part, were much more backward than the Japanese, and having a hundred-dollar watch was, apparently, the next thing to heaven. Having two watches was something out of this world. The Japanese guard with whom we had formerly done our "swapi-changi" business sent a young Formosan around to take up where he had left off. I was terrified of the Formosans. I was afraid of the Japanese guards, but I always felt that they had a modicum of honor—if they made a bargain they would stick with it. The Formosans were an entirely different kettle of fish. One felt that they wanted the watches, and resented very much having to put out anything in return for them. Not only were they afraid of their own Japanese officers, they were obviously afraid of us, and that made the situation very much more ticklish, for *they* had the guns. When they came into our cubicle they never set their guns down, and that fact alone spoke more loudly than words.

Though it paid little in the way of beans and sugar, we could at least trade the sugar for more beans, and it *did* make a difference. Jerry and I had known we were playing a dangerous game, and we had felt that some day very probably we would have to kill a guard, or be killed. Having reached that decision, my outlook on life was to change once again. It seemed to have a hardening effect on my thinking that nothing can ever quite soften again. I feel that one can never be quite the same person after one has killed, or made up one's mind that one can, if necessary, kill a human being. There was only one thing that really worried us in this matter. When a guard has set a gun down everyone has a fair chance. When the guard keeps his finger on the trigger, one does not have a fair chance.

After much haggling we made our first deal with the young

Formosan. We weren't at all happy about the new situation, and felt that it was about time to give up the swapi-changi business. However, when we tried to explain to the Formosan that all the American watches were gone, he did not understand, and wasn't pleased with what he did understand. The guard insisted that he would like to have one more watch. Actually we did have one more watch, but we were willing to give up [the swapi-watchi business] while we still had our heads tucked on. After much bickering, we told the guard that we would try to get one more watch and that he should come back two nights from then to get it.

"Tomorrow-tomorrow" came, and with it the Formosan. He came stomping in, surly, filthy, and uncouth, but with a dirty five-pound bag of sugar under his arm. For the sugar he wanted a 21-jewel Bulova watch. Since the Formosan had said that he would also bring beans (and he obviously hadn't) Jerry told him he had not been able to get the watch. As a matter of fact, we had been so concerned about the attitude of the guard that we had scouted around and found a missionary who had spent time in Formosa and spoke the language, and had asked him to come in and interpret for us this night. Our own missionary friend brought the Formosan-speaking missionary (who all too obviously wanted no truck with us, the guard, *or* the situation) and all of us were getting jumpy when the guard, who was acting much more formidable than usual, said he would throw in two cans of sardines "and watch he better be here next night." After all the haggling, the squabbling, and the interpreting were finished the guard asked if he might leave the sugar and fish with us until he came for the watch. Asking us to guard the sugar and fish was like asking us to sit down at a banquet table and not touch a bite. Finally we agreed to take care of the things for him. All intercourse with the Formosan had been done in a flickering half light, in whispers, so that the neighbors would not hear us. The whole situation completely jangled my nerves.

For hours after the deal was settled, and they had all left our cubicle, Jerry and I lay on our couch and I shook and shook and cried and cried. I felt absolutely dirty and contaminated from being fouled up in a shady situation which had to be carried on at night, in whispers. I think that I was more morbid that night than I need have been, for everyone with enough intestinal fortitude was in the swapi-changi business with the guards, as indicated by the presence of so many watches on so many Japanese wrists. In our own case, we simply had had more dealings with the guards than many of the other internees. In the beginning we had had only one watch, one ring, and one pen between us, so it behooved us to be the middlemen for those with more jewelry and less courage than we had. I was horribly ashamed that we had let ourselves get pushed into such a nasty business, even though our lives had depended on it. That night we decided that there would be no more of it, come what might. With our decision we went to bed, and to sleep. Later in the night Jerry went to the bathroom, and when he came back he awakened me and said "Do you know what those damned fools are saying in the bathroom? They are all hepped up, and saying that the Japs are leaving. They say they're taking all the shovels." We smirked to ourselves, in the dark, and I thought "Shovels, indeed–," and again we went back to sleep. For three years a day never passed that people hadn't speculated wildly or otherwise about how our deliverance would come about. Some of the guesses were wild, too. There were people who kept themselves alive and sane by never admitting that we would be in camp for more than "two more weeks."[33]

We hadn't been asleep long this time when our good friend Doc burst in. He had blood all over his hospital gown and said, "For Christ's sake, get up. They're gone!" I couldn't believe it, and yet I could hear people racing up and down the hall, lights were beginning to come on, fires were being lit in cook shanties.

33. "These people could function in camp in a reasonable way as long as they thought they only had to stand it for a couple of weeks at a time" (MS to LB 8/11/87).

Something had happened, certainly. Jerry just lay in bed and said "Hell, you've all gone stir crazy. Go on back to bed and let me sleep." Nothing we could say or do would make him get up and look around. Doc went away then and in a few minutes the fellow who was shacked up with a Russian girl who had the end cubicle arrived from the bachelor barracks. Immediately he started pounding on the wall, and in a minute put his head over the partition and said "You remember what I promised? I said when the Japs left I'd open my last cans and we'd have a real chow." With that Nadia and he came over with coffee, canned milk, and Spam. My first thought was "The sugar, five whole pounds of it under our bed, AND THE DAMNED JAPS ARE GONE. God is good!" With the coming of the coffee Jerry got up. We had no more than gotten the water hot when Doc burst in again and said, "Jerry, your time has come to rise and shine. For God's sake, break out your receiver and let's see what's going on." My first thought upon hearing that the Japanese were gone had been sugar under our own bed, some people's first thoughts had been looting the Japanese barracks. Then came the news.

How can I ever hope to picture the wild excitement of that dawn? Our neighbors were dumbfounded when we produced the radio, and I was amazed that we really had been able to keep it a secret, for there were times when I had been sure they had looked at us askance. Probably it wasn't the radio they were thinking about, however. Things happened so fast in the next two hours that it is hard for me to remember them in their correct sequence. I do remember that, through no effort of Jerry's, both the radios that had been left behind in the Japanese barracks were in Jerry's hands before the day was over. The radios were brought to him by people who had looted them and wanted them repaired.[34] Naturally there was wild looting at the guards'

34. "Jerry had a lot to do—remember, he was trying to work during a typhoon—and didn't fix them. He would have needed the parts to make a transmitter, or to fix one" (MS to LB 8/11/87).

barracks as soon as the Japanese were gone. The first thought Doc had when they left was their pigs! Result, blood all over his gown.

At dawn a storybook ceremony was enacted, and all the time I kept saying to myself, "This can't be true." And yet, just as the sun rose, we were singing our own beloved *Star Spangled Banner*. The words have never been so significant, and the flag which had been kept hidden somewhere has never looked so proud or meant so much. People all over the camp cried unashamedly, and two or three women even fainted. A member of the central committee made a speech over the loudspeaker, and announced that "We are now in communication with our armed forces." It was Jerry's and my turn to nearly faint, for it was not true. We merely had a radio, which could only tell us what our armed forces were doing. Jerry immediately insisted that they retract that statement and say instead, "We are now getting the news of the war, because the Japanese left a radio behind when they left our camp." As things turned out it was great good fortune that he had insisted on that statement being made, for everything that was said was written down and kept as a record of what happened during the following week.

That was the most hectic week we shall ever know. It was amazing what people looted from the Japanese barracks. The commandant's kimono, his bicycle, his dishes. The second day of our false liberation, as I shall call it, a third radio came over the fence to Jerry. It was also to be repaired. One of his Filipino boys from Cavite had heard that he was in Los Baños, and had brought it all the way to him. We were simply filthy with radios! It began to rain that day and rained most of the following week. Almost immediately the central committee, with Doc as their intermediary (Doc was a member of the committee, and they apparently found it convenient to forget that Jerry had been in ill repute), set Jerry up in the communications business once more. This time he was in the commandant's barracks. Before he could get organized in the office, however, the committee sent "reporters" to our cubicle to get the news in shorthand as it came over the radio. It was then typed and put on the bulletin board for the consumption of the entire camp. Nothing could have made me more happy than the complete surprise with which the "reporters" greeted our cubicle. They were amazed that anything so nice could have been made from what might, a few months before, have passed as a horse's stall.

The reason for the guards abandoning us soon became apparent. The Japanese had sighted an American convoy off the coast and thought the Americans were going to make a landing in the south. Naturally they went north as fast as they could go. However, it wasn't long before they discovered their mistake, for the Americans had landed in the north.

Within two days after the Japanese were gone, Jerry had his equipment all carried over to his new "office" and was installed as the new communications department. The third day certain factions within the camp were beginning to be jealous of Jerry's sudden burst of popularity, and had decided among themselves that all of his equipment and his radio were *really* camp property; "Hasn't he gotten them while he has been in camp?" News of this sort has a way of getting home, but Jerry is more charitable than I am and said he'd stick it out for a few days. However, when the central committee began to be persuaded that perhaps all Jerry's things really *were* camp property, Jerry decided that enough was enough. While the committee was in session, trying to come to some agreement about how to go about taking his things away from him, Jerry crawled under the fence (a high fence surrounded the Japanese barracks), went into his "office," and dragged every single piece of equipment that belonged to him out to the fence. He shoved it under the fence to James, who was waiting on the other side. Together they came "home" with the things. Jerry went back then and told the committee they could get the news any way they saw fit, but it would not be from his radio they heard it. Then he retired into silence once more.

During that entire week, when almost every other soul in camp had been making deals over the fence with the Filipinos,

Jerry had spent his every waking moment at the communications department and had not taken time to get any extra food for us. A Filipino whom he had known in Cavite sent him a small parcel of gabi (a native root, somewhat like potato), but that was the extent of our take for the week. I was furious at the whole situation. I couldn't go scrounging for food, for it rained almost constantly and I had to take care of the children, and besides we had spent all of our money at that time. Jerry had a perverted sense of duty, I thought, and didn't go scrounging because it was dark before he quit at the "office." The seventh night, I think it was, the Japanese returned as quietly as they had gone. They had left the sentries, who kept the camp surrounded after they had abandoned us, and they had warned us that we were not to leave the vicinity. The Japanese army was still there [throughout this time].

I believe a sense of apathy and a fear of the unknown (to say nothing of the fact that we are brought up to do what we are told, and never under any circumstances to be different from our neighbors) had too strong a hold on us internees at that particular time. Life is much easier if we don't fight back. We were told that there was a fully equipped garrison of Japanese soldiers just outside the fence. (There was: over the hill.) Perhaps the never-ending rain had something to do with it. If we had gone over the fence, where could we have gotten in out of the rain with our children? A few of the unattached bachelors did go, and came back later with the guerrillas. People are desperately afraid of the unknown. We knew that within the camp we at least had roofs over our heads. Outside the fence there was no telling what we might find. It has something to do with what is undermining the nation, *security*. We have sold our heritage of freedom for security.

In the night the whispers started—"The Japs are back"—and the sense of thankfulness which Jerry and I felt because his radio and all his gear were carefully stowed away under the floor was overwhelming. The night before, they could have walked in and taken over everything that Jerry had worked hard for three years to collect. As it was, we were considerably worried about the neatly stacked news bulletins which the committee, not knowing the Japanese would return during the night, had left for them to read. We were thankful to remember that Jerry had asked the committee to change the wording of their first address, because it was all written down for the Japanese to read. "In contact with" and "getting news of the war" are two entirely different things.

After our week of false freedom, life picked up in tempo, for the Japanese were back and they had lost very much face in having left us. Face, to an Oriental, is all-important. We suppose they had been reprimanded by their superiors, for in no other way could we explain the stern measures they took with us. Food rations went down, the commandant was furious because his kimono and his bicycle had been taken, and "Where is the radio to which you have been listening?" "You *must* bring back the radio," said he.

Jerry and I shook in our boots, We knew where *all* the radios were, and we had no intention of taking any of them back. In the first place, we couldn't! During the week the Japanese were gone Jerry had very carefully taken both Japanese radios apart, one to get spare parts for his own radio, the other to get parts for a transmitter. The cases we had destroyed. Late one night we very quietly placed all the broken pieces in the garbage pit, under the garbage.

The second night after the Japanese returned prominent members of the central committee kept the path to our door hot. They came over during the night so that they wouldn't be seen talking to us, for they seemed to think it inevitable that the Japanese would soon know that Jerry had been the "communications department" in their absence. Apparently they did not want to be associated with us in any way. In a way it was amusing, for we certainly had no intention of telling the Japanese anything if we could help it. Who then, was going to tell them about Jerry? Everyone was trying desperately to think of a way out of the situation. The Japanese were being very tough with the committee about the fact that a radio, any radio, had to be produced or someone would most certainly get shot. We knew very well that if we produced our radio someone *would* get shot. And we knew who it would be. When the Japanese left, the committee gave Jerry their blessing and complete support in regard to building a transmitter. When the Japanese came back, several of the committee members came sneaking over in the night and said, "For God's sake, forget that a transmitter has ever even been mentioned. We're in enough trouble as it is." One week the committee was all buddy-buddy and "anything we can do for you, Jerry" and the next it was, "Get the damned radio back together, Jerry, or we'll have to turn you over to the Japs." We were able to keep in close contact with what went on within the committee room through Doc, and as a result we knew that our chances of survival were becoming slim, for the Japanese had given the committee an ultimatum. The radio, or else. . . .

During the night that followed that particular committee meeting, a man whom I had known for several years came to see me. He was a mining engineer, and had been at the same mine with us in the Mountain Province. He had been very nice to me during the past year. Perhaps he was still being kind to me in his own way, who knows? In Los Baños he was a member of the police department, his camp detail. When he came in I thought he had come as a friend, but I soon realized that he had come on business. He said, "Margaret, I hope you will forgive me but I may have to carry out orders which I am not going to like. I have heard from one of the committee members that I may have to turn Jerry over to the Japanese, and I hope you aren't going to make it hard for me when I come for him." I could not possibly write of the wild fury that nearly choked me. That night I abandoned all pretense of being a lady. I told him that if he ever *dared* come into my cubicle to take Jerry away I'd kill him with my bare hands, if necessary. And I told him a few other things that weren't nice, but seemed necessary. I honestly had no intention of killing him; how could I? I could barely toddle around under my own weight, let alone kill a man twice as big as I was, but the sincerity in my voice must have been unmistakable, for he was very hurt that I took his kindly meant warning in that way. From that moment we ceased being friends. "No one has ever threatened to kill me before," he said and though I am sure I couldn't have, if it had become necessary for me to carry out my threat, I certainly would have tried with every means at my command. A lion at bay had nothing on me.

One of the committee members, and I would love to give him the opportunity to read this, and let him recognize himself for the heel that I think he is, was almost able to sway the committee into handing Jerry over to the Japanese. Said he, "I have a wife and family in the States whom I must think about, and besides everyone knows the kind of trash Jerry and that Sherk woman are." But for the common sense of two men on that committee, Doc and Alex Calhoun,[35] Jerry would have been handed over to the Japanese. He would have been shot and my story would have ended there. Doc and Calhoun thought that handing Jerry over to the Japanese, particularly after the committee had given him their blessing the previous week, might look quite ugly in later years to unbiased judges.

The following day a member of the Japanese office force came to the committee and told them that the Japanese had maneuvered themselves into a position from which they could not back out without losing face. This they were not willing to do. He said, "However, if you can produce a radio, *any* radio, and put it in the office I think the matter will be considered closed." And so, another God-given opportunity was at hand. One of the committee members came to tell Jerry, and of course we did have another radio, the one the Filipino had sent in to Jerry to be repaired. Without a doubt there was no one else in that entire camp as brave as Jerry was. As soon as it was dark he put the Filipino's radio in a gunny sack, slung it over his shoulder, and

35. Alexander D. Calhoun was the "distinguished, aloof" vice president of the National City Bank in Manila. He had been a member of the central committee in Santo Tomás before being transferred to Los Baños, where he assumed a major role in camp leadership (Stevens 20, Arthur 26).

went striding off into the dark with it. I am sure that no other man in camp would have done it. Jerry walked straight over to the Japanese office, took the radio out of the gunny sack, and left it for the Japanese to discover before midnight (which they did). I died a thousand deaths while he was gone, for fear he'd run into a guard and get himself shot for his trouble, or for fear they might be waiting for him in the dark, but he was back in a few minutes and we breathed a sigh of relief.

The relief was short lived, for we had another visitor that night. The guard who had left the sugar and sardines with us "for protection" had returned with the rest of the guards and he was in an ugly frame of mind. He was the very last man on earth I wanted to see, for the sugar—a great part of it anyway —had gone down the little red lane, and I knew of no way to get it back. Since we could produce neither the watch *nor* the sugar, we were in another spot. We managed to talk ourselves into a couple of days' grace, but there was no sleep for us that night.

Apparently the Japanese were dumbfounded when they discovered the radio at the office that night. They realized that it was not one of their radios. Presumably they felt that there must be a radio in every cubicle if, out of the hat as it were, we could produce an entirely different radio than the ones for which they were looking.

While we waited for the situation to simmer down to a slow boil, Doc persuaded us that the hospital would be the best place for the radio for the time being. Since Doc was a member of the central committee, he felt that the hospital would be the last place the Japanese might look for it. Jerry and I thought it was a good idea, too. As soon as it was dark Jerry carried the radio over to the hospital, where he and Doc listened to "the man." Afterward, while no one was around, they very carefully and quietly put it up in the attic. During siesta the next day Doc thought it might be a good time to get the radio down and listen to Tokyo Rose, or whoever happened to be on at that time of day. A few minutes later he burst into our cubicle and said,

"Did you get your radio, Jerry?" Jerry and I were struck dumb, for of course Jerry had *not* gotten it. We had considered it almost as safe as if it were under our own floor.

For a few minutes we were all too crestfallen to think, or to talk coherently. Finally Jerry said, "Hell, Doc, you must have just missed it up there in the dark." Since hope *does* spring eternal, they both went back together to make a more thorough search. Very soon they had to admit that it simply was not there. Their first thought, naturally, was that the Japanese had discovered it and taken it. On second thought it seemed impossible that the Japanese would take it and not arrest someone. The more they thought about it, the more they thought that it was an inside job. There have never been two more frustrated or furious men.

Upon investigation Doc discovered, through the nurses, that a man from the electrical department had been called in that morning to repair something that had necessitated going up in the attic. He saw the radio, understood the situation immediately, and took the opportunity for which he had been waiting. He was the fellow who had walked off with Jerry's first radio, and an unsettled grudge had been festering there for more than a year. As soon as Doc learned who had been in the attic, the whole puzzle fell into place. An enraged bull would have quailed before him. Doc told Jerry to let *him* handle the situation. He felt that he personally had been robbed, since the radio was his to protect for the time being. Doc immediately found the fellow, confronted him with the situation as it appeared to us. Doc told him that he'd beat him to death if he didn't get the radio for him immediately. Doc is a big man, and a stern man when he needs to be. As if by magic, the radio was back in Doc's hands. That night Jerry brought the little sewing box back home to the cubicle again, and we rested more easily knowing that it was under the bed. It was at that point that we decided not to let it out of our sight again.

For no accountable reason that we could ever see, it was that day that the same eminent member of the committee who had

advocated turning Jerry over to the Japs decided that the internees should steal rice from the bodega. There may have been
some sound reasoning there, but not much. By not using every
grain of rice that we were allowed for each day's ration, we had
saved one hundred sacks of rice. The rice was our own, therefore, and it had been saved the terribly hard way. With the return of the Japanese and the cutting down of our daily ration,
we were all afraid that they would take the rice away from us.
We internees had been saving it for the day when they wouldn't
allow us *any* rice. As it was, we were being given approximately
a handful of rice per day per person. It was not enough to sus-
tain life in a bed patient in a hospital, we were told by our doctors. It was decided that two men from each barracks should
sneak over to the bodega at midnight and carry the rice away.
That way the rice would be well distributed throughout the barracks, two sacks for each barracks. Jerry, of course, was one of
the men chosen from our barracks. There were a very limited
number of men who were willing to do anything that might very
conceivably get them into trouble.

Jerry and I thought it a silly idea, but it just might work;
who could tell until we had tried it? The men got the rice all
right, with no one being caught going to or from the bodega,
but the next morning when its theft was discovered by the guards
another ultimatum went out. "Either the rice comes back or
Mr. B., the author of the idea, gets shot before night." Silly
how the tables turn. The rice was carried back, in broad daylight this time, with everyone feeling very shamefaced about the
situation. I must confess that Jerry did not carry his sack of
rice back. "Let them shoot him" was our motto. Yesterday Jerry
would have been turned over to the Japanese if Mr. B. had
had his way. Today it was Mr. B.'s turn. I'm afraid the milk of
human kindness was running pretty thin in our veins at that
point. We had learned from experience that turning one's cheek
merely got another slap on the other cheek. We had also learned
that there is a decided difference between a slap on the cheek
and a shot in the head.

Almost every day we could hear bombing now, and often several times during the day we would see American planes overhead. The first American planes we had seen, in October, were two P-38s. They were so very high in the sky that they looked like tiny silver squares. We couldn't think what they were, but we were *sure* that they were American. Jerry had a long glass, another forbidden item, and he could just make out part of the insignia. He couldn't understand it, however, for the insignia was no longer what it had been when we had lived in the United States. Everyone in camp had his own ideas about those planes and that insignia, and no two people agreed about either. Jerry came closest to guessing what it really was, for the long glass gave him an advantage over the rest of the internees.

Every day now the planes came lower and lower, which could mean only one thing to us. The situation must be fairly well in our hands. When Americans bombed a near-by sugar refinery they knocked down the power and transmission lines which fed electricity into our camp. Thereafter we had no electricity, for the Japanese were much too busy to put it back. As a result, the radio-receiving business took a sudden turn for the worse.

A committee member for whom we had great respect came around to see us one night after blackout and told Jerry that, "Feud or no feud between you and the central committee, the immediate welfare of the camp depends upon our finding out what is going on in the war." A few nights before the electricity was gone for good, Jerry had succeeded in getting his transmitter in working order and actually made contact with the American forces. Jerry called an army net on Marinduque Island that was operating around six megacycles. The first night they answered him, and he tried to answer them and yet not disclose the fact that he was in a Japanese internment camp, for fear the Japanese might be listening too. He tried to identify himself through former Navy officers who had been associates of his in Cavite. The Americans received his message that night, he is sure, but thereafter refused to answer, and he overheard a conversation within the net in which they seemed to think he was a "darkie." The fact that they thought him a Japanese—we presumed that that is what they meant—ended all possibility of help through that route.

After the electricity went off Doc kept prodding Jerry. He told Jerry that we needed the news now more than we had ever needed it before. For a few days Jerry was sunk about the whole situation, for his batteries had long since gone dead, and though he had been able to revive them for awhile, they were now beyond recall. To make their own electric supply seemed almost out of the question. Before the present impasse Jerry had borrowed a 1/4-inch Black and Decker drill from a man in our barracks. They had put a hand crank on the chuck and used the gears in the drill to increase the motor speed. Electrically it worked fine, but the noise was unbelievable, and no one was strong enough to turn the crank for more than a minute or two. As a result they were forced to look for another compound-wound motor which could be used as a generator. It was at this point that Doc came over to our cubicle and offered Jerry any motor that they had at the hospital: refrigerator, washing machine, centrifuge. . . .

When Dana mentioned centrifuge, it opened a whole new train of thought for Jerry. However, the next problem that reared its ugly head was how to turn the generator. They tried various hand crank systems, but they all ran into too much horsepower on our limited diet. Jerry made some remark about "foot power," and Doc suddenly remembered that he knew the man that had stolen the commandant's bicycle. And that did it! It meant yet another man in on the operation, but it had to be. Unfortunately they were in such a hurry to get under way again that they neglected to tell the bicycle fellow the alibi, just in case they were discovered. This man had let his beard grow for the three years of internment. Dr. Nance and Jerry had drummed up a sort of story, but one never goes into too great detail with an alibi. One just goes on the assumption that one will not be caught.

During siesta time Doc, Jerry, the bearded one, and the fellow who owned the drill decided that all was in readiness, and that they would go over and give the thing a trial spin. They had enough power to make a hundred-watt bulb light up beautifully. They thought the best place to try it out would be the carpenter shop, the farthest barracks, which would be empty during siesta hour. It had been several days since we had heard any news, and I was as anxious as anyone else to find out what had been happening. Terrific bombing could be heard in the direction of Manila, and at night we could see the glow of great fires on the horizon.

Jerry put the radio, which was still in its original sewing box, inside a bayang, put on his straw hat, and set off. Shirtless, shoeless, just a pair of worn-out shorts, his hat, and his radio. I could count every rib as he walked away, and every instinct in me wanted to take care of him somehow, but I could do nothing except wait at the cubicle and pray. He hadn't been gone more than half an hour when I looked up from the cook shack where I had been cleaning rice, and there he came striding very quickly down the path, with his bare radio in his hands.

Two American planes had just given us a zoom job, and I thought perhaps his face looked so white from something about them. When he said "They caught us" I could hardly believe my ears, for here he was with the radio in his hands. So how could they have caught him? Very quickly he explained it to me. They'd gone to the barracks, each man appearing with his share of the bargain. Bicycle, "generator," and radio were in readiness. Jerry was to work the radio, for no one else could; Doc and the other two men were to take turns pedaling the bicycle. At that last moment Jerry had decided he would take the radio into a small tool room at the end of the barracks, just on the off chance that a guard might come snooping around. He tapped into the electric line which ran into the tool room, closed and locked the door, and got himself settled. He had heard the first words of the announcer from KGEI when suddenly the thing went dead. He started to shout at Doc to pump harder on the bicycle, when the God-given sixth sense told him to keep quiet. The wall was made of sawali, so it was easy enough to peer through a crack. What he saw was Doc perched on the bicycle, with one foot up in the air, looking dumbfoundedly at a Japanese guard who had come in to see what the noise was all about. Probably the Japanese was as surprised as the Americans were. In any event there was very little to be said. Finally the fellow with the beard, who had stolen the bicycle, said "Want to swapi-watchi?" It broke the spell, and immediately the guard turned around and ran to call his brother guards. At that exact moment the two American planes flew very low over our camp, and Jerry picked up his radio and went straight through that sawali wall. Any other time in the world he would have been caught, but the Japanese were always frightened of American planes and hit the dirt every time they flew over our camp. Occasionally they even dived into a handy cook shanty when planes went over. We knew they weren't after *us,* but apparently the Japanese thought each and every one was after them, and *this* time would be it. While the Japanese guards were in the ditches waiting for the Americans to let them have it, Jerry made his escape. By the time the rest of the guards got back, the other three men were gone too.[36]

At this point the most awful suspense that I have ever known began for us. We stewed and fretted and worried, and eventually had our fingernails chewed off. Jerry made immediate plans for going over the fence. The plans were simple. Put on both pairs of shorts, and be sure to wear his dungaree jacket and his shoes that were out at the bottom. He decided to wait for dark, and then if there was the slightest inkling that the Japanese knew of his part in the setup, he'd go. If we hadn't heard anything to

36. Margaret's account differs in significant particulars from Arthur's account of the same incident (217–18). Indeed, Arthur provokes Margaret's explosive reaction, "Arthur's account is in almost NO WAY accurate. *The way I told it is the way it happened.* In fact, the radio belonged to Jerry, the generator belonged to Jerry (the idea was Jerry's and he had built the generator with the help of Rube Levy's centrifuge), and the footpower was meant to come from Dr. Nance, the fellow whose drill Jerry had tried to use, and "Chum" Hughes, who had stolen the commandant's bicycle. *No* one except these men were involved. No central committee, no nothing," contrary to Arthur's report (MS to LB 11/10/87, 12/14/87).

the contrary, he'd wait for awhile, but there was no doubt in either of our minds that he would not stick around and get himself shot if either of the men talked. And we had very little doubt but that one or the other of them would be forced to talk. It is simple to be made to talk, and I for one can understand and forgive it. It seemed certain to us that the Japanese would soon know of Jerry's part in the setup, and as soon as we knew that *they* knew, it was time for Jerry to leave. I felt that I would probably never see him again if he did go over the fence, for there were miles of enemies between us and the guerrillas. We were horrified with ourselves for not having given the bearded chap the alibi, such as it was, for of course he was the most easily identified man in camp.

Within minutes after they picked him up, we knew that the man with the beard was in the Japanese office for questioning. The next news we got, by way of Kathy, who was doing double duty between Doc's office and our cubicle, was that Doc had been taken to the Japanese office. Jerry was really getting itchy feet by this time, but it was still daylight and there was very little use trying to escape at that time of day. Night came, and they had not yet called Jerry. We had not heard from the hospital for a couple hours, but the coming of darkness let us breathe more easily anyway. What a blessed thing is the dark, sometimes. During the afternoon I had come to another grave decision. If we were fortunate enough to get through this scrape with our heads still in their original places, we were going to give up the radio business! That I was sure of. From the beginning I had given it my 100 percent approval and help and cooperation. Suddenly the whole business turned sour. As long as I felt that we had even half a chance I was all for it, for it seemed terribly important to us, but each time we had a scrape it seemed to me that they got a little closer to us. This afternoon I could definitely feel them breathing down our necks. We had never gotten anything except abuse from our friends, the internees, about the radio (at the least they thought we were crazy, at the most they thought we "endangered the camp"), and suddenly I didn't like the radio business any more. Especially I did not like it if it meant Jerry having to go over the fence.

That night, long after roll call, Doc and Kathy arrived and told us all that had transpired during the afternoon. The fellow with the beard was easily identified by the Japanese, and he had been called to the main office within minutes after the guards got back to the carpenter barracks and found the men gone. By a strange coincidence he came through with a story that was similar to Jerry's and Doc's, and seemed to be acceptable to the Japanese. Since he was in the electrical department, he told them that he was trying to make a generator for the hospital, just in case they had an emergency operation at night. The Japanese were satisfied with the story, and they let him go. Then they sent for Doc.

For many reasons Doc had the respect of the guards, but when he walked into the commandant's office, sat down and put his feet up on the desk, the commandant went into a temper tantrum about Doc's lack of respect for authority. Finally he calmed down and started asking Doc questions. He wanted to know if Doc knew the man with the beard, to which Doc replied that he did. Then the commandant asked if he had talked to him recently. Doc said "Yes, I saw him on the road the other day and stopped to talk to him." The commandant then said "Did you tell him anything?" Doc took a chance then and said "Yes, when I saw him last week I told him that we were likely to have a night operation any time, and I wondered if it would be possible to make some sort of a generator that would give us enough electricity to perform an operation." With that they turned Doc loose. We assume that they discovered a tube which Jerry left behind in his hasty exit, since he could not find it when he went back later. The tube was coated inside with mercury, and since there was no other trace of the radio, we have always thought they probably did not know what it was. As far as we know they never did find out that Jerry had any part in the episode. After we had hashed and re-hashed the details of the afternoon and our narrow escape, Doc and Kathy went back to the hospital, and Jerry and I, since our immediate danger was over, remembered how hungry we were and how little time there was between us and starvation.

We sat on and on that night on our little board walk, and made plans for our eventual escape if the situation did not take a turn for the better, and it certainly did not look as if there was any chance of that. Just before Christmas I had opened the last little can of oatmeal for Gerry Ann (which I had bought before she was born), and it was now gone. The Lees had given Gerry Ann and David each a cookie at Christmas, and the sight of Gerry Ann shaking all over at the exquisite taste of a tiny sugar cookie will never leave me. That night we decided that it would be better to be shot and killed quickly than to wait and watch the children die slowly. Decidedly, the war's tempo was quickening again, for it was a tremendous effort to walk as far as the bathroom now. We no longer let David run and play, for running took much-needed energy away from him, and I could not stand having him watch every bite of food I put in my mouth. All up and down the barracks these days children were crying, crying, crying for the food which their distracted and hungry parents could not provide for them. I knew I would go mad when David started it. Gerry Ann had always cried, for her hunger had never been entirely satisfied, but somehow I could stand it better than to have David start, for she at least could not talk, and I comforted myself by thinking, "Maybe she doesn't know why she is crying." That night as we sat and made our plans we thought of all that we would do for a tiny ten-cent hamburger, the kind we had once been able to buy in the United States. More than half seriously we decided that if we were given a choice, we would gladly give one finger, or two toes, just for one hamburger, right then. No doubt it seems silly, it does even to me at this point, but at that moment we were sincere in wishing that we could be allowed to give a finger for a hamburger.

At this time, approximately two weeks before we were liberated, everyone almost without exception, was suffering from two diseases, one of the mind, the other of the body. All over camp great swollen knees and ankles were appearing. In the morning our faces would be terribly swollen, in the evening our legs were. Beriberi was beginning to make real headway among us. Countless people had great oozing, painful sores on their extremities, particularly their legs, and it was almost impossible to make them heal.[37]

The disease of the mind I did not recognize as such, though I was one of its most acute sufferers. The biggest thrill I could have was to find someone who had an old tattered and torn magazine which had pictures of food in it. If there were colored illustrations I was practically beside myself. I found myself spending every spare moment I had searching out people who might have rare and exotic recipes. It didn't matter in the least what kind of food it was. The more butter and sugar there was in it, the better I liked the recipe. Jerry was provoked with me, for he did not want to look at the pictures of food and wouldn't even consider reading what was in the recipe. I still have a great

37. Beriberi is caused by dietary deficiencies, especially vitamin B1; it was exacerbated among the internees as their diets became progressively more inadequate. A report on the internees' hygiene and sanitation for October, 1944, apparently prepared by Dr. Nance (see Arthur, 107–8), says, "The general health of the Camp has shown a sharp decline during the month of October. From the beginning of the Camp in May, 1943 to September 30, 1944 only 12 cases of clinical beriberi had been diagnosed in the Clinic. 77 new cases of beriberi were diagnosed during October together with 113 new cases listed as avitaminosis and 162 as asthenia, both of which conditions are diseases of malnutrition and could be classified as incipient beriberi," making a total of 380 new cases attributable to malnutrition during October. The overall total of cases treated for the effects of malnutrition was 1,126, "showing that more than 50% of the Camp has clinical signs of starvation.

"The daily average calorie value of food served from the Main Kitchen has fallen during the month of October to the appalling figure of 881, . . . starvation rations. The October figures have declined to 65% of the 1345 calories issued daily in September. The writer sees little point in writing these monthly reports if they do not result in any improvement in the diet of the Camp which is so desperately needed. They only serve as an indictment of the inhuman treatment of civilian internees by the Japanese authorities. November 1, 1944." (Margaret Sams collection. Margaret comments, "I, for one, did not go to the clinic to be treated" 11/10/87.)

many of the recipes I collected, and the most amazing one is a terribly rich Lobster Thermidor—and I can't stand the sight of lobster! Indeed, I must have been going a little wacky on the subject of food.

After the last scare with the radio, Jerry had carefully bundled his radio and all the gear together. One night after dark he crawled down in the garbage pit and craftily concealed the things under a lot of dried leaves and twigs which he placed in a fairly dry corner of the pit. The things had been down in the pit three or four days and we were beginning to worry for fear the moisture would ruin them. Nothing further had come of Doc's and the other fellow's interviews with the Japanese, so we were beginning to breathe again and to think that perhaps we had been scaredy-cats. We were going crazy wondering what was happening in Manila. We heard dozens of rumors, but no one knew for sure what was going on except that somehow, from somewhere, an American dollar bill had come into camp. The Americans were here—but where?

Jerry and I had made pretty definite plans for going over the fence when we got a nasty surprise—Jerry came down with bacillary dysentery. We were on the verge of rescuing the radio when Jerry was taken to the hospital. Again the radio, and all it might have to tell us, was completely unimportant. The only thing that was important in the world was for Jerry to get well. After Jerry had been in the hospital for three days, where he got the same castor oil treatment that I had had, he was ravenous. We had one small can of baby food left. It wasn't much of a decision to make. First things had to come first. If Gerry Ann had been sick, it would have been hers, as it was intended to be. If David had been sick it would have been his. As it was, it was Jerry's. I made one tiny can into two delicious bowls of pea soup.

Every day as Jerry got better he became more worried about his radio and finally, the night before he came home to the cubicle, James Lee and I went stealthily to the garbage pit and rescued the things. It was a bright moonlight night, and I remember well crouching down low on the ground (James was down inside the pit ready to hand the things up to me) as a guard marched down the road. The moonlight gleamed on the polished steel of the bayonet at the end of his rifle. But he went on by and we breathed a sigh of relief.

With Jerry out of the hospital, so terribly much thinner, with the Japanese giving us nothing now except a handful of palay a day, we knew that our time had come. Palay is unhusked rice, fed to horses in the Philippines. It can no more be eaten with husks on it than can oats. For two days we worked hard trying to get the husks off of our rice. But rice is not like oats or wheat; rice has a husk that sticks to the kernel like glue, and it takes a decided pounding to get the kernel free from the husk. However, if one pounds it, one breaks the kernel of rice, and loses half the rice. We had not one single grain to spare.

I could not bear to look at the new babies, those who were three or four months old.[38] They looked like tiny little rats, all head, and eyes, and stomachs. We knew that within days Gerry Ann was going to look like those babies. They looked like all the pictures of starving babies that one has ever seen. At that time I had seen only pictures of those from Spain, and there was a decided resemblance to our internment babies. Among the Igorots I had seen terribly thin, undernourished, pathetic-looking little babies. I knew that I would far rather be dead and have my baby die quickly than have her starve to death.

All day, the day of February 21, [1945,] Jerry and I made plans for our escape. We had to have help, and as usual it was our friends the missionaries, and Doc and his two companions, who came to the rescue. We knew that we were going to run into trouble for, physically, it was almost more than we could do to walk to the hospital. A path, well-known by a few mestizo boys, led through the fence behind the hospital and eventually to the

38. Minutes of the Los Baños Administrative Committee reveal wartime totals in the Los Baños camp, May 1943–February 23, 1945 of 12 marriages, 14 births, and 20 deaths (Margaret Sams collection).

guerrillas. Doc was to contact the "guides" who were not at all enthusiastic at the request. Guiding a few brave bachelors, one at a time, was one thing. We took every possible precaution. I gave all of our extra clothing, sheets, etc., to a family in our barracks. The woman, another missionary, had been nice to me, and I knew that she was going to need everything that she could get her hands on, for she was pregnant.

We made a will. In case both Jerry and I were killed Gerry Ann was to go to the Lees. They had wanted a little girl very badly, and they adored her. We knew that she could have no better parents.[39] David was to go to the States to his Grandmother, if we were killed. The Lees did not want us to go at all; in fact, they kept coming over all day trying to persuade us to wait just a few more days before we tried to leave—if nothing else, to wait until we had no moon, for the moonlight made the night as bright as day, and they felt we stood little or no chance of making it. However, whether it was wise or not, we had made our decision and we knew that in a few more days we would not be able to crawl to the fence, let alone walk through it. Not only would we have to carry Gerry Ann, we would have to help David, and we had to have a few clothes and a blanket and a mosquito net. Also, Jerry wanted to take his radio, for at the time of the false liberation the guerrillas had sent in to *us* to find out about the news.

Doc had promised to give Gerry Ann a shot of something-or-other which would make her sleep while we were going through the fence, for we knew that the slightest sound from her would fix us right up, but good. We thought we could impress David enough with the seriousness of the situation so that he would be a good little boy. We put the children to bed early that evening so they would be sound asleep by the time we had decided

39. "I knew Gerry Ann would get a fair shake with the Lees. I didn't know whether my mother would accept her because at the time she didn't even know I'd had a baby" (MS to LB 8/11/87).

to make the break, for we thought there would be less chance of them making any noise that way.

James and his wife came over and cried, as we were getting our things tied together to go, and said they hoped we wouldn't mind if they went right back to their cubicle and prayed for us. We didn't mind, of course; we needed prayers—the more the better. Night came, and with it a full moon shining brightly. We awakened the children and walked stealthily through the barracks and to the hospital. I was panting and shaking from the exertion of walking, and as the time drew nearer and nearer for us to escape I was shaking all over, inside and out, from a combination of fear, hunger, and exhaustion, three formidable opponents.

Doc and Kathy kept saying that they wished we would stay just a few more days, but when it became apparent that we were going to go through with it, Doc gave us thirty pesos, and gave Gerry Ann her shot. She screamed mightily when he gave it to her, and for the next two hours she continued to scream. We waited and waited and *waited* for her to stop crying and go to sleep as she was supposed to, but again, though we certainly did not know it at the time, Fate, or God, or the Lees' prayers, or something kept us from going over the fence. Finally, after Doc promised to give her "something different the next time, something that will really put her to sleep," we went back to our barracks, and I don't believe that Jerry and I have ever, together, felt as lost and hopeless as we did that night. We had built ourselves up to a terrific pitch—after all it does take a little "building" to go through with an action that may end in you and your children being shot within the next few minutes—and here we were going back to our barracks, carrying a crying baby. Such depths we hit that night. It seemed as if everything in the whole world was against us. To this day, the Lees are absolutely certain that it was their prayers that kept us from making the break that night. As far as I was concerned it was Gerry Ann crying which did it, but who knows the inscrutable ways of Providence? I do know that she cried all that night, every minute of it. Doc told us the next day that occasionally [the drug] had that effect upon certain people.[40] He was telling us! He assured us again that he'd give her something else the next time we tried it, which we planned to do that night.

Morning finally came, and Jerry and I went back to our rice husking. We've always given the Japanese credit for having a perverted sense of humor. They could just as easily have given us husked rice, but it must have seemed highly amusing to them to see every single able-bodied individual in that camp, some 2,000 of us, all working like mad to eke out a few grains of rice which could do nothing more than stave off the inevitable a few more days. Why do people try so hard, I wonder? Does life *really* have that much to offer? Every family had a different way of husking the rice. Some rubbed it between two boards, some put it in a bottle and pounded on it with a stick, some just picked, grain by grain. . . . All that day we worked on the rice. Again there was no time to wash. Grain by grain, very slowly and methodically (we finally decided that was the best system for us), if we kept at it and didn't stop, we were going to have one cupful of rice for the next day's three meals. Three meals for four people.

During the afternoon, as was not unusual now, two lone P-38s appeared out of nowhere and lazily cruised around just looking the situation over. Jerry and I looked up at them, and for the first time I actually felt malice. "So there you are, you beautiful American boys, just cruising around while we sit down here and starve to death." Need I say that I am now ashamed I ever felt that way? By Japanese edict, we were supposed to get under cover, and not even look up when an American plane appeared in the sky, but this afternoon I didn't care in the least what we were supposed to do. Suddenly, with no warning, while we were watching them, they peeled off and we could see the bombs begin to fall. We had been husking the inevitable rice in our cook

40. To this day the Sams are not certain whether Dr. Nance meant to prevent them from leaving by giving the baby medicine that he knew would make her cry. They suspect he knew or had intimations of an imminent liberation attempt, but they can't prove it.

shanty when they came over, and I said to Jerry "To hell with the Japs, let's watch this." For the next fifteen minutes or so we sat and watched one of the most beautiful shows that I have ever seen performed. Two P-38s made run after run on our beloved enemies, and we watched every bomb that fell. And when they were finished with their bombs they made a circle and strafed them, time after time, until there was no more ammunition and then, still without a scratch, they flew off. Part of our three-year tour of duty had been vindicated that afternoon. The excitement that ran through the camp was absolutely electric in its impact. One could positively feel it in the air. That night we had no roll call, and we were told that most of the guards had gone over the hill to see what damage had been done to their brother Japanese. It seemed incredible to us that we could have been planning to go over the fence that very night, for certainly the afternoon's bombing had wiped out all thought of trying it that night. For the first time we had proof positive that the Americans were on the way!

The morning of the 23rd of February dawned bright and clear, much as any other morning in the dry season. Gerry Ann was thirteen months old that day. My first thought upon awakening was "I wonder if they'll have roll call this morning?" On the off chance that they might, we were beginning to stir around when James Lee called from across the way, "Jerry, where's the axe?" Jerry called back "It's in the cook shack, come on over and get it." He had no more than said it when James said excitedly, "Jerry, come here!" Jerry called back, "I can't, I haven't got my pants on yet," and this time James yelled "To hell with your pants, come here!" With that Jerry bounded out the door, for we are sure it was the first and last time that James has ever sworn in his life. A second later Jerry shouted, "Margaret, come here." And there it was, the most beautiful sight I shall ever witness.

Paratroopers from the Eleventh Airborne were gracefully floating down out of a blue-blue sky. From nowhere a plane appeared with huge lettering on its sides, "This is your liberation." As if we needed to be told. Almost instantly, savage firing burst from all sides of the camp. I said to Jerry "I'll bet we'll be out of here in two days," and Jerry laughed and said "Two days, hell, if we aren't out of here in two hours I'll be disappointed." With that he ran for his long glass, and raced down the aisle of the barracks and climbed up in the peak of the roof, and looked down on what he described later as a "rather pathetic sight." Apparently the paratroopers had caught the Japanese just as they were getting up, and as fast as they came tumbling out of their beds they were shot. Just as Jerry was really becoming engrossed in watching the battle, a shot went through the barracks, just under his perch. Deciding that the sights might be slightly higher the next time he suddenly realized that the best place for him would be with the children and me in the drainage ditch just outside our barracks.

We lay there for a little less than an hour and had a grandstand seat at a battle we had been longing to see for more than three years. During the entire battle there were planes buzzing and swarming overhead. Once one of them came unusually low. Gerry Ann jerked loose from her "breakfast" just long enough to stare up at it with a "How dare you interrupt me?" look, and then she went right back to her favorite pastime. There was little doubt that going outside the fence into the world meant nothing to her.

Suddenly the shooting became less intense and we looked up in time to see what looked like a pair of dirty pants sneaking down our hall. We felt sure that it was a guard trying to make his escape, but just as Jerry reached the hall he gave us a big wink and we looked again and recognized, through the dirt and filth and grime of battle, a Filipino. Not only was he on our side, he was generous. He gave Jerry an egg that had come through the thick of things—unbroken. One lone egg, but such a lovely sight, and we hadn't had it ten minutes until it was cooked and Jerry was forcing me to eat it. And to think that that day we had been counting on the hundred grams of rice which we had managed to get husked, and two tiny treasures in the form of cocoa beans!

The fighting had hardly died down when we saw a long, long line of the most wonderful-looking American boys I have ever seen. They came marching down the path between the garden and our barracks, and they were chanting as they came striding along, "Get ready to move, get ready to move, get ready to move." So we got ready to move. While I rolled up a bundle of clothing I insisted that Jerry and David take the pictures out of the albums, albums that I had saved from the Suyoc days instead of being smart enough to save the silver, as most of the rest of the women had done. As a few last sporadic shots rang through the camp we got ready to move.

Such wild excitement I shall never know again, and it is just as well, for I couldn't take too many of such days. The strange rumbling, of which we had been only slightly aware during the last hour, suddenly materialized, and up the road, between the barracks, came amtracs (amphibious tractors), though we didn't realize what they were at the time. Standing up on the front of one of them was Doc, proudly leading the way. Later in the day I saw him, and he grabbed me and hugged me and said, "You see, I *knew* you weren't supposed to go over the fence that night."

Very shortly then, we were lined up in the road waiting for our turn to climb up into a tank. Finally it was my turn, and I felt most inadequate when I had to have help getting up into it. The barracks were beginning to burn as we went down the road.[41] I shall never forget the sight of an old man, with long

41. The Eleventh Airborne Division of the U.S. Army had already set fire to the barracks of the Japanese guards and before leaving set fire to the barracks in which the internees had been living, as well. Lt. Gen. E. M. Flanagan, Jr. discusses the strategy of the raid and evacuation in his authoritative and highly readable *The Los Baños Raid: The 11th Airborne Jumps at Dawn* (Novato, California: Presidio, 1987): "[Lt. John M.] Ringler also noticed that the internees [near the guards' burning barracks] were moving ahead of the fire toward the amtracs. [Major Henry A.] Burgess seized on the burning barracks as the answer to the question of how to move the internees. He told Ringler to go to the south side of the camp, up wind, and torch the other barracks.

"'The results were spectacular,' Burgess remembers. 'Internees poured out and into the loading area. Troops started clearing the barracks in advance of

white hair, a man who had worn a sort of dress during internment, go dashing back into a burning barracks. They dragged
him back out before he was burned alive, but I've always wondered what he was going back to retrieve. What could have been
so precious to him? Pictures, perhaps? I wish I knew. We met
Mrs. Lee and her two small sons, and very proudly, out where
everyone could see, she was carrying the radio which we had promised to give to them when we were liberated.

Always at this stage, so I read, people look back and see a
kaleidoscopic picture of their lives up to that point. I'm afraid
I don't even remember looking back. I was much too eager about
the future. Now, at long last, thank God, Jerry and I could begin to straighten out the tangled skein of our affairs. At that particular point I don't believe I was aware of anything except that
very moment.

We were in a tank that had big, beautiful, blond American boys
in it. They looked like young gods from another planet, and they
were doing a heavenly job of taking care of us. I didn't know
where we were going, and I didn't even wonder about it, nor
care. I felt sure that *they* knew, and I was entirely willing to leave
it all in their hands.

We had been riding in the tank for fifteen minutes or so, when
all at once the machine guns mounted around the edge of the
tank burst forth in a very decided language all their own. We
were being sniped at by Japanese who had climbed up into coconut trees, and this was the Americans' answer to them. I admit

---

the fire and carried out to the loading area over 130 people who were too weak
or too sick to walk'" (174).

Although both Flanagan and Arthur (250–51) say this extreme measure was
adopted to force reluctant internees to leave, as does the U.S. Army film of
the 11th Airborne rescue, the Sams say that people knew perfectly well that
they were supposed to leave in a hurry, and did so to the best of their ability. "Of course we did not know," says Margaret, how *imperative* it was for us
to *HURRY, HURRY, HURRY!* We were already in an amtrac and had started
down the street when I saw the first barracks on fire" (MS and JS to LB 8/11/87,
MS to LB 11/10/87 and 12/14/87).

that curiosity got the best of me, and instead of hitting the bottom of the tank as they told us to do, I simply had to watch the boy—all the Americans seemed very large to us—who was manning a machine gun at the end of the tank. From the look on his dirty face, I am positive that he was enjoying himself hugely. And he wasn't thinking about a thing on earth except using that machine gun to the very best of his ability. The machine guns were spewing hot, empty shells down into the bottom of the tank, with no discrimination as to where they fell. One fell inside David's shorts, as he lay on the floor of the tank, and it brought him to in a hurry. During the excitement, Gerry Ann acquired a nasty burn on one of her tiny, bird-like little hands. Abruptly the machine gun fire ceased and we were riding as smoothly as if we were on a paved road in a high-powered motor car. When I looked over the side we were out in the bay, and I was horrified for fear this iron monster that we were in would sink. It could float, or sail, or whatever, for in approximately an hour after the boys had shared their C-rations, their cheese, and their cigarettes with us, we landed on the far side of the bay, inside American lines. And may it be said proudly, during that entire day I did not hear one single child cry!

For an hour or two we stayed on the beach and talked to the rejoicing Filipinos who had come down to the waterfront to welcome us. The Filipinos brought coconuts, mangos, bananas, all the things we had wanted for so long. If one had money one could buy the fruit, and we managed, somehow, to buy two bananas and a few cincomas. While we waited we heard many stories of Japanese atrocities among the Filipinos. The most pathetic story still remains with me. An old grandmother, several younger women, and girl children came over to talk to us. A few days before, in a raid on a sugar plantation not far from there, every male member of their family had been executed. The grandfather, the father, the young men, and all the boy children had been killed on the same day. The quiet resignation on the faces of those women has sometimes made me ashamed that I cannot without putting up a terrific fuss, accept life on its own hard terms as those women had done.

We stood in a long, long line that night and eventually were served a bowl of celery soup and a cup of milk. We were again inside a fence (Muntinlupa had formerly been a prison), but with what a vast difference. We again slept on a floor, but it didn't matter this time, for our liberators were outside sleeping on the ground. In any event, we were much too keyed up to sleep. Jerry was still weak from his recent bout with dysentery, so he slept, but I could not, and I spent most of that night and the following one just walking and walking and listening to the boys. I felt as if I'd never be able to sleep again.

Breakfast of the second day in Muntinlupa we were standing in an endless line, when suddenly almost the entire line broke ranks and ran. For a second we weren't sure what was happening. Were the Japanese attacking? Should we run too? Or should we stick it out for breakfast which wasn't more than half an hour away? Then we, too, saw the reason for the stampede. The kitchen was throwing away empty five-gallon cans! A tin can had been all important for entirely too long for us to pass up an opportunity like that. And tin cans were still important, for washing still had to go on, and what could be more wonderful than a five-gallon tin can for washing one's clothing?

The next night Jerry and I sat on the steps of our dorm and I knew that we were really among Americans again, for the most delectable of all odors permeated the night air. The unmistakable smell of freshly baked bread made us realize more than anything else could have, that we were among friends, for we had not tasted the staff of life for three long years.

As usual the American Red Cross came through in a big way. Each internee was given a small tube of toothpaste and a toothbrush. The men were given shaving gear and there was either powder or lipstick for the women, whichever they preferred. We couldn't have cared less about these. There was nothing we didn't need. Later, David was given a pair of pajamas, contributed by the Mexican Red Cross, and Gerry Ann received a beautiful little dress, contributed by the Filipino Red Cross. Still later, but we had gone by then, the remaining women were given wool suits— poorly made and badly fitting—for the long, cold trip home to the States, but they were required to turn in the suits as soon as they got home. When I was in Leyte, each female ex-internee was given two cotton dresses, so skimpy and shapeless that we were not required to turn them in when we got home. I must not forget, either, that we were given free doughnuts and coffee as long as we were in Leyte—this distribution gave the Red Cross girls the chance to flirt with the GIs.[42]

Jerry gained twenty-five pounds during the first week we spent in Muntinlupa, which seems unbelievable, but he ate four or five times a day, and worked long hours for Army communications. That week I almost decided that I had made a sad mistake in my judgment of him, in spite of all that I knew to be true. When Jerry and I were becoming acquainted we had discussed drinking, along with a thousand other discussions we had on various subjects, and he had assured me that he didn't drink. An occasional "social drink" he said, which was all right with me. The first morning after arriving in Muntinlupa, Jerry sought out the Army communication people and they immediately put him to work. Until we left this camp he continued to work with

42. Margaret's critical attitude toward the Red Cross is typical of that of many civilians interned in the Philippine Islands during World War II who saw the Red Cross as providing the wrong things, too little and too late, from a mean-spirited policy intended to enhance the public image of the organization rather than the lives of the recipients. Although internees credit the Red Cross packages with providing life-saving food and medicines, many Red Cross shipments were looted or siphoned off by grafters at the port of entry and never reached their intended recipients. Each internee in the Baguio camp, for instance, received only one 47-pound Red Cross package throughout the duration of the entire war, and got that because their humane commandant, Rokuro Tomibe, sent armed guards (including a number of internees) directly to the dock in Manila to protect the shipment. See Crouter, *Forbidden Diary*, 263–77.

them almost every day. Jerry became acquainted with the officer in charge, who invited him to join him and his staff each evening to swap war stories. They were as interested in our experiences as he was in theirs. Each evening they gave him a cold beer. That beer had a tremendous effect on him, since he had not tasted anything alcoholic for more than three years. One bottle of beer and he was seeing the world through rose-colored glasses. I felt absolutely sick and bitter and disillusioned and let down; in climax I thought, "Here I am, much as I love him, stuck with a drunkard." Today it seems ridiculous that I felt that I wanted to scratch his eyes out every time I saw him, but I did, and for the first week after we were liberated I continued to lose weight, and I thought that I most certainly was going mad.

The first constructive thing that I did in the way of rehabilitation for us was to write to my mother and tell her about Gerry Ann. It was a letter that I had been dreading having to write. Now I could no longer put it off. Though I had mentally written that letter a thousand times it came no more easily than it had the first time I had tried to think of the proper way to tell her the story without shocking her to death as she read it. Needless to say, the final result was anything but satisfactory. In the end I told her the facts, exactly as they were. I told her that I realized perfectly that she lived in a very small town which had known both Bob and me for many years, and that I knew they did not condone what I had done. I told her that if I did not hear from her before we sailed for the States I would consider that she thought it best, for everyone's sake, to consider me dead. And I fully expected her to think it best for everyone, for I knew the way I had been brought up, and I knew the small town where I had lived when I was growing up, I knew Bob's family —and I knew my father, had he been alive, would probably have considered it his duty to shoot Jerry. For all I knew, my brothers might feel the same way about it. God knew what Bob would do about the situation when he got home. After the letter was sent I felt as if I were drained of all feeling. I waited for an an-

swer that did not come. I also wrote to my best friend and received an answer by return mail.[43]

We had been in Muntinlupa almost a week when a man whom
I had first known in Santo Tomás, Bob Merrill, came to me one
day and said he wanted to talk to me. I couldn't think what he
might have to say to me that required our being alone, but I
soon found out. With no preamble he told me that Bob was
dead. He had been killed on a Japanese transport on its way to
Japan, when the ship had been bombed by American planes.[44]
I couldn't believe him at first, for I couldn't picture a situation
so fantastic. A prisoner of war for three years, and then to be
killed by our own Americans just a month before he would have
been liberated. How could there be any justice in the world, and
have that happen? That I had given him a death blow the year
before will always be my cross to bear. If he could have come
home and found a new life, and new love, my conscience would

43. "Sue Bywater Hoppe was my best friend from high school days. She
wrote back saying, 'Honey, if it's all right with you, it's all right with me.' I
later learned that my Grandmother told my Mother, 'If it's all right with Margaret, it must be all right.' My Grandmother was ahead of her time in practically everything" (MS to LB 8/11/87).

44. The ship, the *Meiyo Maru* left Manila for Japan on October 29, 1944,
loaded with 1,600 American prisoners of war who were to be put to work in
mines in Japan. George Weller of the Chicago *Daily News* Foreign Service wrote
a series of some 20 articles on the fateful cruise, based on information gathered from the 300 survivors of the ordeal, who were in "prison camps, rest
camps, on hospital ships and at U.S. bases in the Pacific." The 17th article of
the series begins with this account of the deaths of Bob Sherk and his brother
Jack, Mickie's husband:

> Even in the filth, thirst and starvation of the prison ship, decency would
> send up timid occasional shouts. The Shirk [sic] brothers, Robert and
> Jack, had been mining engineers in Manila [actually, Bob was in Suyoc
> and Jack was in the South Islands] when the Army crooked its finger and
> gave them commissions. Jack fell sick first, grew worse, and finally the
> corpsmen saw that he would not live.
>
> They removed him from the sick bay and laid him out on the hatch,
> where he soon died. Having stripped his body, they were about to tug
> it roughly from the dying to the dead side of the hatch, when a corps-

have had a chance to heal. As it is, my conscience will always grill me, no matter how devotedly I love Jerry.[45]

The next afternoon, during siesta hour, a woman came into the room and told me that a man was asking for me at the door. Since Jerry had gone to Manila I couldn't think who could be wanting me. When I went to the door I still didn't know who it was, for he was a complete stranger to me. A tall, thin man in navy greens and flyer's goggles stood before me. He'd apparently been driving a long way, and he was tired, but when he saw me he smiled and said, "Hello Margaret, it looks like you don't remember me; I used to be Bill Windon back in Beaumont, but now I'm Commander Kauber. When I went in the navy I had to take my father's name."[46] He had his glasses off by that time, and I could begin to see the skinny, freckle-faced young boy with whom I had gone to high school so many hundreds of years before.

"Come on outside and let's talk," he said. I went, never suspecting that he was going to stab me right through the heart. We stood out in the road in that blazing sun, and he told me more about my father's death than I had known before. He said he'd heard that Tommy was "in the navy and doing well." I said "What about Edward? What have you heard about him?" He looked at me then and said, "You haven't heard about Edward?"

---

man looked up and whispered: "Hey, handle this one with a little extra care. His brother is watching us from that upper bay."

When they had laid Jack Shirk with the others, Bob Shirk climbed painfully out of his bay. He went and stood a little while looking at his brother, his matted head bowed. Perhaps he prayed. At length he shook his head slowly and went back to his own bay, where he too died.

("The Voyage of a Death Ship, When Snow Fell, the Prisoners Caught What They Could in Their Messkits." c. December 4, 1944. *Chicago Daily News*, c. Dec. 6, 1944.)

45. "My conscience will never let me be totally at ease about having hurt Bob so much, even now" (MS to LB 8/11/87).

46. "Bill had been living with adoptive parents, the Windons, in school and used their name, but the Navy insisted that he use his biological father's legal surname, Kauber" (MS to LB 8/11/87).

The sun stopped shining then, and I was cold, for I knew before he said it that Edward, the most wonderful of all brothers, had been killed. Edward the dynamic, Edward the lovable, Edward, though four years younger than I, always my superior, and I his very willing slave. From the time he was born, Edward had always been "my baby." I couldn't have loved him any more if he had been my own child, instead of my brother. It was a hot, sticky, ugly afternoon in that dusty prison yard, and it was the second death in two days.

It seemed my turn to tell him things then, so I told him about Jerry and me, for I like knowing where I stand with people. His was a gentleman's answer (and he had a story of his own); he asked then if I'd like to go to Santo Tomás, in his jeep, and pick up Jerry who was due back that day. Mrs. Lee volunteered to take care of the children for me, so I got a pass and we were off.

The sight of Manila that day is one that veterans of European wars saw many times, I presume, but I believe that Manila must have looked as bad, or worse, than any of the European cities. The queerest, most eerie feeling I have ever known, was to drive down through a part of the city with which I had been familiar before the war and not be able to recognize anything. How could a single war so completely alter the face of a city? One would think that it would take a thousand years of wars to create the complete havoc that we saw on all sides of us, or at the very least, an atom bomb. One street in particular, was fantastic, lined with the remains of walls of what had been tall buildings. Now, no wall was more than four feet high, and they were all jagged and grayish and crumbly-looking. Isolated Japanese were still holding out in various buildings left standing around the city. The street had been cleared of enough rubble to allow a jeep to pass, and everything seemed to be cement-colored and gritty, as if the buildings were already turning back to the original sand and cement mixture from which they had been made. Nothing was alive on that street. I was very glad to get to Santo Tomás, though we missed Jerry.

Bill and I went up to the old landing, which held so many memories for me. There we found Robert Merriam, much heavier than he had been the last time I had seen him, for the army had been feeding them well. We ate bread and cheese with him, just to help along our own waistlines. A little later we found Gretchen, who had been outside in a hospital during the heavy bombing. As a result of cancer, which she had developed during the previous year, she had had one breast removed. For three days she had lain on the floor, below the range of Japanese fire. Since then she has died of that same disease.

Bill had two or three of his crew members with him. Since Bill and his boys had been traveling all day they were tired, so we trekked wearily back through Manila, and arrived at Muntinlupa after dark. Jerry was there ahead of us, and he and Bill immediately formed a mutual admiration society. We stayed up most of that night, telling and listening to sea stories. Bill was the skipper of a "Black Cat" Squadron of night fighters, dubbed "fat cats" because they looked fat and low in the water.[47] We thought he and his crew members were wonderful. Each had a good story to tell, and we lay on the grass and enjoyed a relaxation that none of us had known for three years.[48]

47. "These.were PBYs—patrol bombers, painted black, whose duty it was to prey on night shipping" (JS to LB 8/11/87).

48. Margaret recalled in 1987, "There are three stories I remember from those nights that we spent with the armed forces. The first two stories came out of the China-Burma-India theatre. These pilots generally flew only "The Hump." They were taking supplies into China, but occasionally they had passengers as well. If there were no passengers they could pretty well make their own time schedule. Sometimes they didn't feel like flying when there was a passenger, so they worked out a system. In that case, the two pilots took off their collar emblem wings and exchanged them for the crossed rifle emblems of infantrymen. They'd go aboard twenty minutes before flight time with a bottle or so. They'd be loud and whoop it up, and pretty soon one of them would say, 'Can you fly one of these things?' the other would reply, 'Yeah, I can fly anything. I once took a couple lessons.' Pretty soon one of them would say, 'Let's give 'em five more minutes, and if the pilots aren't here let's take 'er up.' Five minutes passed, the two 'infantrymen' went up to the pilots' compartment and

Movies were in order every evening at the camp, but as yet I could not sit through one. Life had recently been too grim. I could not understand how the boys could watch such drivel; it seemed unmitigated nonsense to me at that time, but the evening spent with Bill and his boys made me begin to come out of the trance that had held me captive for so long.

For the first few days before Bill came we had been behind the lines. Food was flown in to us by DC-3s and dropped by parachute. It was dangerous to be out from under cover during the time they dropped the food, for there was no telling where it would land. People seemed to think that it would be heaven to be killed by falling food, though—indeed, one man was so killed—and no one except mothers was too worried about the hazards of the manna from heaven. I did get a bang out of seeing a man covered by the parachute from one crate of food while

---

started up the engines, at which point half of the passengers would bail out. Then they would taxi out to the end of the runway and rev up the engines, and the rest of the passengers would jump out. No passengers, no fly the Hump today!

"Story 2: Originally the planes that flew the Hump were C–47s—eventually C–54s. Passenger runs had WACs as stewardesses. The C–54s had a door that went directly from the outside into the pilots' cockpit. They also had a passenger door, of course. Practically every new stewardess got the 'treatment.' The pilot would come aboard and say to the WAC, 'By the way, when the co-pilot comes aboard send him right up.' Shortly after takeoff the pilot would call the stewardess and tell her to 'send the co-pilot up front.' 'But sir, there's no co-pilot back here.' 'WHAT, you let me take off without a co-pilot?' Naturally the stewardess was very distressed. Upon landing, the co-pilot would go out the pilot's door (while the WAC was getting her door open) and just as she got the door open he would drop to the ground and gasp, 'Another mile and I wouldn't have made it!' Regularly, at this point, the stewardess fainted—so they said.

"Story 3—Bill's own story: When the war started, Bill was ferrying a plane from the Philippines to Hawaii. In Guam he had taken on some bombs. Somewhere between Guam and Hawaii he 'saw a big fat Jap cruiser.' He decided to go down and participate in the war. He tried to bomb the cruiser, but missed, and the cruiser made absolutely no effort to defend itself. However, the second run was different. They let him have everything they had—but they

trying to dodge another crate that was descending at a terrific rate of speed. He came clawing his way out from under that parachute as if the devil himself were after him.

Each day we were given a cigarette and chocolate ration. David dearly loved the chocolate, but we were cautioned not to eat too much of it, because it was unusually rich. Every day I gave him the amount that they told us would be good for us, and then I put the rest away under the makeshift bed, which was an army blanket wound tightly around the framework of a single steel bed frame. Jerry had been taught how to do this when he was in the Marines.

David was terribly upset with me for not letting him eat all the chocolate he could hold, and we had several scenes about it. Once he got into it and ate so much that he made himself sick. He vomited all over the floor, while I was out of the room, and someone else had to clean up the mess. Naturally we weren't either of us very popular as a result of that.

One day when both children were asleep, I thought, I went

---

missed him. At this point his better judgment recommended (inasmuch as he was flying a PBY) that he'd better get on the way to Hawaii. When he got there he reported all this to headquarters. They asked him a few questions and thanked him for trying—and he went on his way. A few days later they called him back and said 'Tell us more about that Jap cruiser again.' It seems it was an *American* cruiser and the Americans were not at all happy about the attempted bombing. They, too, had reported it to headquarters. Bill lost a lot of "face," but had no serious trouble about it.

"Not long after that he was in Australia and *almost* had serious trouble. Naturally he found a beer joint and it was loaded with American sailors. As he went in they were talking about a 'dumb bastard that tried to sink our ship right out from under us—between Guam and Hawaii two or three days after the war started.' They went into some detail about what they would do to him if they ever caught him. Since he wasn't ready to be strung up yet Bill did what any good red-blooded American would have done—agreed that the pilot was a dumb bastard and really *should* be strung up.

"I am absolutely convinced that one of the reasons we won the war was our American sense of humor. Today *nothing* is funny to the younger generation. Fifty years ago lots of things were funny. [Later]—I've decided that isn't exactly true!!" (MS notes 2/87, 11/10/87).

to do my laundry. I had no more than gotten started when I remembered something I had intended to wash, so I went back after it. I could have dropped dead when I saw David, my David, walking down the street in front of me. I ran to catch up with him and found his pockets simply bulging with chocolate and cigarettes. Chocolate was all over his face, and another bar of it was in his hands. When I asked what he was doing he said "I'm running away from home, 'cause you won't give me my chocolate and cigarettes." Drastic action seemed necessary, and spanking had done no good. We walked on over to the fence and sat down in the broiling sun. I made him eat three bars of chocolate. When he looked as if he were going to gag if he ate another bite I insisted that he smoke a cigarette too. After all it was his ration, he had told me so, and obviously he had felt as if he were being discriminated against. I had expected to be up all night with a violently sick child, but I was disappointed. To date he has not "run away from home" again, however.

When Bill left Muntinlupa he said he would be back in a few days to pick us up in his PBY and take us up to the air strip where he was stationed in Lingayen. Jerry and I couldn't believe that this was really happening to us, but we went through a long procedure at the headquarters office, signed our lives away it seemed, and finally got ourselves released. On the day that we were to meet at Nichols field, we found a command car going in that direction and hitched a ride. We were early, or Bill was late, and while we put in time David had the first ice cream that he could remember. He said "It's good Mommy, but why do they make it so cold?" He had not tasted anything cold since we had left Santo Tomás, and he had forgotten the sensation.

The rubble, the craters in the runway, and the demolished Japanese planes were still very much in evidence and we almost felt apprehensive about Bill landing when we at last saw a "Black Cat" in the distance. (An Army man once brought down the wrath of the entire Navy on his head when he called Bill's plane a "Fat Cat.") We took Bill and his entire crew to our hearts. Gerry Ann and I rode up in the front cockpit with Bill, and I had to

make myself believe that I wasn't dreaming. The last three years
had been much the most real experience of our lives, and all that
had happened during the few days since liberation seemed like
dreaming. The other was real—not this!

Bill flew us over Manila, then over Los Baños. As far as we
could see, on three sides of Los Baños the coconut groves lay
glistening in the sun. If we had only been allowed one millionth
part of the coconuts on those trees, the last year of starvation
would not have been at all necessary. Many dead internees would
have still been alive.[49] Why, how, can a human mind be so devil-
ish? Shooting, kicking, beating, almost anything I can understand
except deliberate, malicious starvation.

But starvation was behind us, for we ate almost all the way
to Lingayen, and Bill was sure that we would be sick all over
his plane. We weren't, though, and landed at dusk, in time to

49. Hartendorp, Stevens, and Flanagan, using the same census, list the Los
Baños population as 2,122 at the time of liberation. Since Los Baños was intended to house around 2,000 internees, the interned population, though near
starvation by the war's end, essentially survived except for the murders of Pat
Hell and George Lewis, discussed earlier. The 20 deaths, less than 1% of the
population, are no greater in numbers than would have been projected in
peacetime. (See Martin Bloom and James Halsema, "Survival in Extreme Conditions." *Journal of Suicide and Life Threatening Behavior* 13.3 (1983): 195–206.)
However, the Japanese Eighth Infantry Division, Saito Battalion of the Seventeenth Regiment, commanded by Colonel Masatoshi Fujishige, systematically destroyed the village of Los Baños after the Americans had been liberated.
On the evening of February 23, 1945, Japanese forces had tied nearly 1,400 Filipinos to the stilts that held their houses above the ground and then set fire
to the houses, and to a church in which people had sought sanctuary, burning the entire village—"the stench of the carnage was beyond description." Los
Baños Internment Camp commandant, Lieutenant Sadaaki Konishi, was tried
and convicted of war crimes perpetrated between February 28 and March 6,
1945 which consisted of permitting Imperial Japanese Army troops under his
command to kill over 100 noncombatant Chinese and Filipino civilians in the
town of Los Baños, and to burn and destroy their houses and personal property. Both Konishi and his superior officer, Colonel Fujishige, were hanged for
their crimes; shortly before his death Konishi became a convert to Christianity
(Arthur 257–61).

eat steak and pie with the Navy. Not only that, Bill had two tents: one for us and one for him. They were right beside a cemetery which was honeycombed with foxholes into which we were to crawl in case of an emergency. And wonder of wonders, he had scouted around and found us a real, honest-to-goodness bed, with springs and a mattress.

I felt as if we were among the privileged few the week we stayed with Bill and his men, for we were allowed to see things, and hear things, that we would never otherwise have known. To hear and to see planes warming up for an early morning strike, and to have their dust nearly suffocate us, and their noise deafen us, seemed a distinct privilege then, and still does. It helped a little to erase the memory of Japanese planes flying at will over Manila. The sight of a returning plane coming in low and making crazy antics over the field, to indicate that the pilot had just shot down two Japanese planes, was pure joy. The pilot, who obviously was proud of himself, was not nearly as proud as I was of him. Every plane had a symbol painted on its nose or side. Artistry and humor were all I chose to see there, and I enjoyed both. The yearning, the longing, the occasional pathos, and above all the humor of the pictures on those planes was a thing that gave my downtrodden spirit a great lift.[50] This was America. This then, was what we had been waiting so long to see, and but for an accident of acquaintance we might never have seen it. One day we flew all day, down low, and up high, and the look of tiny, emerald green islands ringed with glistening white beaches still lingers with me. The water was so clear and blue that we could almost count the fish, and it was very satisfying to see an

---

50. "The C–47 rescue planes had painted in big sloping letters, 'YOUR RESCUE.' What a waste of paint—we knew what they were for. Pin-up girls were popular on planes; the design was chosen by consensus of the crew. The best picture was not on a plane but at the Officers' Club on Leyte, a 20′ by 10′ painting of a Japanese officer going to the bathroom, with a million planes descending on him and the caption, 'Caught with your pants down'" (JS to LB 8/11/87).

occasional Japanese ship on its side, half submerged, a symbol left to rot.

One night that week we even went to a native dance. It was an old fashioned "box-social" and I, because I was the only liberated American woman there, was the belle of the ball. The Filipinos had not seen a white woman for three years, and many of the American men there that night had not seen a white woman for an equally long time. I was nothing to brag about, being a skinny bag of bones (though I had already gained twenty pounds), but I was a white woman, and a Marine paid forty pesos for my box. My dancing wasn't worth it but I was pleasantly flattered, although I appreciated every angle of the situation. We had jeeped for miles through, over, and around rice paddies, to get to the dance and we danced to the strains of "Planting Rice." For the first time in years it was almost fun to be alive.

Time marched on and Bill was transferred to Samar, just across the way from Leyte, where we were to wait for a ship to take us home. We packed our duffle bag and went with him. We stayed in Tacloban for a month and under different circumstances it could have been fun. As it was I loathed it. Jerry and David were in one camp, and Gerry Ann and I were in another camp twenty miles away. I was more or less ostracized, which didn't really matter, and yet I couldn't help being a little lonely after the one friend I had left for Australia. Gerry Ann and I were alone in a tent, which I liked (had the other women realized it), but still, it gave me too much time to dread going home and having no one to welcome me. I still had not heard from my mother, and other people were getting letters daily, so I felt certain that I had cut myself off from everything in the world except Jerry. When Jerry was there it was fun, but on the days he didn't come over I wanted to blow my brains out. The army nurses who were at that camp gave me the usual "treatment."[51]

51. "The army nurses were not about to associate with civilian women. The army nurses and the Red Cross girls were officer-oriented; why spend any time

Hospicio had taught me to expect it of them, but they constantly referred to Gerry Ann as "that brat," and I wanted to kill them with my bare hands. There was one nice nurse, however, and she gave me a silk slip the likes of which I had not seen for years. David got acquainted with a WAC in his camp, too, who sent over a pair of slacks and a shirt for me.

David spent his seventh birthday in the camp in Leyte, and immediately stopped wetting the bed.[52] Jerry and David stayed in a rotation camp, and Gerry Ann and I were in a camp full of hospital patients. They were not bed patients, but they were not well enough to be at the front.

Easter was coming up, and since Gerry Ann had no shoes we decided to hitch a ride in to Tacloban and see if we could find a pair of native shoes for her. David's WAC friend had given him a pair of her shoes. The fact that they turned up at the toes didn't matter in the least. They would keep his feet warm on the long, cold trip home.

As we walked along looking in the ship portholes, we suddenly saw an old orange peeling lying in the gutter, the first one we had seen for more than three years. At the mere sight of it we practically choked to death on the saliva that started flowing. Jerry and I both thought about the refrigerator ship that was riding at anchor in the bay. We abandoned the shoe idea immediately and started for the pier. We found the refrigerator ship all right, but the entire crew was busy getting ready to sail, so we had to give up the idea of eating an orange that day. We thought we might as well stand around and see the ship sail.

Wherever we went we talked to the soldiers, the sailors, the marines, anyone who would talk to us and tell us about home. Before we knew it we had quite a group around us, all swapping sea stories. A great tall, blond sailor who hadn't spoken before

---

on women? There were only a few navy nurses, all of whom we knew and liked. They seemed to be a different breed" (MS to LB 8/11/87, 11/10/87).

52. "I think he stopped not because the war was over but because he was finally growing up. Three of our four children (not Kathy) were bedwetters" (MS to LB 8/11/87).

said, "You know, I once had a cousin out here in the Philippines somewhere. Her name was Margaret Coalson. I wonder if you might know her?" And so help me it took me a full minute to realize that Margaret Coalson had once been *my* name. I looked at him then, really looked at him, and I could see family resemblances, though I had to guess at which one of the baby brothers he had been when I last saw him. And then it came to me. "Why, you're Junior!" but Junior certainly did not fit him now. Junior said that he had been on one of the small landing craft tied up along the pier when he saw us walking down the pier, and he had bet one of the sailors that I was his cousin. I have the family legs, and he recognized them. Mill posts, my grandfather called them! The rest of the afternoon we spent in catching up on family gossip. He cabled his mother (my mother's oldest sister), "I've found Margaret."

The rest of the stay in Leyte was better, for Junior managed to get over to see me most evenings. Sometimes we went to the movies, where we sat on coconut palm trees which had been cut and laid down as benches. A time or two we went to a dance. At one of the dances we met Lanny Ross and I enjoyed seeing him, for my mother had always loved hearing him sing. I have never forgotten the impression he made on me. He was beginning to get gray and he had a good and serious face. He looked like any man in uniform who has seen a war. When we first came home I could tell in one glance whether or not a man had been in the war. I can still tell it somewhat, for there is a look in the eyes that is unmistakable, a look that nothing except a war can put in a man's face. I doubt if years ever entirely erase the look. Not long ago I turned the radio on just in time to hear Lanny Ross say "I am going to sing a song for you that I learned in the Philippines during the war." He sang "Planting Rice," and for a few minutes I was back in Leyte.

Jerry became acquainted with a group of army doctors who invited us to their quarters for chow and the inevitable sea stories. We enjoyed their company, and I think they enjoyed us. All the men enjoyed seeing the children, I know, and it seemed wonderful to have people like children again. I had almost come to the conclusion that all people really hate children; at best, they merely tolerate them. Dozens of men during our stay in Leyte asked if they might take Gerry Ann's picture. Naturally I was very happy to oblige them. After all, except for one crayon drawing for which I had traded two packages of cigarettes, we had nothing to show us what Gerry Ann had once looked like. Several of the men were nice enough to send copies to us.

Roosevelt died during the time we were in Leyte, Truman became President, and eventually it was time for us to sail for home. We were taken out to the ship in a torrential downpour, stayed out in the bay all night, and finally sailed for home the next morning. We were escorted part of the way, went through endless zig-zag maneuvers, but on our trip home saw nothing more than planes practice-diving off the coast of Honolulu. The war in Europe was officially declared finished while we were en route home, and I am still puzzled at the lack of excitement that it stirred in us.

Early one morning in May we sighted San Francisco, and as we four stood on deck, as we eased our way under the Golden Gate Bridge, I felt that God had indeed been good to us. We were all relatively healthy, and we had lived to see the United States of America again. Even Jerry, who never shows emotion, had tears in his eyes. We slid into our berth and I felt as eager, as reluctant, as hesitant, as a virgin on her marriage night. I wanted to know what tomorrow would hold, and yet I was afraid to know, for I knew now that my mother had really cast me off. There had been no letter from her in all the long weeks since we had been liberated and though I did not blame her, I could not help being just a little disappointed. I knew, too, that there were months, perhaps years, in front of us before Jerry and I could have smooth sailing.

There was much filling-in of forms, much questioning, much ado about not very much, when we arrived (among other things we were given a ration book), and by the time a shipload of us had been put through customs, several hours had elapsed. Gerry

Ann and David had had their pictures taken by a newspaper woman (they told us) while I was filling out forms. I had completely lost track of Jerry. Finally, the very last person on the ship, I was finished and ready to go down the gangplank on to American soil. I had worked all the trip home to get us looking half-way presentable when we arrived in San Francisco. I had no idea where we would go, or what we would do, but as we started down the gangplank I felt much as an immigrant must feel as he steps off at Ellis Island. "What now?" And then I heard someone say, "There's Margaret now!" and looking up I saw my mother, grey now and lined with worry, my aunt Maude, my brother Tommy, so very handsome in his Navy uniform (he sailed for Japan the second day after we got home), and another tall, nice-looking blond boy whom I did not recognize but felt sure must be my little brother Stanley. They were all waving, and smiling and crying. The Prodigal had returned. I knew without asking that the fatted calf would be killed for me.

One may talk, think, feel, reason until one is blue in the face about the relative importance of a piece of paper called a marriage license, but in our society, which is based on marriage, unless one is the proud possessor of that same piece of paper, one is an unhappy individual, an outcast, a prey to age-old conflicts. At the same time one is an outcast, one realizes that unless a marriage is held together by more than that piece of paper, unless one is truly married in one's heart, unless one is truly willing to give one's life for the loved one, one has missed the real meaning, the true joy of life.

Although Jerry and I would have lived together a lifetime, if necessary, without ever being married, we were finally granted the opportunity we had sought so assiduously. Then, having waited so very long, we waited yet a few more days. We wanted to look at it from all its angles, we wanted to savor its every blessing. We knew that we had been truly married for three years, but for the sake of our children, our grandchildren-to-be, our families, convention, and custom we were finally, legally married. Though that day marked the culmination of many things, it can never be the anniversary which we celebrate. Not to have to worry every time the phone rings, the doorbell trills, the mailman comes, a stranger appears, has been a never-ending blessing to my innately conventional soul.

Being all too human, we invited the internment people in our area to our wedding. They, being also human, forgave us much that day, and were glad in their hearts for the moment, perhaps, that our story had ended happily. Robert and Louise, our dearest friends, were there too, and it completed a cycle. They had stood by me in my darkest hours, and they were still standing by, and Jerry and I were on our way to becoming a normal family; and, as the marriage service says, we've had it all, "for better, for worse, for richer, for poorer, in sickness and in health."

Internees prepare to leave Los Baños on Liberation Day.

Margaret and her cousin, "Junior" Sutton, the skipper of a small Navy landing craft, who was part of the U.S. liberation force

The first photo of the Sams family, taken in the Philippines three weeks after liberation. Everyone had gained considerable weight during that time.

Margaret at the army camp on Leyte, regaining her strength and waiting to be returned to the United States

Gerry Ann's graduation from high school was also a reunion for the former internees pictured here. (Front row, left to right: Louise Miller Meskovsky, Gerry Ann, Mabel O'Toole, Margaret and Jerry. Back row: David, Frieda Magnuson, Robert Miller, and Bob Merriam.)

In February 1987, Margaret and Jerry returned to the Philippines with a group of sixty former internees. Here they are visiting Baker Hall, the gym of the internment narrative.

Margaret and Jerry on Corregidor during the 1987 trip

Afterword

We interpret ourselves through interpreting our experiences; as Emerson observed, "Man is only half himself, the other half is his expression." Most former internees have tales to tell about this major experience of their lives. Some recount military strategy, others resort to fiction, and still others become the central characters of their personal narratives, oral or—in many cases—written. Whatever the emphasis, as William Gass explains in "On Talking to Oneself," "Yesterdays are gone like drying mist. Without our histories, without the conservation which concepts nearly alone make possible, we could not preserve our lives as were the bodies of the pharaohs, the present would soon be as clear of the past as a bright day, and we would be innocent arboreals again" (209).

Writing an autobiography is an act not of innocence but of experience. Gass's choice of metaphor is revealing, for the pharaoh's mummified body has been transformed into a stylized work of art in the course of preservation—a process analogous to that which the skillful storyteller employs in transforming the phenomena of a life into the artistic work of autobiography. The subject of an autobiography becomes both artifact and artificer; a written life, however candid, is a revised life. As Annie Dillard observes about her own autobiographical writing: "If you spend a week or two laying out a scene or describing an event, you've

305

spent more time writing about it than you did living it. After you've written, you can no longer remember anything but the writing. . . . After I've written about any experience, my memories . . . are gone; they've been replaced by the work" (70–71).

Because Margaret Sams's natural mode of expression has from childhood been storytelling, her decision to write a memoir of her wartime experiences as soon as she had gained sufficient perspective to do so is natural and inevitable. Five years' postwar reflection enabled her to recognize the magnitude of her wartime watershed experience, forever significant. The passage of time reaffirmed the psychological rightness of her romantic choice, which she had not fully explained to her mother or others who knew her in her postwar role of—not surprisingly—bourgeois wife and mother. Telling the love story would not only reconstruct it, but would interpret it in a way to justify her violation of social norms ("our love has been good; therefore we should not be judged in haste") without encouraging anarchy in her own children (see p. 23). Margaret's natural impulse to candor would have both artistic and didactic dimensions—the appropriate blend for an *apologia*.

Telling the love story in the total context of life in two internment camps would be not only cathartic, but therapeutic. Margaret could deal there with the social opprobrium (slights exaggerated, perhaps, in her hypersensitive state in internment camp, but real nevertheless). In her memoir, through a combination of candor, good humor, and a plethora of highly specific details, Margaret could reveal herself as an attractive character demonstrating an abundance of virtues. She was an extraordinarily good mother, a meticulous and resourceful housekeeper even under conditions of extreme privation, a hard worker, and a good manager. Such a person, however, might be too dull and predictable to warrant a book, were not Margaret's redeeming features the very ones that got her into trouble; she was thoroughly romantic, adventurous, risk-taking. Though these characteristics might cause some to view her through scarlet-colored glasses, for others they become the rosy lens that makes her transgression both human and forgivable. Seen from this humanizing perspective, *Forbidden Family* becomes as much a tribute to Bob Sherk, Margaret's first husband, as to Jerry Sams, for in this triangle there are no villains, only good people, lovers all. Thus this book lays the ghost, allowing Margaret to publicly make peace with the good man who died with no opportunity for reconciliation, just as it publicly celebrates her new love. As Margaret herself explains, "Writing it all down had been wonderful therapy for me; I was OVER internment."

With her usual perspicacity, Gertrude Stein says, "I write for myself and strangers." Although Margaret's primary audience is composed of people she knows—her mother, her children (and potential grandchildren), friends, and casual acquaintances—behind these familiar figures looms a larger audience, the strangers for whom the author wants to recreate the most profound experience of her life.

The long-term effects of a watershed experience are, more likely than not, played out in a familiar context, for after an all-encompassing war the restorative spirit is strong. In peacetime, people seek to return to pre-scripted roles enacted on a familiar stage, rather than to continue with the uncertain, improvisatory guerrilla theater of wartime. They want to go home and get on with their lives. Those whose prewar jobs and communities had been destroyed and otherwise disrupted, as was the case with most Americans in the Philippines, could not go home again. There was no home, anymore. So they had to start anew and, more often than not, in a new place, for the postwar Philippine Islands were in a turmoil. Most Americans who had resided there before the war returned to the United States; it never occurred to Margaret and Jerry to go anywhere else, or to play other than traditional roles.

To start afresh was easier for Margaret and Jerry than for many. With no prewar life together anyway, they had no choice but to begin anew. The Prodigal Daughter was welcomed back into her family; its circle, shrunken by the deaths of Margaret's father and brother Edward, expanded easily to include Jerry and Gerry

Ann. Jerry's divorce from his first wife was accomplished with dispatch, leaving the couple free to marry, which they did, on January 26, 1946, in McLean, Virginia. (However, they consider September 13 their anniversary, and celebrate the day they met in 1942.) Margaret could continue being a "nice wife" and mother, her lifetime ambition the ambition, avowed or understood, of nearly every other young woman in postwar America. That this "feminine mystique" was in the 1960s to be condemned so severely by Betty Friedan and other militant feminists, was of no consequence to Margaret then or later on. A happy, comfortable existence with the great love of her life and, ultimately, four children (Ned was born in 1946 and Kathy in 1954) was to fulfill not only Margaret's desires but the Great American Postwar Dream.

Unlike many American internees whose material assets had been wiped out by the war—businesses destroyed; savings used up, confiscated, or rendered worthless by inflation; income nonexistent for three years—Jerry Sams was in excellent financial shape. The navy paid him back salary and overtime for the entire period of internment. Jerry had approached his postwar career with foresight. Realizing that his electronics knowledge would stagnate in internment camp and be outdated when he was released, he decided to become an expert in a new field, guided missiles, which needed engineers with a background in electronics.

The family arrived in San Francisco in May 1945. They were young and in relatively good health. Upon release from internment, Jerry weighed 120, down from his prewar weight of 180;[1] Margaret weighed 100, down from prewar 142; David, 7, weighed forty pounds, and Gerry Ann, at 13 months, had attained a remarkable seventeen pounds—a testament to the benefit of breastfeeding even when her mother was on a starvation diet. Unlike some internees who never fully recovered from the effects of chronic

1. Margaret's figure. Jerry disputes this, and says he weighed 90 pounds at the war's end, though in view of others' weights, this seems unlikely (JS and MS to LB 8/7/89).

malnutrition, Margaret, Jerry, and the children seemed to suffer no permanent damage except that David, although he reached an adult height of 6'1'', had lost all his teeth by the age of 25. On an adequate diet, the adults quickly recovered their vitality, and within a year (as photographs reveal), their prewar weight.

By the beginning of July 1945, Jerry had a job with the navy in special communications in Washington, D.C., working on—fittingly enough in light of his wartime activity—"speech privacy" (scrambling speech to ensure secure communication), "single side-band" (radio teletype), and "data links" (remote control of radio transmitters and receivers). They moved to the first of the large, spacious houses that have ever since the war been their antidote to cramped confinement, buying a mansion on Old Dominion Drive in McLean, Virginia. "At night when I sat there in that big beautiful house I thought I'd died and gone to heaven," laughs Margaret. Whenever possible, each new job was accompanied by the biggest and best house the Sams could afford, never for the sake of show, for they are not ostentatious, but always for the space they so valued. Between 1947 and 1969 Jerry, as a special-ist in the national missile program, held a number of jobs which involved frequent moves: to the navy's test center at Point Mugu, California, as chief of external instrumentation; to the Signal Corps Lab at Fort Monmouth, New Jersey; to the Pentagon; to Florida as assistant technical director at Cape Canaveral; to California as chief of the Missile Evaluation Division at the Naval Ordnance Laboratory in Corona. Jerry eventually became man-ager of Polaris instrumentation at Lockheed's Missile and Space Division in Sunnyvale; then joined the Stanford Research Insti-tute for five years, and spent another two with IBM's Federal Systems Division. Stanford sent him to Sweden for a six-month tour to help solve the engineering management problems of a Swedish firm; he finished early, and Margaret joined him for a "very belated European honeymoon."

In the Bay area the Sams bought a house in Atherton, then as now a residential community of handsome houses and lush vegetation adjacent to Stanford University. The imposing, white-

columned dwelling they called "The Big House" represented another fulfillment of the American Dream. The 10,000-square-
foot house had ten bedrooms, five baths, a 40 × 25 foot living
room, and a foyer and library of equal size. Margaret, always an
excellent cook, supervised the household with the part-time help
of Carmen Rincon, from 1959 until they sold in it 1972. Two years
later Jerry retired as president of Data Optics, the small, innova-
tive high technology firm he founded in 1969 after leaving government work. "Data Optics was," Jerry says, "ahead of its time.
Its principal product was a laser system that could detect intru-
sion when someone or something crossed its fixed line of sight.
It could be adapted to measure navigational distances aboard ship
or to count traffic. It also had military applications, for instance,
as a means of providing detection-free communication between
one aircraft and another." After retirement, Margaret and Jerry
moved to a smaller, 2,800 square foot, house with light and airy
rooms they built themselves on their 153-acre ranch near Chicago
Park, California.

In some ways the Sams represented the quintessential Christmas card photographs of the American family of the 1950s — handsome parents, four attractive children (with Gerry Ann forever
an elfin blonde), and a series of photogenic dogs, living in more
than comfortable surroundings, traveling cross-country in the family station wagon (with ritual stops at the national parks), going
on picnics or to Sunday school together. Indeed, with both daughters and their families living on the Sams ranch since their marriages (Gerry Ann's to Heiner Schwede in 1967, Kathy's to Randy
White in 1973), and Ned and his family less than ten miles away,
the Sams to this day remain an unusually close extended family,
with almost daily visits from the grandchildren and frequent
communication among the adults — including sharing of tools,
equipment — and on the Sams ranch, scarce irrigation water in
dry years.

This physical, and in many ways temperamental closeness (like
their parents, the children are energetic, vigorous, and are accomplished mimics and storytellers) does not imply unanimity

of attitudes and views, but it does imply tolerance and great love, expressed with a fair amount of joking, as well as respect. Data Optics was for a time a family business, employing Heiner Schwede (who met Gerry Ann when they were undergraduates at Stanford; he also earned a master's degree in biomedical electrical engineering) as an engineer, David Sams also as an engineer, and his first wife, Dorothy, and Kathy Sams as assemblers. Ned Sams was a salesman, and his first wife, Ruth Harrington, was Jerry's secretary.

Gerry Ann and Ned and their families are far more religious than are their parents. All their children, the three Schwede daughters, Dana, Amy, and Martha, and Ned's stepson John David and his two sons, Eric and Gabriel, by his second wife, Gisela Bourdeaux, attend the fundamentalist Forest Hills Christian School, and both families are active in the church. Gerry Ann is a substitute teacher in the school, sings in the choir, teaches Sunday school; she and Heiner are sponsors (and sometimes surrogate parents) of the youth group. Ned, now a successful salesman for a paper company, plays on the church softball team, and other sports in season; he and Gisela are likewise involved in a myriad of church-related activities. In accord with church teaching, these are traditional families; the husbands are the breadwinners, the wives are the homemakers.

But there are other inevitable differences, as well. Although both Gerry Ann and Kathy attended Crystal Springs School for Girls, an imposing private day school in Hillsborough, California, Gerry Ann is the only Sams child to graduate from college. Ned spent one year at Montana State, one year at a junior college, and another year at art school, but went to work as an insurance salesman without graduating. Kathy married at 19, had three children (Becky, Cori, and Steven) in five years, and after working full-time for many years in a pharmacy, is now a receptionist in a doctor's office while her husband is employed as a machinist by the Grass Valley group, an electronics firm where Heiner Schwede works as an engineer.

David's life has been the most divergent from the family pattern. In 1954, at 17, he enlisted in the navy, against Margaret's better judgment but with her reluctant permission, and married Dorothy Heleson soon after. He later earned a high school diploma, and for years thereafter he took courses in community colleges and by correspondence; he was an aviation fire control specialist. After retiring from the navy, he worked for Data Optics for a time, and then reenlisted. In 1981 he changed his name from Sherk to Sams. Now, retired for the second time from the navy, he works for an aviation firm and lives with his second wife, Joni (Deal), and the youngest of her three daughters in rural Louisa, Virginia, coincidentally near the location of the original Sams home in the seventeenth century.

Except for writing the manuscript of *Forbidden Family* (which Jerry finally read in 1987, when it was being edited for publication), for most of their lives Margaret and Jerry did not dwell on their experiences in internment camp. They soon learned after the war that "all the civilians wanted to know was whether or not Margaret had been raped. When she said she hadn't they didn't want to hear any more," even though, as Margaret says, "Many things can happen that are a lot worse than rape." Moreover, Jerry's work was exciting, their children were growing up, their lives were focused on many other matters. "A large house," says Margaret, "brings lots of adventures. People simply gravitate toward it"—a reflection more of its owners' welcoming spirit than its size, for the Sams hosted American Field Service exchange students from Sweden, Cambodia, Germany, and two Stanford students from India. Margaret also helped to teach English to foreign wives affiliated with Stanford, including two young Japanese women of whom Margaret became very fond and "never ever mentioned the fact that I had been in a Japanese internment camp."

Retirement on the ranch is also busy, though more focused on the immediate family community than on the world at large. Margaret does all the laundry, housecleaning, and cooking, three gourmet meals a day, breakfasts and after-school snacks for visiting grandchildren, and frequent meals for company. Jerry does all the work on the house and outbuildings—two sheds where he works on electronic equipment, care of the dog and the resident chickens (enough to keep the Sams in eggs) and the faithful horse, Abner, that dogs his footsteps and serves as a patient sentry by the shed door while Jerry is at work. He waters the yard, does the heavy outdoor maintenance, and shares the gardening with Margaret. They travel throughout California for reunions with Margaret's family and old high school friends; Margaret tried to see her mother in Riverside every four months until she died, in 1985. They have recently taken long trips—to Alaska and to Hawaii, among other places.

In retirement they have once again begun to assess the meaning of their internment experience. Jerry bores the grandchildren with a two-hour videotape of the Eleventh Airborne rescue of the Los Baños internees; its repetitious narrative has become a family joke to all but the perpetrator. They usually attend one internee reunion a year, in California. Through their longstanding friendship with Dana Nance they met Jim Halsema, whose keen appreciation of the literary merits of Margaret's manuscript has led to its publication. In 1987 they returned to the Philippines with other former internees for a look at Los Baños and Santo Tomás. Margaret, ordinarily not given to tears, was overcome with emotion when she walked through the front door of the main building at Santo Tomás and began to read the plaque commemorating the wartime internment.

Through the years Margaret and Jerry have remained best friends, as well as lovers. The wartime ambience remains omnipresent, *sotto voce,* in their contemporary Western household. They dance the length of their 52-foot living room to tapes of 1940s big band music, the same tunes Jerry broadcast on the internment loudspeaker. They listen, every fifteen minutes day and night, to the chimes of Westminster Abbey's Big Ben, tape recorded and emanating from a loudspeaker mounted on an empty Polaris missile casing at the edge of the canyon—a comforting reminder of the wartime BBC broadcasts. They still get most of their news from television, a newsmagazine, and the radio, now in full view, rather than from newspapers. The unusual and enduring legacy of wartime internment for Margaret and Jerry Sams resides in the gift of each other, and their children, recorded here in *Forbidden Family*.

Works Cited

Allied Geographic Section Southwest Pacific Area. *Terrain Handbook 44*. Brisbane, Australia: Lucena, 1944.

Arthur, Anthony. *Deliverance at Los Baños*. New York: St. Martin's, 1985.

Bloom, Lynn Z. "The Diary as Popular History." *Journal of Popular Culture* 9.4 (1976):794–807.

Bloom, Lynn Z. "Introduction." In *Forbidden Diary: A Record of Wartime Internment, 1941–1945*, by Natalie Crouter, xi–xxvi. New York: Franklin, 1980.

Bloom, Lynn Z. "Until Death Do Us Part: Interpretations of Wartime Internment." *Women's Studies International Forum* 101 (1987):75–83.

Bloom, Martin, and James Halsema. "Survival in Extreme Conditions." *Journal of Suicide and Life Threatening Behavior* 13.3 (1983):195–206.

Crouter, Natalie. *Forbidden Diary: A Record of Wartime Internment, 1941–1945*. Ed. Lynn Z. Bloom. New York: Franklin, 1980.

Dillard, Annie. "To Fashion a Text." In *Inventing the Truth*. Ed. William Zinsser, 53–76. Boston: Houghton, 1987.

Donnelly, Ann Tipton. "Memorial to Robert Minssen Kleinpell, 1905–1986." *The Geological Society of America Memorials*. 18, 1–3. Boulder, Colo.: Geological Society of America, 1987.

Egan, Susanna. *Patterns of Experience in Autobiography*. Chapel Hill: University of North Carolina Press, 1984.

Flanagan, Jr., E. M. *The Los Baños Raid: The 11th Airborne Jumps at Dawn*. Novato, Calif.: Presidio, 1987.

Gass, William H. "On Talking to Oneself." In *Habitations of the Word*, 206–16. New York: Simon, 1985.

Hartendorp, A. V. H. *The Japanese Occupation of the Philippines*. 2 vols. Manila: Bookmark, 1967.

Hartendorp, A. V. H. *The Santo Tomás Story.* New York: McGraw, 1964.

Hyland, Judy. *In the Shadow of the Rising Sun.* Minneapolis: Augsburg, 1984.

Irons, Peter. *Justice at War.* New York: Oxford University Press, 1983.

Kane, Samuel. *Thirty Years with the Philippine Head-Hunters.* London: Jerrolds, 1934.

Kerr, E. Bartlett. *Surrender and Survival: The Experience of American POWs in the Pacific, 1941–1945.* New York: Morrow, 1985.

Miles, Fern Harrington. *Captive Community: Life in a Japanese Internment Camp, 1941–1945.* Jefferson City, Tenn.: Mossy Creek, 1987.

Moule, William R. *God's Arms Around Us.* New York: Vantage, 1960.

Newman, John Henry. *Newman's "Apologia Pro Vita Sua": The Two Versions of 1864 and 1865: Preceded by Newman's and Kingsley's Pamphlets.* Ed. Wilfrid Ward. London: Oxford University Press, 1913.

Petillo, Carol M. "Introduction." In *The Ordeal of Elizabeth Vaughan,* vii–xix. Athens: University of Georgia Press, 1985.

Reports by Provinces for Census of Population. Census of the Philippines: 1939. 2 vols., I, 3:9. Manila: Commonwealth of the Philippines Commission of the Census, 1940.

Santos, Vito C. *Vicassan's Filipino-English Dictionary.* Manila: National Book Store, 1986.

Sayre, Francis B., Letter to the Hon. Charles A. Wolverton, Chairman of the Enemy Property Commission. U.S. 80th Congress, Hearings before the Committee on Interstate and Foreign Commerce. In *Enemy Property Commission Report,* 153. Washington, D.C.: Government Printing Office, 1947.

Shaplen, Robert. "Letter from Manila." *The New Yorker* (26 March 1979), 99.

Siebenschuh, William R. *Fictional Techniques and Factual Works.* Athens: University of Georgia Press, 1983.

Smyser, Dick. "A Name for Oak Ridge to Remember." Editorial. *Oak Ridger* [Tennessee] 19 June 1987:4.

Stein, Gertrude. *Everybody's Autobiography.* 1937. Rpt. New York: Vintage, 1973.

Stevens, Frederic H. *Santo Tomás Internment Camp.* N.p.: Stratford, 1946.

Taylor, Vince. *Cabanatuan: The Japanese Death Camp: A Survivors* [sic] *Story.* Waco, Tex.: Texian, 1985.

Vaughan, Elizabeth. *The Ordeal of Elizabeth Vaughan.* Ed. Carol M. Petillo. Athens: University of Georgia Press, 1985.

Weintraub, Karl Joachim. *The Value of the Individual: Self and Circumstance in Autobiography.* Chicago: University of Chicago Press, 1978.

Weller, George. "The Voyage of a Death Ship: When Snow Fell, the Prisoners Caught What They Could in Their Messkits." *Chicago Daily News,* 6 December 1944.